PAST LIVES

PAST LIVES

Unlocking the Secrets of our Ancestors

IAN WILSON

A Seven Dials Paperback

CONTENTS

AUTHOR'S PREFACE

Over forty years ago, when taking entrance exams at a Cambridge college, I was allotted a room normally occupied by a medical student. It was my first ever stay away from home on my own, and greeting me as I opened the door was a human skull, accompanied by a thigh-bone. The three-day experience of living with those bones taught me a lifetime's respect for so structural an element of our being.

For, as Galen remarked, 'As poles to tents... so are bones to all living creatures, for other features take their form from them'. Bones define structure so clearly that, via a variety of techniques, a skull can now be 'refleshed' to reproduce its original owner's living likeness – and with considerable accuracy, even after tens of thousands of years. To me the ultimate in recapturing a life from the historical past is to come face to face with that individual – hence my fascination with such techniques, and the inspiration for this book.

Clearly no one, least of all myself, can be an expert in the whole vast spectrum of human history and prehistory encompassed in the pages that follow. A further challenge is that some of the examples selected relate to topics currently riven with controversy – particularly concerning the period when the American continent first became peopled, and by whom. Moreover, scientific understanding is changing so rapidly that, as I write this preface, news comes that the standard forensic method used to calculate age from bones may be in serious error. While several individuals are described here as dying at what by modern standards would be a young age, the very latest advice is that such calculations may have erred by as much as thirty years. So life in ancient times may well have been less short, as well as less nasty and brutish, than scientific orthodoxy has long supposed.

Specifically in order to minimise the more avoidable errors, wherever possible I have sought out specialists to check relevant chapters. In this regard the warmest thanks must go to Dr John Prag, Keeper of Archaeology at the Manchester Museum, and to Richard Neave of the Manchester University Unit of Art in Medicine, both of whom from the outset gave the project every encouragement and assistance. Their definitive book *Making Faces* has been a particularly valuable source of reference. Thanks are likewise due to Raymond Evans and Caroline Wilkinson, also of the Unit of Art in

Medicine, for their kindness to my wife and me during a visit to Manchester in 1999. I am also grateful to Dr Dominic Tweddle of Past Forward, York, for his guidance on those reconstructions made by his company several years ago. In the United States, Betty Gatliff of Norman, Oklahoma, Dr Emily Craig of Frankfort, Kentucky, Professor Denis Lee of Ann Arbor, Michigan, Karen Taylor of Austin, Texas, Dr Donny Hamilton and Professor Gentry Steele of Texas A & M University have been immensely helpful with information on, and images of, individual 'American School' reconstructions. Professor Konrad Spindler of Innsbruck provided useful comments about the Ice Man reconstruction, John Follain of Times Newspapers, Rome, sent data on the Roman sailor, while Jean-Claude Bragard, Patrick Gilbert, Sabine Pusch and Petra Collier of BBC TV Manchester, and Bill Jones and Sandra Singleton of Granada TV most helpfully provided data and videos for recent British TV programmes featuring facial reconstructions.

Thanks must go to Carey Smith and Colin Ancliffe of Anaya Publishers, who backed the idea in its first incarnation six years ago, only to be thwarted by a company take-over; to Caroline Knight and Michael Dover of Orion for enthusiastically taking the project on; to Christine Vincent of Toucan for helping it along the way, and to Marilyn Inglis, Margaret Little and the ever conscientious and communicative Tim Whiting, all of Cassell, for so ably and patiently steering it from manuscript to illustrated book. Although I have worked with a number of copy-editors over the years, the dedication and encyclopedic historical knowledge that Elisabeth Ingles brought to this particular task have been without peer. I am also greatly indebted to Caroline Thomas for her immense diligence in hunting down a daunting list of sometimes very elusive photographs. Last but not least, my thanks as always to my wife Judith, whose skills with a recently acquired digital camera proved invaluable, and who unstintingly helped at every stage, from the research trips to checking the completed text.

IAN WILSON
BELLBOWRIE, QUEENSLAND, AUSTRALIA
MARCH 2001

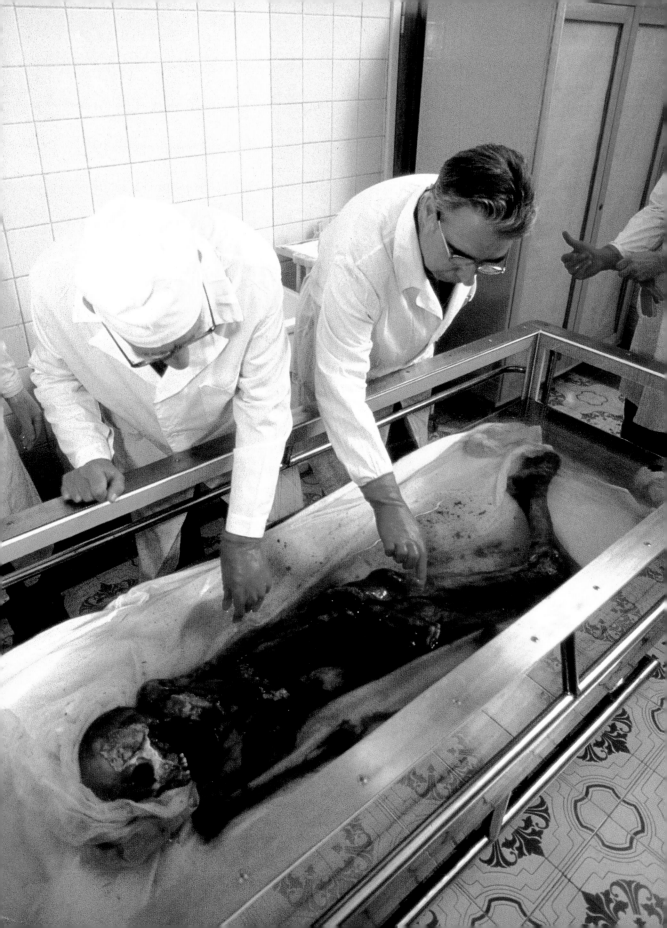

INTRODUCTION
The art and science of facial reconstruction: A history

Opposite title page: Dubbed the 'world's oldest face', the features of this 4500-year-old mummy from Egypt's 5th Dynasty have been strikingly well-preserved thanks to an ancient plastering technique. Today's technologies, however, can enable us to 'see again' such faces from the past even when only the bones have survived.

Left: Today, when an ancient body is discovered, a variety of techniques can illuminate details of the life that the individual led, even his or her facial appearance. Here, scientists in Moscow examine the remains of the 'horse-queen' featured in Chapter 9.

A century or so ago the discovery of ancient human bones was of relatively minor interest to the archaeologist. The opening up of a tomb full of gold and jewels or the uncovering of a gate of ancient Babylon might create world headlines and attract wealthy patrons. But old bones held no such popular appeal. If they did not end up on a spoil heap, they were often piled into a cardboard box, stored deep in some dusty museum basement and all but forgotten. Even the pharaoh Tutankhamun's mummified body, once stripped of its many gold amulets and (by modern standards) perfunctorily autopsied, received less attention than most of the objects found in his tomb.

Today all this has been changed by recently developed techniques that enable an ancient skull, even one in a seriously fragmentary state, to be transformed into a vividly lifelike reconstruction of its owner's face. And this can be done with an accuracy that is difficult to credit until the science behind it is properly understood. Furthermore, recreating the face is but the tip of the iceberg. Drill into the bone to extract a DNA sample and you may well be able to glean important facts about the individual's ancestry. Soon, if not already, you should be able accurately to determine his or her skin colour, hair colour, health defects and much else.

In the case of people who lived since the development of photography, in the relatively recent past, such advances may seem to be of only limited interest. But in the case of more ancient individuals, from cultures with no reliable portraiture, or, above all, those from before the era of descriptive writing, the potential window opened on their lives is nothing less than sensational, with the view from it growing clearer all the time.

And if we ask 'but what's so special about recreating an ancient face?', the answer is 'rather more than may at first appear'. Unless we are blind, we are so familiar with the faces of family, friends and colleagues, seeing them daily, identifying them without a second thought, that we rarely consider just how odd it is that we can recognise them with such ease.

For, if we pause to think about it, each of us has two eyes, two ears and two cheeks, combined with a nose, a mouth, a chin and some degree of hair, all in roughly the same places and in roughly the same proportions to each other. Yet somehow, perhaps without conscious thought, we can pick out a friend's face among a crowd, even sometimes from the merest glimpse, like the animals and birds which recognise their mates or offspring among their teeming herds and flocks. In children we always instinctively look for the characteristic facial features that they may have inherited from parents and grandparents. If we lose a friend or loved one, it will most likely be a picture of their face that we will treasure more than any other keepsake.

A further oddity is that this importance assigned to faces, of both living kin and ancestors, can be traced back for millennia, from the portrait galleries of stately homes to the gravestones of ancient Rome and the colossal statues of Easter Island. From time immemorial, people have sought to perpetuate indefinitely their own and their family's facial likenesses. Nor does it end there. Confronted with a skull, even the most hard-headed and unromantic of us will try to recreate in our mind's eye the living features that it once bore. Our scientifically literate generation is not alone in this imagining. Four hundred years ago Shakespeare had his Hamlet remark of the jester Yorick's skull: 'Here hung those lips that I have kiss'd I know not how oft.' So how far back can our urge to recreate facial likenesses be traced?

What we do know is that the actual practice of 'refleshing' a skull to restore its living features can be traced at least as far back as around 9000 years before Shakespeare's time. The ancient inhabitants of Jericho, which is one of the world's earliest known cities, buried their deceased family members beneath the floors of their houses – a common enough custom among prehistoric peoples, surviving even to modern times in Polynesia. But in certain cases the Jerichoites and their neighbours went significantly further. After they had waited long enough for the flesh to rot away, they then dug down to the skeleton, removed the skull, and carefully plastered over it to recreate the semblance of living flesh. With bitumen and pigments they then painted in facial features such as hair, moustache and beard. As the finishing touch they inserted shells in the sockets in order to give the semblance of living eyes. The British archaeologist Kathleen Kenyon found several examples of such heads during her excavations at Jericho in the 1950s: 'Each… has a most individual character, and one cannot escape the impression that one is looking at real portraits.'[1] There is general agreement that the inhabitants of Jericho set up displays of such reconstructed faces in special gallery-shrines that were devoted to their most revered ancestors, whom they could then consult at times of need.

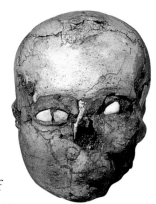

From c.7000 BC, one of several skulls found at Jericho that had been carefully remodelled with plaster in an apparent attempt to recreate the deceased's facial features.

So deep-rooted is the importance of the face in the human psyche that 7000 miles across the world, and at much the same time, the Chinchorro peoples on the Pacific coast of Chile adopted a very similar practice. They too cut off the head, but then they filled it with grass, hair and ashes, and remodelled it as a living face using a thick layer of paste made from ashes, the nearest available equivalent of plaster.[2] As at Jericho, they painted in facial features, mostly in black and red. They even re-attached the original hair, and reunited the head with its body, similarly re-processed. As described by the British bioanthropologist Dr Joann Fletcher, who has recently made a special study of Chinchorro specimens: 'There is the minimum of detail, yet they are incredibly powerful. It's like they have been re-upholstered.'[3] A further 7000 miles across the Pacific, some of the aboriginal tribes of Australia followed suit, seemingly quite independently.[4]

In around 3000 BC the ancient Egyptians began artificially mummifying their dead, as distinct from the earlier practice of merely allowing the hot, dry conditions to preserve the corpse naturally. Although they succeeded in arresting the rotting of the flesh, the salts used in the mummification procedure had a marked shrinking effect on the bodily tissues. So they wrapped fine cloth bandages around the body's contours, then coated these with a thin layer of stucco plaster which dried to follow the deceased's features faithfully, the effect closely resembling a statue.

From the era of Egypt's Old Kingdom, c.2500 BC, the face of Waty, a striking example of early Egyptian morticians' use of plaster to model, and thereby to preserve, the deceased's facial features.

The face of Waty, a very minor Egyptian official of the Old Kingdom Fifth Dynasty (roughly the mid-third millennium BC), found at Sakkara, within a stone's throw of the oldest pyramid, has been dubbed the world's oldest face because it is the earliest surviving example to have been artificially preserved in this manner.[5] Tucked in an overlooked corner of a more illustrious relative's tomb, Waty was fortunate enough to escape the tomb-robbing that destroyed the rest of his contemporaries' remains in antiquity. On his rediscovery in the mid-1970s, it was found that his morticians had not only moulded his face with great skill, they had also shaped his eyebrows and thin moustache in the plaster, and supplied him with a false linen beard, likewise stiffened with plaster. By the same process they managed to preserve for posterity even his fingernails, his testes and a foot callus.

The Old Kingdom appears to have been something of a golden age for this wet-plaster method of facial and indeed body preservation. The principles behind it retained so powerful a significance throughout succeeding millennia that right up to the coming of Christianity virtually all the dead, even the humbler members of Egyptian society, were fitted with coverings in the semblance of a face, albeit mostly of no specific likeness.[6] The masks varied according to the prevailing fashion, but ranged from moulded cartonnage (papier mâché) sarcophagi to Tutankhamun's peerless gold face mask, now in the Cairo Museum, and later, in the Christian era, to icon-like panel paintings that were fastened to the mummy wrappings. Numerous examples were recently found in the so-called 'Valley of the Golden Mummies' discovered at the Bahariya Oasis.[7]

The rulers of Mycenae in ancient Greece in the second millennium BC echoed the practice, using thin sheets of gold hammered into the semblance of the deceased's face. The so-called Agamemnon mask that Heinrich Schliemann found amidst the tombs of the city's grave circle is one of the most evocative examples. The Bosporan kings of the northern coast of the Black Sea perpetuated the practice until as late as the third century AD, as indicated by the splendid specimen of King Rhescuporis preserved in the Hermitage Museum, St Petersburg.[8]

In AD 79 the volcano of Vesuvius in southern Italy performed its own remarkable feat of preserving human likenesses when it erupted, creating natural 'moulds' by spewing out hot ash which settled around the bodies of the citizens of Pompeii overwhelmed before they were able to flee. Nineteenth-century archaeologists discovered these cavities in the solidified ash and lava and found that, by pouring liquid plaster into them, they could often produce a near-perfect cast of the victim's body. When the surrounding ash was removed

the body would be revealed frozen in its last posture. In the so-called Garden of the Fugitives at Pompeii modern-day visitors can view a group of thirteen men, women and children 'moulded' in this way, left *in situ* exactly as found. Many other similar casts are scattered around the site. The casts taken even include pet dogs that had been unable to escape because their owners had chained them up. Recently the Italian specialist Amedeo Cicchitti has developed a 'lost-wax' refinement of this process whereby the cavity is filled with wax instead of plaster. When the wax figure is removed, a new plaster mould is created around it from which the wax is melted and poured out, to be replaced by translucent epoxy resin. Thanks to the resin's transparency it is possible to see otherwise unnoticeable features such as jewellery and any small objects that the victim may have been carrying.

Christianity, when it became an 'establishment' religion, initially spurned any effigy-making of the dead as pagan, but from the Middle Ages right up to the age of photography the practice was partially revived in the form of plaster death-masks of kings and queens made shortly after their expiry. Very probably the earliest English king for whom such a mask was made was Henry III (d.1272). The

From 79 AD, in Pompeii's so-called Garden of the Fugitives, the bodies of thirteen citizens, among hundreds who were overcome before they were able to make their escape from the Vesuvius eruption. These plaster casts were made from moulds naturally created by the eruption's volcanic ash, uncannily preserving the deceased's in-life physical appearance even though the body had otherwise disintegrated to a skeleton.

accounts of his son and successor Edward I record the purchase of 300lbs of wax for an effigy of the dead king's 'exact likeness' wearing 'his most precious robes and the royal crown'.

By the reign of Edward III (1327-77) 'an image in the likeness of the king' made by one Stephen Hadley was absolutely explicit, and has actually survived among several such royal effigies preserved in Westminster Abbey.[9] Although this particular example is of wood, and lacks the original beard and wig together with much of the coloured plaster with which the king's features were built up, close study of the face reveals a curious downward twist to the left side of the mouth and a dead, flattened appearance to the left eye. These are widely interpreted as indicating the final paralysis Edward suffered when, as historically recorded, he lost all power of speech, and his jewel-loving mistress Alice Perrers took the ring from his finger. Whatever the validity of this, by the fourteenth century the casting of exact likenesses certainly became routine for both English and French monarchs when they died.

In the next century the practice spread to the ranks of the ordinary Europeans. The Renaissance art historian Giorgio Vasari reported of Leonardo da Vinci's mentor, the fifteenth-century Florentine artist Andrea del Verrocchio, that he was:

> very fond of making plaster casts, for which he used a soft stone quarried in the districts of Volterra and Siena... During Andrea's lifetime the custom started of doing inexpensive casts of the heads of those who died, so one can see in every house in Florence, over the chimneypieces, doors, windows and cornices, endless examples of such portraits, so well-made and natural that they seem alive.[10]

Verrocchio joined forces with a wax-worker called Orsinoto to create life-size figures in wax of their patron Duke Lorenzo de' Medici, to mark Lorenzo's survival of an attempted coup in which his brother Giuliano was killed. Apparently the figures were painted 'in oils with the hair and other adornments' again so natural that they seemed 'real and alive'. And although they have been lost, something of their impact can be gleaned from the fine bust of Lorenzo that is now in the National Gallery of Art, Washington, DC, and the mask (almost certainly the work of Verrocchio) made on his death in 1482. The death-mask is now in the Museo Medico, Florence, where we can gaze on the actual features of the forceful Florentine who was Michelangelo's first patron.

In the seventeenth century the similarly forceful Oliver Cromwell was subjected to the technique, and the resemblance between his death-mask and a fine Samuel Cooper portrait miniature of him is startlingly close *(see overleaf)*. The same century also saw the method applied to living persons. The entry for 10 February 1669 in Samuel Pepys's diary duly recorded:

I to my wife, and with her to the Plasterer's at Charing Cross that cast heads and bodies in plaster; and there I had my whole face done, but I was vexed at first to daub all over my face with Pomatum [a grease enabling the mask to be eased off without discomfort]; but it was pretty to feel how soft and easily it is done on the face and…by degrees, how hard it becomes, that you cannot break it.[11]

In commenting on the procedure, which gave him 'little pleasure', Pepys omitted to describe the crucial means by which he had been enabled to breathe. Most likely this would have been via quills or straws inserted in his nostrils, the method employed by later practitioners such as Madame Tussaud. Whatever was used, when Pepys later revisited his 'Plasterer' to view the bust made from the mould, he described it as 'most admirably like'[12] and promptly ordered a second copy.

Sadly, neither Pepys's bust nor innumerable others of the time have come down to us. There is, however, one little-known exception, a wax effigy of the wool merchant and philanthropist Sir William Turner, who was London's Lord Mayor in the very year of Pepys's visit to the plasterer's. Preserved in the chapel of the Sir William Turner Hospital, Kirkleatham, Cleveland, in northern England, this historic waxwork is so exact that even stubble can be seen on Turner's chin.

In Pepys's time, women were unheard of as makers of waxworks, but by the next century the field was full of them. London's leading practitioner was a Mrs Mary Salmon (1670-1760), proprietor of a Fleet Street business that sold 'all sorts of moulds and glass eyes' and exhibited 140 waxwork figures 'big as life'. Indicative of just how slick the taking of 'life-masks' had become is the story of how in 1746 Mrs Salmon and her daughter were persuaded by the madcap Duke of Montagu to make a mask without the sitter's knowledge. Montagu's chosen victim was the unpopular German-born operatic manager John Heidegger (immortalised by Henry Fielding as 'Count Ugly'), whom the Duke persuaded the Salmons to 'plaster' when he was too drunk to notice. From this Mary Salmon skilfully created a lifelike face-mask, which Montagu arranged for an actor to wear when King George II was at the opera. As the King made his grand entrance, before Heidegger could give the normal signal for the orchestra to strike up 'God Save the King', quick as a flash the actor appeared as Heidegger himself, loudly calling, in the latter's heavy German accent, for 'Over de Vater [water] to Charlie'. With the fugitive Bonnie Prince Charlie a topical and popular figure, the audience was reduced to helpless laughter.

Another woman practitioner, a generation later, was the American spy Patience Wright, who after 'plastering' the faces of King George III and Queen Charlotte, chatting with them as she did so, was able to send back across the Atlantic reports of

Oliver Cromwell (1599-1658), from a portrait miniature by the contemporary artist Samuel Cooper (1609-1672). Cromwell famously insisted that artists should portray him 'warts and all'.

their inmost thoughts on the American revolutionary war. Then, in 1802, there arrived in London, hotfoot from her work on the victims of the French Revolution, a certain Madame Marie Tussaud to found a waxwork business that, despite the coming of the age of photography and television, continues to flourish to this day.

While the science and art of creating a lifelike waxwork as perfected by Tussaud – most notably the making of prosthetic eyes, wigs and make-up – had important implications for what would follow, all the attention (with the notable exceptions of the ancient plastered skulls of Jericho and Chinchorro) was focused on moulding faces that, living or dead, remained fully fleshed. It was not until the very end of the nineteenth century, or later still following a proper scientific method, that anyone began seriously to revive the idea of recreating lifelike faces from skulls that had long lost all their flesh.

Death mask of Oliver Cromwell, created in 1658, as preserved in the National Portrait Gallery, London. This shows the close likeness that artist Samuel Cooper achieved in his portrait version reproduced opposite.

It was the German anatomist W. His who was the pioneer. Around 1895 he took the first proper measurements of facial tissue depth in cadavers by driving a pin through a piece of soft rubber, then pushing the pin into a key point on a cadaver's face until it was stopped by the bone. He then lowered the rubber to the skin surface, and by measuring the distance between it and the pinhead calculated the tissue thickness from the length of pin still buried beneath the skin. Repeating this procedure at several key points on the faces of more than two dozen cadavers, male and female, His was able to draw up a complete table of the average tissue depths at each point, so that by modelling clay over a skull to the same depths the face of the living could be recreated.

When His demonstrated this using a skull thought to be that of Johann Sebastian Bach, the reconstruction received great acclaim as a convincing match to known portraits of the composer. Soon His's work was followed up and expanded by the Swiss anatomist J. Kollman and his sculptor colleague W. Büchly, who produced a much more extensive set of tables for average tissue depths, based on twenty-three different points on the face. Using these tables they made the first truly scientific three-dimensional facial reconstruction of a man from the early Stone Age.[13]

There followed a flurry of early twentieth-century reconstructions of pre historic and historic skulls, all theoretically based on 'scientific' methods. One anatomist, Welkeld, claimed to have identified the skull of the painter Raphael by comparing his reconstruction with the artist's self-portraits. Another, Geiss, did the same for the remains of Kant and Haydn, and produced a second version of Bach. Then it was observed that different sculptors were producing widely differing faces based on the same skull and data. Not surprisingly, the method soon became seriously discredited, probably well deserved since the sculptors too often followed their own artistic inclinations rather than the scientific guidelines provided for them.

Thankfully, a twentieth-century Russian palaeontologist, Mikhail Gerasimov, saved the method from being abandoned altogether.[14] Gerasimov noted that paying particularly close attention to the musculature of the face and neck, as determined from the strength or otherwise of the muscle attachment points on the surviving bones, played an important part in achieving the best possible result. In 1950 he founded a laboratory which was devoted to creating what can be termed the 'Russian method' of facial reconstruction. Soon this laboratory was turning out reconstructions of prehistoric ancestors that included 'Peking man' (then so-called), various Neanderthal specimens and a number of well-known historical figures such as the sixteenth-century Russian tsar Ivan (IV) the Terrible and the eighteenth-century German dramatist and poet Friedrich Schiller. Gerasimov also produced about a hundred reconstructions for criminological work successful enough to show that his historical versions had credibility. Although he died in 1970 his work has been continued and expanded by his former pupil Galina Lebedinskaya, and his laboratory still exists at the Institute of Ethnography and Anthropology of the Russian Academy of Sciences in Moscow.

The Russian palaeontologist Mikhail Gerasimov, pioneer of the 'Russian method' of creating facial reconstructions from skulls. The Russian reconstruction method pays particular attention to muscle attachment points. (For Gerasimov's remarkable Ivan the Terrible reconstruction, see p.189)

During much the same period the technique was developed independently in the United States; because of the Cold War the American and Russian practitioners had no contact with each other. As early as the 1940s the anatomist Dr Wilton Krogman developed a criminological version of the method. He provided a professional sculptress with the skull of a forty-year-old black and the average statistics on soft tissue depth available at the time. She duly applied a lattice of clay strips to the skull, carefully built these up to the statistically determined tissue depth, then modelled the features to suit, producing a reconstruction of the man's face that was declared 'readily recognisable'.

The method has since been further developed by Betty Pat Gatliff of Norman, Oklahoma,[15] the revered doyenne of most of the small band of Americans who are working in this field at present. Now retired, Gatliff is noted for the 140 or so facial reconstructions that she has undertaken to help US police in criminological cases, and which have contributed to some 105 positive identifications. Her historical reconstructions have been a spin-off from this work. The procedure – what may be termed the 'American method' – involves first mounting a cast replica of the original skull on a stand in what is called the 'Frankfort Plane', the natural, upright way of holding the head. Cylindrical rubber markers are then individually cut to the lengths prescribed for eighteen key points on the skull, according to the average tissue thickness known to pertain to the particular anthropological type, gender and group to which the skull's owner belonged (already determined by bone analysis and other indications). The markers are glued to the skull at the prescribed points, plaster balls inserted into the sockets to serve as 'eyes' and strips of modelling clay worked all round the skull up to the depths indicated by the markers.

The mouth 'barrel' is then formed according to certain prescribed rules, such as the width, covering the front six teeth, and the vertical thickness of the lips, corresponding to the gum-line depth of the teeth. Similar rules govern the modelling of the nose, its projection being reckoned as three times the length of the nasal spine bone. As there is no bone in the external section of the ears, reconstructing these is more conjectural. Gatliff's rule of thumb is that the ear and nose should always be approximately the same length, while the skull's external acoustic meatus, or ear aperture, determines the points to which the reconstructed ears should be attached, and the ears are always slanted back at approximately 15 degrees from the vertical.

A typical example of a Gatliff or 'American' reconstruction is the artist-anthropologist Sharon Long's recent rendition of the face of a 9400-year-old mummy

The 'American method' of creating a facial reconstruction, as exemplified by these stages in Sharon Long's recreation of the face of a 9400 year old mummy found in Spirit Cave, Nevada. The American method relies more heavily on average tissue thickness tables than on facial musculature calculations.

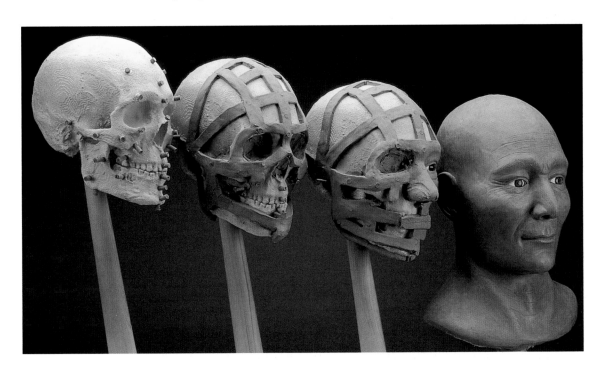

– North America's earliest known example of mummification – found in 1940 in Spirit Cave near Fallon, Nevada.[16] Visitors to the Smithsonian Museum of Natural History, Washington, DC, can see reconstructed faces of an Early Bronze Age couple who lived *c.*3200 BC at Bab edh-Dhra in the environs of the Dead Sea. These are accompanied by explanatory photographs showing how the busts were built up stage by stage.[17] Besides Betty Pat Gatliff and Sharon Long, other current 'American School' practitioners include Professor Denis Lee of Ann Arbor, Michigan; the forensic anthropologist Dr Emily Craig of the Kentucky Medical Examiner's Office, Frankfort, Kentucky; the anthropological artist John Gurche of the Denver Museum of Natural History, Colorado; and Karen Taylor, forensic artist of the Texas Department of Public Safety, Austin, Texas.[18]

But although the United States is a world leader in so many fields, this particular one may be an exception, thanks principally to some arguably more advanced techniques that have been developed independently by Britain's Richard Neave, anatomical artist at the University of Manchester Medical School.[19] After spending many years at art school, Neave went on to observe dissections being performed at hospitals in London and Manchester. While this gave him the necessary grounding for his subsequent career producing medical illustrations, in the 1970s he had little knowledge of his Russian and American counterparts' work in facial reconstructions. He entered the field when the Manchester Museum Egyptologist Dr Rosalie David asked him to reconstruct the faces of two ancient Egyptian mummies from the museum's collection, the half-brothers Khnum-Nakht and Nekht-Ankh, who lived around 1900 BC. At that time Neave had only the Kollman and Büchly soft tissue thickness tables, then seventy years old, as his guide. With no proof of the method's reliability, he first tested it using four cadavers that were about to be dissected by that year's class of medical students. He arranged for the cadavers' faces to be photographed while still complete, and the photographs were then locked in a safe; he saw neither the photos nor the cadavers. After the students had reduced the bodies to skeletons, Neave collected the skulls, some incomplete because of the dissections, and reconstructed them to the best of his ability.

The reconstructions produced some striking resemblances to the subjects photographed, and Neave has since been able to follow this up with similar work on criminological cases, the results of which effectively prove his method's accuracy. For instance, when in 1983 a female skeleton was found in the grounds of Blenheim Palace, near Oxford, Neave's reconstruction enabled British police immediately to recognise her as the missing Finnish nurse Eila Karjalaimen, whose passport they had found abandoned two miles from Blenheim.

Similarly, in 1989 South Wales police asked Neave to make a reconstruction from the skull of a young woman whose badly decomposed body had been found in a

Richard Neave of the Manchester University Medical School creating a facial reconstruction from the cast of a skull, using his own specialised method. Note the pegs inserted at key points as a guide to tissue thickness, also the method used for determining the rake of the nose.

Cardiff back garden; the pathologists' estimate of her date of death was anything from five to nine years before. When Neave's clay model of her was publicised via posters and the BBC TV programme *Crimewatch*, two social workers telephoned independently to say that she closely resembled Karen Price, a teenager who had run away from a children's home and had been missing since 1981. A check of dental records confirmed this identification, and after further police work Karen's killers were caught, tried and found guilty of murder.[20]

When it is applied to ancient skulls, Neave's method, as it has now evolved, is almost invariably preceded by a forensic appraisal of the whole skeleton conducted by his Manchester Medical School colleagues, which may throw light on any deformities or injuries of special interest. He also works in close association with Dr John Prag, Keeper of Archaeology at the Manchester Museum, who advises on historical aspects. The condition of the skull may pose some logistical problems, particularly if it has been cremated, crushed, deformed or broken into pieces with portions missing. In such circumstances special methods have to be applied to overcome these difficulties.

Neave's work proper then begins, much like Gatliff's, with the making of a cast from the original skull, or its fragments. In his view it is always preferable, not least for damage limitation reasons, for a reconstruction to be built up on a cast, rather than on the original bones. If the skull is in pieces, the casts of the fragments are patiently assembled in jigsaw style, and missing portions reconstructed until a workable complete skull cast has been achieved. Although the two halves of faces are rarely if ever absolutely symmetrical, they are close enough for mirror images of missing elements to be scientifically acceptable. Holes are drilled into the cast at a series of standard key points, and pegs inserted and trimmed to the exact length stipulated by the tissue thickness statistics. In the case, for instance, of a female of Caucasian or 'white European' type, these are 3.5mm over the forehead; 4.75mm over the eyebrows; 5.5mm over the eyes; 8.5mm over the upper lip; 10mm over the lower lip; 10.5mm over the jaw and 5.75mm beneath the chin.

Thereafter the Neave method begins to differ significantly from its American counterpart, instead taking something of a cue from Gerasimov. Rather than merely overlaying the cast Gatliff-style with somewhat crude, lattice-like strips of clay, Neave carefully moulds his preferred working material, Cornish pot clay, to replicate individual facial muscles. A crucial element in his method is that he takes into account the relative strengths and positions of those points on the skull that formed the anchor for these muscles. In addition, a forensic estimate of the individual's age at death is important in determining the correct degree of elasticity that should be given to the muscles, so differentiating a youthful face from one on which a lifetime of stress has taken its toll. The order in which Neave assembles the clay muscle replicas is first the temporalis muscle on each side of the upper skull, then the masseter on the side of the cheek, then the smaller muscles. The build-up is somewhat similar to professional model ship construction, in which the model vessel will be constructed much as the original, strut by strut and plank by plank, rather than just as a solid block of wood carved into shape.

The line of the mouth, technically a sphincter muscle that contracts over an opening, is set at one third of the way up the top teeth. Much like Gatliff, Neave determines the approximate shape and size of the nose geometrically by extending the direction indicated downwards from the lower third of the nasal bone, which projects below the forehead, and outwards from the angle of the nasal spine above the upper lip, which determines the degree of uptilt of the nose. Here he follows a useful rule of thumb. If the skull has a long, narrow nasal opening the individual had a long, narrow nose, while if the opening is wide this means a wide nose, as the width of the skull's nasal opening is approximately three-fifths that of the 'fleshed' nose.

One of the last stages of Neave's method is to spread broad strips of clay over the exposed 'muscles' to simulate the outer layers of subcutaneous tissue. If a high degree of finish is required, the clay bust will be cast to make a waxwork, to which a wig, prosthetic eyes and make-up will be added. But, as is evident from a visit to Neave's studio, a clay model alone can be quite realistic enough.

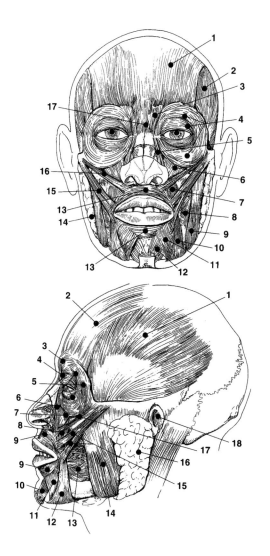

The musculature of the face, upon which Neave carefully bases his reconstruction method. Beginning with clay renditions of the temporalis (2 & 1) and masseter (9 & 14) muscles, he then adds more overlying muscles, such as the major and minor zygomaticus muscles (15 and 16 & 15 and 17), which help control facial expression.

The accuracy of Neave's reconstructions demonstrated by his criminological work gives very good reason to regard his ancient cases as similarly reliable. His ground-breaking reconstruction of Lindow Man, a victim of a Celtic human sacrifice whose body was thrown into a peat bog in Lindow Moss, Cheshire, epitomises his pain-staking methodology. Because this was an instance in which there was no direct access to the original skull – to this day it remains covered with facial tissue, and is distorted from its long immersion in peat – Neave had to recreate its original appearance step by step from X-rays before re-fleshing it with a lifelike countenance.

This was one example that he brought to a high degree of finish as a waxwork, the likeness that he achieved having all the more claim to authenticity thanks to the data still available from Lindow Man's surviving hair and tissues.

Furthermore, the know-how accompanying the Neave and related methods has advanced quite spectacularly during the last three decades. For instance, average tissue depths need no longer be obtained by the laborious and rather grisly pin and rubber method used by His, Kollman and Büchly. Ultrasound now enables much more accurate measurements to be made without breaking the skin, so that even living subjects can be used. The much greater volume of data thereby produced has led to widespread recognition that tissue depths can vary point by point between the different racial types, as well as between the genders. So for Caucasians, for Afro-Caribbean Negroids and for Mongoloid orientals[21] such as Japanese, different tables of averages have been drawn up, and the relevant one needs to be consulted once the racial type and sex of a skull has been determined. The basis of this racial differentiation according to cranial formation is expanded further on page 23.

Another advance is that, whereas Neave was obliged to use X-rays of the facial bones when he worked on Lindow Man in the late 1980s, he can now use computer tomography (CT) scans. The disadvantage of X-rays is that, like conventional photographs, they are two-dimensional, so that any structures which they show appear superimposed on top of one another, often making interpretation difficult. In CT scans, however, the rays pass through at different angles, thereby eliminating any superimposition, enabling bone and other varieties of structure to be viewed selectively and in 3-D.

Remarkably, CT scans can selectively 'see' through the bandages, cartonnage and surviving tissues of ancient Egyptian mummies that have never been unwrapped, producing high-quality three-dimensional images of the body that, because the data is in digital form, can be fed into a computer. So when the living tissue data for a modern control face of the same racial type, gender, age and bone structure are also fed into the computer and digitally 'morphed' or 'wrapped' around the CT-scanned mummy skull, an on-screen reconstruction of the ancient face can be made. No one need ever have physically touched the original skull, or gained direct access to it.

The British Museum, in collaboration with the Medical Physics Department at St Thomas's Hospital, London, and the Institute of Laryngology and Otology at University College, London, has in recent years done much pioneering work with mummies that have not been unwrapped.[22] Similar strides have been made on the other side of the Atlantic by researchers at the Biomedical Visualization Laboratory of the University of Illinois at Chicago. In collaboration with colleagues in Zurich, the Chicago specialists CT-scanned a Neanderthal child's skull of which one third was missing. Using a process called stereolithography they laser-scanned the skull and produced a 3-D model of it in plastic resin, from which they filled in the missing fragments by computer mirror-imaging.

Once a complete skull has been made by this means it can be copied digitally onto a computer, then overlaid with the image of a modern face which can be 'morphed' to conform to the requisite average tissue depths as already independently fed into the computer. If desired, a milling machine can be linked to the computer to carve a three-dimensional reconstruction of the head mechanically from a block of polystyrene, which needs only to have the finishing touches of hair, prosthetic eyes and so on added by a professional sculptor and/or make-up artist. While some of the reconstructions produced by this method do not yet have the characterful qualities of the altogether more hands-on Neave School versions, with computer technology's ever more rapid advances no doubt the results will continue to improve in this still very young field.

In fact facial reconstruction, whether it is by the Russian, American or Manchester methods, is merely one of the ever-burgeoning means now available for regenerating details of the physical appearance, characteristics, infirmities and life-styles of people from the past, even from the evidence of the bones alone. While to the layman a skeleton may seem completely inert, *Gray's Anatomy* defines its

CT scan technology being applied to the facial reconstruction of a Neanderthal skull. By using such technology an ancient face can be reconstructed virtual reality-style on a computer screen. Then if the computer is linked to a milling machine it is also possible to create a highly accurate three-dimensional replica of the skull, or of the face as reconstructed from this.

constituent bone as 'a highly vascular, living, constantly changing, mineralized connective tissue'.[23] And when it is recognised as such, its capacity to embody an impressive array of information about the individual it once carried, however long ago, can be altogether better appreciated.

Thus even if a skeleton is not complete, study of an adult skull or pelvis is usually enough to determine the individual's sex, even where no other information is known. Although individuals inevitably differ one from another, in males the mandible or jawbone tends to have a sharp angle of near 90 degrees to its rear corner, whereas in women this corner is mostly gently rounded, and with an angle of about 120 degrees. When this same bone is viewed from below, in men it tends to be squarish, while in women it is more rounded. Likewise, the large gap at the base of the hip-bone, known as the obdurator foramen, is oval in men, whereas in women it is smaller and more triangular. In general, male bones tend to be heavier and with more pronounced muscle attachments than their female equivalents.

When trying to determine age, it can be more difficult to be exact. Estimates within five years are about the closest possible, except in the case of children, in whom the degree of union of the so-called epiphyses, or points where bones grow to join each other, provides a very useful guide. Obviously, if many teeth are missing or badly worn, and there is degenerative disease evident in joints, the individual is likely to have been elderly, but the age at which these changes occur can vary from culture to culture.

Height can be calculated reliably enough from measurement of bones such as the femur. For these there exist osteometric formulae that translate the bone's length into its owner's estimated overall height, subject to certain variables such as sex and race, for which different formulae are applied.

Bones are also, of course, an indicator of race, that is, a group of peoples having a certain set of genes that give distinct physical features in common. The head forms vary according to the flatness of the face, the projection of the jaws (so-called prognathism), and the head's overall length and breadth, called the cephalic index in a living person and the cranial index in the case of a defleshed skull. If the head's maximum breadth is x and the maximum length y, then its index is:

$$\frac{x \times 100}{y}$$

A skull index of 80 or over is defined as broad or short-headed (brachycephalic), from 75 to 80 as intermediate (mesocephalic), and under 75 as long or narrow-headed (dolicephalic). Those of Mongoloid type are generally regarded as having the broadest heads, those defined as Negroids having the narrowest.

Following the discovery of DNA in the 1950s, DNA analysis of the bones of ancient human remains has been revealing a breathtaking wealth of new data, and this is likely to accelerate still further with the recent successful mapping of the entire human genetic code.[24] As is now well known, when each of us was conceived we received half of our DNA from our mother and half from the fertilising sperm of our father. From this act of union every cell of our body is programmed with a particular sequence of DNA pairs that not only determines our humanness, as distinct from other animal and plant species, but also the physical peculiarities and individualities that we have inherited from our parents, from their parents, from their parents' parents, and so on back into infinity. The really exciting advance, however, is that, because certain peculiarities are shared by large population groups, all of these traced back to a particular common ancestor in whom the peculiarity was first manifested, the background details of this inheritance are now proving far more traceable than anyone might previously have contemplated.

But the method is far from perfected. While any living person's DNA can be sampled very easily and painlessly by taking a swab from inside the cheek, getting DNA from ancient bones is more difficult. With the degradation of body proteins over time the DNA degrades similarly, the chains comprising it breaking into shorter and shorter sequences. Fifty thousand years old seems to be about the maximum limit, with cooler climatic conditions more favourable to survival. Furthermore, stringent precautions are needed to guard against modern contamination from such sources as breath or dandruff.

Nevertheless, by drilling into, say, an ancient skeletal molar in a strictly controlled laboratory environment it is often possible to obtain reliable, meaningful DNA. Of this DNA, the mitochondrial variety, which passes only through the maternal line, tends to survive better, since each cell has 500-1000 copies of it compared to only two copies (in the nucleus) of nuclear DNA. And as we will see from examples to be featured later in this book, when ancient DNA even in comparatively short sequences is compared with that of modern populations, fascinating insights can be gained into who is related to whom, and how little or how far some human populations have moved geographically over the millennia.

What is apparent is that a quite extraordinary revolution is occurring in our ability once again to 'see' people who lived thousands of years ago. Suddenly – and most unexpectedly – we can put real faces to people from the historical past. This is particularly valuable in the case of individuals from cultures that have left us no images of themselves, such as 'prehistoric' peoples, for whom we have little or no record of any kind. Fascinatingly, what is becoming clear is that, contrary to how the writers of history books even a few decades ago tended to perceive them, these peoples were rather less 'nasty and brutish' and rather more like ourselves.

I

BEFORE RECORDED HISTORY

Historical Introduction

From earliest beginnings to the age of the first farmers

The fact that our bodies lack protective hair implies that our earliest beginnings were as tropical animals, evolving in a tropical climate. By general agreement we are descendants of a species of pre-humans, *Homo habilis*, which walked upright and lived between 2.2 and 1.6 million years ago. These hominids used crude stone tools, but they seem never to have left the warmth of East and South Africa, the only locations where their all too sparse remains have been found. They were followed by *Homo erectus*, taller hominids with larger brains who definitely did venture out of Africa. Perhaps through the challenge of Ice Ages they are widely thought to have learnt to make fires, though some serious doubts have recently been expressed on this.[1] But certainly half a million years ago they were crafting pieces of stone to kill and butcher animals at locations as far afield as Boxgove, Sussex,[2] and Zhoukhoudian, China.[3] The latter location was the haunt of our face number 1.

Between 200,000 and 100,000 years ago there emerged a shorter, stockier variety, *Homo neanderthalensis*, or Neanderthal man, who roamed from Gibraltar to Uzbekistan, wherever the Ice Age ice-cap and the movements of their animal quarry allowed. Characterised by a flattish skull, receding forehead and chin and thick brow ridge, Neanderthals were rather more intelligent than their looks (as pioneeringly reconstructed by Mikhail Gerasimov) or the derogatory associations of their name suggest. They crafted stone scrapers and spears. They made purposeful arrangements of stones. They definitely made camp fires. They seem to have been musical, at least on the evidence of a flute made from a bear's thigh bone found in a cave in Slovenia in 1995.[4] Not least, they appear to have been 'cultured' enough to bury their dead with ritual. In a cave at S. Felice Circeo, Italy, a Neanderthal skull was found in a neatly arranged circle of stones. At Teskik Tash in Uzbekistan a young child was 'crowned' with five pairs of ibex horns. In another cave, at Shanidar in northern Iraq, a male corpse was strewn with flowers, the pollen evidence showing that eight different varieties were used.[5] These findings have been disputed in recent years. But, notwithstanding that particular debate, Neanderthals are now generally regarded as a dead-end offshoot of the human family tree, rather than direct ancestors of our own species. Around 31,000 BC the last of their number died out in seaside caves in Spain in circumstances that are still far from clear, though extermination by a rival species cannot be ruled out.

For in the meantime there had emerged around 100,000 BC, and again out of Africa, *Homo sapiens sapiens*, the species that we recognise as ourselves. These new-comers were characterised by longer skulls, straighter foreheads, stronger chins and markedly less heavy eyebrow ridges. They were fully modern humans, even though individual 'breeds' from them would have the height, colouring and variations in physiognomy that today characterise what we call, with greater or lesser political circumspectness, 'race'.

Giving some unexpected new viability to the biblical 'Adam and Eve' story, it seems there were initially very few individuals of *Homo sapiens sapiens* – according to one recent estimate merely some ten 'Adams' and eighteen 'Eves'.[6] Further, geneticists now doubt that they mixed their genes by sexual contact with Neanderthals. Yet from this tiny handful of early Africans – according to DNA studies by Dr Michael Hammer of the University of Arizona the Khoisan bushmen of the Kalahari are genetically the closest living human beings to them[7] – there sprang every one of the 5000-odd million of us alive today. Again, thanks to DNA patterns, geneticists can even determine the approximate dates when branches of the family split off to become a 'race', the dates coinciding reassuringly closely with independent archaeological findings.

Around 60,000 BC a group of these highly mobile people moved into Asia, particularly eastern Asia, to become ancestors of the Mongoloid peoples. As a type Mongoloids tend to be dark-eyed, stockily built, and medium to short in height. Their head hair is almost invariably black or dark brown, lank, straight and quite coarse. They have little or no facial or body hair, and their skin colour is mostly a yellowish mid-tone. Their skulls are often brachycephalic, or short, and they have fairly wide faces with prominent cheekbones and medium broad noses, the wide appearance often heightened by an excess of fatty tissue. The upper so-called epicanthic fold of the eyelid usually droops over to give the eyes the distinctive slit-like appearance, a trait otherwise absent except among the Khoisan bushmen,

Reconstruction of the camp of Khoisan bushmen of South Africa, a people regarded as genetically closest to the earliest *Homo sapiens sapiens*. Displayed in the South African Museum, Cape Town, this diorama was created from body casts of living Khoisan that were made in the early part of the last century (for further details see p.204).

neatly corroborating their ancestral status. So it is reasonable to infer that 60,000 years ago some ancestor or ancestors of the Mongoloids had much the same characteristics.

Another group spread into Europe and western Asia around 40,000 BC to become ancestors of present-day Caucasians. As a type Caucasians tend to be dolicephalic, or long-skulled, with longish noses, narrowish faces, and much wider variations of hair, eye-colouring, hair-colouring and build than among the Mongoloids. The hair varies from dark to bright red to blond, and from straight to wavy, with adults of both sexes having armpit and pubic hair and adult males substantial facial and body hair. The skin ranges from very pale to deep olive-brown. Again, it is reasonable to infer that 40,000 years ago different ancestors of modern-day Caucasians had various of these characteristics.

In the African heartland there remained the ancestors of today's Negroid peoples, with the Negroid characteristics of dark skin, dark eyes, skulls of the long variety, and hair tending to be short and curly. Although heights vary among these peoples, from the exceptionally tall Dinka to the exceptionally short pygmies, common to most is what anthropologists term prognathism, that is, the jaw jutting out from the face. Not all of this type remained in Africa: some with many of these characteristics definitely migrated eastwards, as far as south-east Asia and beyond to Australasia.

We can be virtually certain that these ancestors of ours were already talking to each other in a language or languages. This can be deduced from the 'genealogies' of the world's 10,000 or so different languages as these can be tracked back through time.[8] Certain words that are common to a great number of languages also reflect a prehistoric, hunter-gatherer life-style, no doubt arising from the messages hunters needed to exchange when co-operating to trap dauntingly large animals such as the mammoth and mastodon, then still extant.[9] The Russian prehistorian Boris Frolov has pointed out that native North American peoples, Siberian peoples and Australian aboriginal peoples all label as the 'Seven Sisters' the group of stars we know as the Pleiades. Since the aboriginals are of the Negroid type (whereas the others are Mongoloid) and moved into Australia at least 60,000 years ago this common appellation – one difficult to attribute to coincidence – must have originated before that split occurred. It also attests to very early observation of, and comment on, stellar movements in the night sky.

Homo sapiens sapiens, in a major advance over the Neanderthals, had learned the art of making projectiles, first in the form of spears, then throwing-sticks akin to the boomerang, then bows to shoot finely crafted stone-tipped arrows, such new technology dramatically reducing the number of injuries previously suffered from trying to bring down any large animal, or hostile human, at close quarters.[10] Rather more incontrovertibly than the Neanderthals, they also buried their dead with ritual, many of their burials being found covered with, or lying on, large quantities of red ochre, possibly intended as a preservative or to symbolise life-blood.

From at least as early as 40,000 years ago many of the *sapiens* groups scattered across the world were living in rock shelters and caves, hunting-lodges that gave them vantage points to observe their animal prey. These rock haunts they decorated with lively paintings depicting the animals and also, though more rarely, themselves. Australian aboriginals are notably among the earliest peoples to do this. Among the rock paintings were pictographic signs that could be said to presage the invention of writing. For shelter, some in more temperate parts built wigwam-type huts supported by poles and covered in skins. The fires that they made to keep themselves warm were carefully lined with stone, in the manner of true hearths, rather than the crude camp-fires of their predecessors. Since they crafted fine bone needles and used hooks for fishing, we may be sure that they had developed thread (and also string and rope). It is likely therefore that they were tailoring weatherproof clothing to protect themselves from the Ice Age cold, though only a few hints of their needlework skills, such as lines of ivory beads sewn on for decoration, have survived.

They were certainly making basketry, perhaps to contain food or as a lining for shelters, as is evident from impressions of woven fibre on clay recently found at a camp-site at Dolni Vestice in the Czech Republic. No boats of such antiquity have survived, but the ancestors of Australian aboriginals must have used them because Australia was separated from Asia by at least forty-three miles (68km) of deep water long before humans evolved (evident both geologically and from the fact that Asian mammals such as monkeys, tigers and elephants are not found in Australia nor Australian marsupials in Asia), and the earliest evidence for human occupation of Australia is now thought to date from around 60,000 BC.[11] Anthropologists are generally agreed that at least two culturally quite distinct groups made the crossing from Asia to Australia, one a delicate-featured tribe that settled at a very early stage around what was then Lake Mungo in the south-west corner of New South Wales, another of rather more primitive, beetle-browed appearance that settled in northern Victoria's Kow Swamp region.[12] It was from the combination of these two (from whom there developed an astonishing 500 different languages or dialects) that today's aborigines descended. It seems that some aborigines even managed to voyage all the way across the Pacific to South America, this being the startling conclusion that has recently been drawn regarding the owner of our face number 2.

We must remember that until 20,000 BC Ice Age polar glaciers extended as far south as the Alps and the Pyrenees, thereby confining human activity to the warmer zones to the south of Europe. Precisely because the ice was so widespread the world sea level was much lower than today, so there was no sea separating Britain from Europe, and Sicily was still joined to Italy. Likewise, the American continent was at that time still joined to north-east Asia by the Bering land bridge, which was still thickly covered with ice.

Around 13,000 BC, when cave painting had reached its acme in the Lascaux Caves in south-western France, a change in world weather patterns caused the ice sheets steadily to retreat, this new moister, warmer phase soon creating lush conditions. What is today the Sahara desert became the haunt of elephant, rhino, giraffe and antelope, which we know because the people of the area hunted these animals and skilfully recorded them in the Tassili rock paintings.[13] Although there was a temporary return to a cold period between 10,500 and 9400 BC (the so-called Younger Dryas or Miniature Ice-Age period), thereafter the ice retreated more or less permanently to roughly its present-day Arctic and Antarctic confines.

At this point groups of people living in north-eastern Asia spread across the Bering land bridge and into north America, pursuing the abundant grazing animals which had made similar migrations. These were the ancestors of today's native American Indians, and the bison and other animals that were available to them meant that many had little incentive to progress beyond hunter-gatherering. Such, we must infer, was the case with the young woman whom we feature as our face number 3.

Meanwhile, other peoples inhabiting western Asia north of the present Syrian and Iranian deserts embarked upon a spectacular developmental phase. As in north America, the northern ice cap's retreat had opened up vast tracts of grassland – not just any grass, but emmer and einkorn, edible varieties ancestral to our wheat. Again as in north America, this abundance of fodder attracted large herds of grazing animals, though in greater and more manageable varieties here, most notably wild asses, horses, sheep, goats, gazelles and cattle.

To the human population this must have seemed almost too easy a larder and would certainly have prompted them to think of ways of using it all to better advantage. For if a strong animal such as a wild ass or horse can run faster than you, why not capture it when young, fit it with some rope for control, and make it carry you on its back wherever you want to go? If one strain of sheep provides better meat than another, why not round them up, breed them selectively for better quality, and persuade them to trust you by regularly feeding and watering them? If one particular strain of grass grows more abundantly than another, why not try scattering its seed over ground you allot for this so that you can fatten your animals on it? And if this same grass provides good nutrition for the animals that you eat, then why not try eating it yourself, perhaps grinding up the seeds, compacting, moistening, and cooking the result to make it more palatable, thereby creating bread?

There is no existing written evidence behind these developments, because writing as such lay a few millennia in the future. But it is clear from the archaeological record that some resourceful western Asians did indeed begin domesticating cereals and animals along these lines some time around the tenth millennium BC. Other peoples, however, such as those in Britain, would stay hunter-gatherers for a few millennia longer, like our face number 4.

From correct dating of the sites at which the earliest domesticated plants occur it is possible to tell where the first organised plant cultivation began, and where it spread to. Plant DNA fingerprinting can also help: the DNA of the earliest domesticated einkorn wheat, found in the earliest farming villages, was recently found to match a wild variety still growing in Anatolia.[14] Domestication can clearly be seen to have begun in western Asia and spread across Europe. Rye and barley, broad beans, lentils and peas all followed in the wake of emmer and einkorn, with rice doing much the same across Asia. It only needed one successful experiment of a specially planted grass variety producing a useful crop for other varieties to be tried, whereupon it seems the spread was almost breathtakingly rapid.

An indication that the first domestication of animals began in Asia and spread westwards to Europe is the fact that Europe's oldest variety of domesticated sheep is descended from the Asiatic species *Ovis vignei*, native to Turkestan and Afghanistan.[15] The earliest known evidence of goat-herding is the high incidence of goat bones at Wadi Madamagh, near Petra in Jordan, a site dated to about 11,000 BC. Though no doubt wild dogs had been hanging around settlements looking for scraps for many tens of millennia, more formal domestication of these is thought to have begun around 11,000 BC, with pigs, cats and cattle following two or three millennia afterwards, and donkeys, ducks and geese later still.

With better methods of cultivating the edible grasses came the first flint hoes and sickles. The first simple houses appeared, clustering in village-like encampments. The first crude pottery vessels for containing water and other commodities were fashioned. And from the first villages there quickly evolved the first towns, complete with communal facilities, soon to be followed by the development of metal implements. Even so, some peoples would continue to live as hunter-gatherers such as our face number 5 who, although he lived about 3000 BC, provides us with our best glimpse of the equipment associated with the old hunter-gatherer life-style.

But these technologies will be considered later. For now, we should remember that however many thousands of years we are removed from prehistory, it was a period in which real people, actual ancestors of ours, dreamed up ideas, made them happen, and went on to improve upon them repeatedly. And quite revolutionary for us, thanks to the facial reconstruction experts, forensic scientists and others, is that for the first time we can give at least some of these people back their faces and 'see' them again. Although they have not left their biographies in words, their bones and their accoutrements enable us to read a remarkable amount of detail concerning the lives they led, the ailments they suffered and the misadventures that befell them.

A Butcher from Beijing
*c.*500,000 BC

Dim though our picture is of the life of *Homo erectus* some five hundred millennia ago, there is at least one activity of his that we can see with some clarity. That is his purposeful shaping of a hand-sized stone into a sharp tool by chipping off flakes to make a cutting edge. By creating this simple tool, of which many examples have been found, he was able to butcher the animals whose meat he needed as food. This enabled him to divide up manageable hunks of the meat between family or clan members.

Much changed though it is today, we are also able to see the landscape where one *Homo erectus* in particular carried out this activity, hill-caves set high on a sheer cliff at Zhoukoudian,[1] some thirty-seven miles (60km) south-west of Beijing (formerly Peking), China. Thanks to the particular version of facial reconstruction technology developed by the York Archaeological Trust, we are able to see with an astonishing clarity the very face from which he would have gazed out of those caves hundreds of millennia ago.

Immediately evident from this face-to-face encounter, in particular from the very prominent eyebrow ridges and sharply sloped-back forehead, is that he was not quite one of us, a *Homo sapiens sapiens*. But equally clearly, he was very far from being a brutish ape. As his name indicates, he stood fully upright. We have already noted that he knew how to fashion implements from stone. And although there has recently been some controversy on the matter, he probably did know how to light and control fires for the purposes of warmth, cooking and warding off animal predators.

Our hominid and his fellows definitely lived in communities, of which there was a particularly sizeable and long-established one at Zhoukoudian in the form of a complex of hill-caves at different levels. From this vantage point, the prehistoric equivalent of a hunting lodge, the colony could survey the north China plains, then abounding in sika deer, horses, elephant, bison and rhinoceros. Although today the Zhoukoudian region has very hot summers and very cold winters, five hundred millennia ago it is thought that both seasons were a little warmer, with predators

Humankind's longest-lived invention - the so-called 'Acheulian' flint hand-axe. For hundreds of thousands of years, from *Homo erectus* to the development of *Homo sapiens sapiens*, the design of these cutting tools remained surprisingly uniform, suggesting a skill that was carefully handed down from generation to generation.

such as bears, leopards and sabre-toothed tigers inhabiting its nearby forests, and cheetah and hyena roaming its plains.

We know that the deer, sheep, horses, pigs and cattle which also roved the plains were staple fare for *Homo erectus* because the bones of these creatures have been found in abundance among the settlement debris. From the finds of what were said to be huge accumulations of burnt bones and stones, ash and charcoal at every level of Zhoukoudian's human occupation, the evidence for their use of fire for warmth and cooking has also long seemed overwhelming, until quite recently when a team from the Weizmann Institute for Science, Rehovot, Israel, took a series of 'hearth' samples from the site. On finding a lack of the unique chemical signatures that they expected from fires, the Israeli scientists concluded that the 'ash' was not ash at all, but simply accumulated organic debris.[2] This team seems, however, to represent those who view archaeological evidence from an almost impossibly 'minimalist' perspective, and since evidence of fire has been claimed at other *erectus* sites elsewhere in the world their findings are as yet far from being fully conclusive.

Although our hominid's skull was found in China, it was in fact in Java that the first *erectus* discovery was made more than a hundred years ago by a Dutchman, Eugene Dubois. Inspired by Darwin's theory of evolution, Dubois gave up his teaching job at the University of Amsterdam and took his family to Indonesia (then the East Indies) specifically in the hope of finding a 'missing link' between apes and modern man. Four years later, in the autumn of 1891, he believed this ambition achieved when, from gravels at Trinil on central Java's slow-flowing Solo river, he unearthed a cranium of impressive size but clearly not *Homo sapiens sapiens,* followed shortly after by a remarkably complete and modern-looking thigh bone. From these bones Dubois correctly deduced that their owner had walked fully upright, as a result of which he labelled the find *Pithecanthropus erectus,* or 'upright ape-man'. But when he returned to Europe his findings, which were not associated with any stone tools (possibly because the Javan *Homo erectus* used long-perished bamboo implements), were for many years ridiculed by the scientific establishment.[3]

From 1921 onwards further discoveries of *erectus* remains, vindicating Dubois's findings, were made at Zhoukoudian by the Canadian anatomist Davidson Black,

700,000 BC – *Homo erectus* begins moving out of Africa

500,000 BC – 'Beijing' *Homo erectus* lived near Zhoukoudian, China

700,000 BC   600,000 BC   500,000 BC   400,000 B

head of the department of anatomy at the Peking Union Medical College ('Peking' was the accepted transliteration at this time). Between 1927 and 1937 Black, and on his death in 1933 his successor, the German anatomist Franz Weidenrich, found crania, fragments of skulls, jawbones and other bones, representative of about forty individuals. The skulls of seven were in something approaching a state of completeness, and one of them, our subject, became 'Peking man'. And they were of the same *erectus* type that Dubois had first identified in Java.

By 1940, such was the recognition of their importance that at the outset of war between China and Japan arrangements were made for the Zhoukoudian bones to be shipped to the United States for safety. But although they were packed in boxes and loaded on a train bound for the port of Quinhuangdao, where the US steamship *President Harrison* awaited them, somehow or other they never made it to the ship.[4]

Fortunately much of the seriousness of this loss was mitigated by the fact that Weidenrich had made good casts from the originals. And it was from Weidenrich's cast and his convincing reconstruction of its missing portions that in 1994 the York Archaeological Trust embarked upon the first truly authoritative facial reconstruction of 'Peking man', a work that was sponsored by German television.

First the skull was scanned by a laser and its contours relayed to a computer via a video camera. Then the face of a young volunteer Chinese who lived in York was scanned into the computer and 'morphed' or graphically stretched to assume the same contours as those of the skull with the tissue thickness points added. Via the computer and a milling machine the lifelike face thereby built up was translated on to a piece of hard polystyrene foam, giving it three-dimensional form. The professional sculptor Lynn O'Dowd then recast this head to make it fully lifelike, realistically colouring it and fitting it with artificial eyes and other finishing touches.

The result is remarkable. Unless hair samples survive with the skull (unheard of in the case of 500,000-year-old crania), the colour and other characteristics of any head or facial hair cannot be known, though future refinements of DNA analysis may well make this possible. So O'Dowd omitted any hair from her reconstruction. But particularly striking, and undoubtedly true to our hominid as he would have looked in life, is the back-sloping forehead arising from very prominent brow ridges. The

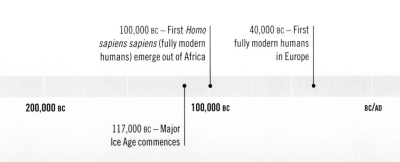

100,000 BC – First *Homo sapiens sapiens* (fully modern humans) emerge out of Africa

40,000 BC – First fully modern humans in Europe

| 300,000 BC | 200,000 BC | 100,000 BC | BC/AD |

117,000 BC – Major Ice Age commences

main reason for this sloped forehead and for the equally evident low vault to the cranium is that the *erectus* species in general had significantly smaller brains than our own – about 70% of our capacity. Probably linked to this is the fact that our hominid's face was not as vertically oriented as ours, and his teeth were much larger.

A more conjectural feature of the reconstruction – directly arising from the fact that a young Chinese was used as its facial 'template' – is the feature of eyelids with the classic epicanthic fold, the genetically characteristic fold of skin that partially or completely covers the eyelids in Mongoloid peoples such as the Chinese and Japanese. From the evidence of the skull alone it is impossible to be sure whether the Asiatic *erectus* already had this characteristic 500,000 years ago, or whether it originated following the emergence of a particular branch of *Homo sapiens sapiens* out of Africa more than 400,000 years later. If the original skull or a suitable replacement were to become available, sooner or later advances in DNA studies might enable this to be determined, but for the present the matter is debatable.

Zhoukoudian, near Beijing, China, where 500,000 years ago a community of *Homo erectus* preyed on the region's then abundant wildlife. This wildlife included deer, bison, elephant and rhinoceros.

One striking curiosity of the Zhoukoudian *erectus* remains is that some twenty fragments of quartz crystal have been found in their vicinity, with others coming to light at similar *erectus* sites in Israel and Austria.[5] Quartz crystals have also been found in much more recent fully human burials, where they are undoubtedly associated with shamanistic and other religious beliefs. So there is at least a hint that our hominid had some kind of religious awareness even at this very early stage – although a more prosaic explanation is that he simply had a magpie-like enthusiasm for collecting bright objects.

Another oddity, which in this instance pertains particularly to the crania found at Zhoukoudian, is that all had lost the underneath surface of the brain case through which the spinal cord passes, a finding which has provoked a variety of speculations. For some the explanation is that this part of the cranium is the most delicate and easily broken. Others have suggested it may be evidence of cannibalism, though anyone seriously minded to eat a fellow creature's brains would surely not have shied from the altogether easier method of smashing the skull right open. Another school of thought, noting the care and deliberation with which the openings were made, has theorised that some religious rite may have been involved, perhaps with the intention of releasing the soul. But yet another prosaic suggestion is that the skulls may simply have been gnawed by scavenging hyenas and rodents.

Following the Second World War more examples of *erectus* were found in Africa, including the unusually complete skeleton of a twelve-year-old boy who lived a million years before our hominid and who was found at Lake Turkana in northern Kenya. From this particular skeleton's completeness the boy's height could be reliably calculated at five feet six inches (1.68m), suggesting that as in the case of our own *Homo sapiens sapiens* it was perfectly possible for *Homo erectus* to reach six feet (1.82m) in height.

Rather less clear is whether *erectus* could talk. Certainly the relative proportions of the tongue and larynx, as deduced from the skulls, indicate that they were capable of a limited range of sounds, similar to those of a modern baby, and therefore that they may have been able to communicate.

Further suggesting this are the surprisingly refined specifications for the making of hand-axes, technically described as Acheulian after the St-Acheul site in France where they were first identified. However crude these stone tools may seem to us, it is important to bear in mind that they were patiently made by generation after generation of *erectus* throughout the period from 1.5 million years to 150,000 years ago. During that time the minds behind the technology gradually improved it, from merely fashioning a single tool from a piece of flint, to hammering with a stone on to a bone or wood punch in order to flake off a series of correctly-shaped blades from an original stone core. These blank blades were then 'pressure-flaked', or refined and sharpened, by chipping off tiny flakes along their edges with a piece of bone or hardwood, first on one side, then on the other. The earliest known purposeful 'serration', this was a giant step towards the precision working that would characterise our own *Homo sapiens sapiens*. So how were these skills passed down from one generation to another if not by some kind of language? Whatever the answer, *Homo erectus* hand-axes represent at the very least the longest-lived technology that the world has ever seen or is likely to see.

Of many matters, such as whether *erectus* wore any kind of clothing, no information survives, though most probably the species went naked. With regard to issues such as diseases from which our Beijing hominid might have suffered, one of the great obstacles to learning more such details is the loss of the original bones. Another is the fact that the Zhoukoudian site, from which it ought to be possible to obtain other fresh samples, is in China. As is not uncommonly the case in Chinese archaeology, three-quarters of it has never been explored. The United Nations organisation UNESCO regards further investigation as a must, not only for China 'but also for the rest of humanity',[6] and already a French team has taken a series of electromagnetic and microgravimetric measurements from which it pinpoints five zones it reckons are ripe for excavation. Chinese officialdom, however, accords the plan a rather lower priority, so Beijing's *Homo erectus* is likely to retain many of his mysteries a while longer.

'Acheulian' hand-axe, clearly exhibiting the pressure-flaking that *Homo erectus* used to fashion it into an efficient cutting tool.

2

AN 'ABORIGINAL' IN BRAZIL
*c.*9500 BC

Modern-day anthropologists classify her as 'Hominid I of Lapa Vermelha IV', but she has rather less formally been dubbed 'Luzia'.[1] She roamed what is today the Lagoa Santa region of central Brazil, notable for a complex of once well-frequented prehistoric caves, shelters and underground water systems, and she died at what modern values would regard as a young age, between twenty and twenty-five. When her bones were found in the mid-1970s, radiocarbon dating of charcoal from the archaeological level, and of carbon from acid washes of her bones, dated her as having lived at least as far back as 9500 BC. This makes her the oldest known individual to have been found anywhere in the Americas.

Another distinctive aspect of her, evident from the fine facial reconstruction recently made by Richard Neave, is that she had facial features, such as projecting eyebrow ridges and a pronounced jaw, of an unmistakably African or Australian aboriginal cast. These characteristics have aroused a hornet's nest of problems for archaeologists and anthropologists that are as yet far from resolved.

For, throughout the greater part of the twentieth century, the perceived scientific wisdom has been that South and North America were the last continents to be discovered and settled by humans, and that their huge landmasses remained empty of any such habitation until after the end of the last Ice Age. Climatologists are certain that a vast cloak of ice blanketed Canada and the northern USA, blocking animal and human migration alike, and that it was only when enough of this had melted by about 10,000 BC that mammoth, mastodon, bison and deer from Siberia began to stream into North America across the Bering land bridge (since broken by the Bering strait), rapidly followed by Siberian/Mongoloid hunters whose food supply they represented.

Consistent with this model, the oldest spear-points found in north America, dubbed as belonging to the 'Clovis' culture, appear at archaeological levels dated around 9000 BC, before which the evidence for any earlier occupation of the sites

Dating between 10,000 and 8000 BC, Australian aboriginal hand paintings from Australia's Murtawintji National Park, New South Wales. Strikingly similar hand paintings, and of similar antiquity, have been found in rock shelters in Brazil, South America.

has seemed non-existent. Ably crafted in stone, the spear-points in question were clearly designed for bringing down even the largest of animals, such as the mammoth. And they are found chiefly in the Middle West, just south of the former icecap line, suggesting that those who fashioned them first settled in these areas.

Likewise, every living native American – whether North American, South American Amazonian 'Indian', or a descendant of the Mayan and Inca peoples – can be seen facially to bear the classic traits termed 'Mongoloid', namely broad, flat faces, lank, black hair and the epicanthic fold to the eyes absent in Europeans. Since these traits are shared with the peoples of Siberia and Mongolia, the general understanding has long been that it was from these north Asian regions that every native American's ancestors originated.

A canyon in the Serra de Capivara National Park, Piaui, Brazil. Some archaeological findings suggest that this and certain other South American sites were inhabited as far back as 50,000 years ago, long before the arrival of the Mongoloid peoples who were the ancestors of today's so-called indigenous Americans.

But if that is the case, how is it that the Americas' very oldest known human remains, Luzia's, have been found so very far to the south, in *South* America? Further, as has been pointed out by the Brazilian anthropologist Walter Neves[2] and his US counterpart Joseph Powell, how is it that the cranium should be of a type that is positively not Mongoloid, but instead more typical of Africans and Australian aboriginals?

It is a problem that has been rumbling among anthropologists and archaeologists for quite a long time. For although Luzia's bones happen to be those of the oldest-known humanoid so far found either in North or South America, French and Brazilian archaeologists working since the 1970s in the same part of north-eastern Brazil have found significant signs of human settlement – for instance, stones with flaked edges, used as tools, and charcoal from open fires – that they have dated as far back as 48,000 BC, that is, well prior to the onset of the last Ice Age.[3] Since 1978 the leading protagonist of these findings has been the Brazilian archaeologist Niède Guidon, who initially disbelieved the radiocarbon dating results. But after her exploration of some 350 sites in the Pedro Furada region, and the evidence found for similarly early dates of human occupation at other sites in South America, she

60,000 BC – First modern humans in Australia

60,000 BC   50,000 BC   40,000 BC

confidently refutes sceptical English-speaking anthropologists[4] who maintain that South and North America were uninhabited pre-Clovis. And Richard Neave's reconstruction of Luzia's skull as 'aboriginal' has now added one further reason for taking Guidon seriously.

There can be little doubt that people related to Luzia, rather than to any later Mongoloid incomers, were responsible for the lively prehistoric rock paintings to be found widespread across the region where Luzia lived, particularly in the São Raimundo Nonato region of Brazil's Piauí state.[5] From these paintings, mostly executed beneath the overhang of vast rock shelters, all the signs are that Luzia and her kindred were a primitive but peaceable people. They portrayed themselves living totally naked amid fauna that included the long-extinct giant sloth, the giant armadillo, deer, jaguar, rhea and much else. Although it is quite evident that Luzia's menfolk hunted many of these creatures, in some instances to extinction, the only evidence of any inter-human violence is to be seen in the very youngest of the rock paintings, probably dateable to around 8000 BC. In these the indigenous people can be seen being ruthlessly clubbed to death by aggressive newcomers. In all logic these latter can hardly have been other than the incoming Mongoloids ruthlessly exterminating the fellow-humans – Luzia's kindred – whom they found already occupying this new land. But the really big questions are: where could Luzia's people have come from, and when, given that they preceded the Mongoloids to Brazil?

As we have earlier noted, our *Homo sapiens sapiens* species is thought to have emerged first in Africa around 100,000 years ago, spreading to the Near East, to Europe and eventually to Australia, which it had quite definitely reached some 60,000 years ago. And as we know,[6] this crossing by ancestral 'aborigines' from southern Asia to Australia can only have been achieved by boat.

In support of this, the Tiwi aboriginals still living on Bathurst and neighbouring islands off Australia's Northern Territory bear a striking affinity to Luzia's facial features as reconstructed by Neave. They are notable, even amongst aborigines, for having lived by boats and sea fishing for as far back as anyone can remember. Furthermore, the oldest painting of a boat known from anywhere in the world, dated back to 40,000 BC, happens to be a rock painting in the remote Kimberly region of northern Australia, an area, just like Luzia's Brazil, with many rock paintings

10,000 BC – Mammoth, bison, etc migrate from Siberia into North America, followed by Mongoloid hunters

9,500 BC – 'Luzia' lives as a hunter-gatherer in Brazil

30,000 BC	20,000 BC	10,000 BC	BC/AD

13,000 BC – in Europe, era of Lascaux cave paintings. Major Ice Age begins to weaken

8000 BC – In Anatolia and Israel, the earliest known town settlements

6000 BC – The earliest known pottery in the Near East

created by its earliest human settlers.[7] As has been pointed out by the Australian rock art specialist Grahame Walsh, even though the Kimberly painting was found far from the coast the boat in it can be seen to have been depicted with a high prow and stern, suggesting that it was designed for ocean-going use. So is it possible that forebears of Luzia's ventured not only across the Timor Strait to Australia, but also made their way right across the Pacific to South America, and gradually eastwards to Brazil?

Whatever the answer, it would of course be folly in the extreme to rest any argument for the earliest settlement of the Americas by peoples of South Pacific (and ultimately African) origin solely on the anthropological evidence of Luzia's skull, or on the striking Afro-aboriginal facial reconstruction that Richard Neave has made from this. Quite undeniable, however, is that one example after another is now coming to light which shows that post-Ice Age America already had a resident non-Mongoloid population before it received its 'Clovis' Mongoloid influx. The so-called Kennewick Man whose bones were found in the Columbia River in 1996, with the remains of an arrowhead in his pelvis, is another example around whom controversy continues to rage.[8]

Yet, ruthlessly genocidal though the incoming Mongoloid 'Indians' would appear to have been towards the incumbent 'aboriginals', it seems unlikely that they could have exterminated the entire population. Some must have fled. This raises the question of whether somewhere in South America at least a few 'aboriginal' tribes might have managed to live on for centuries, perhaps even millennia?

The Brazilian anthropologist Walter Neves and his colleagues have indeed formulated a theory of how and where these first non-Mongoloid inhabitants of America continued to survive.[9] At the point of South America's southernmost extremity, the desolate and chilly Tierra del Fuego, there survived until the early part of the twentieth century a people of a type different from, and more primitive than, the more northerly 'Indians'. Mixed marriages with both 'Indians' and Europeans have probably since wiped them out completely, but when Charles Darwin visited Tierra del Fuego in 1834 during the voyage of the *Beagle* he was astonished to find some of the native Fuegian inhabitants living totally naked, just like pre-colonial aborigines in Australia. And this was despite conditions of extreme cold. In his words:

> The astonishment which I felt on seeing a party of Fuegians on a wild and broken shore will never be forgotten by me, for the reflection at once rushed into my mind – such were our ancestors. These men were absolutely naked and bedaubed with paint… and their expression… wild, startled and distrustful.[10]

When a young mother with a suckling child came alongside the *Beagle* in a canoe, Darwin noted with awed horror how she 'remained there out of mere curiosity, while

Reconstruction of Luzia's facial features, as created by Richard Neave from a cast of her 11,500-year-old skull found in central Brazil. To anthropologists' surprise, Luzia lacked the Mongoloid traits normally found among native American peoples, and instead more closely resembled certain sea-going tribes of Australian aborigines. How she would have styled her hair is unkown, so the reconstruction does not include this.

the sleet fell and thawed on her naked bosom, and on the skin of her naked baby'. Although the evidence remains controversial, Neves' studies of the skulls of Fuegians and Patagonians, preserved from earlier centuries, have strongly indicated that at least some were, like Luzia, anthropologically linked to peoples of Africa and Australia, and were positively not near-kindred of the Mongoloids of northern Asia.

So if Luzia's ancestors were of African/aboriginal origin and her descendants the people of Tierra del Fuego, what sort of life would she have lived? Because of the fragile and controversial nature of the evidence much has to be guessed at, but certainly, just like Darwin's Fuegians, it would have been extremely primitive. Any kind of crop cultivation would have been unknown and – if the more modern-day sentiments of traditional Australian aboriginals are any guide – positively alien to the culture. From stone scrapers that have been found, together with other stone flakes that may have been used as spear-points, it is evident that animals were hunted, and their meat prepared for human consumption. But although the art of making fire was known, hence the hearths that have consistently been found at the most ancient Brazilian sites, there is no evidence for the wearing of any clothes, since no needle, that most vital tool for the making of any garment, has been found.

Yet, as attested by the lively contemporaneous Pedro Furada rock paintings, 'primitive' is a relative term. The climate of Brazil would have been very much more agreeable than that further south in Tierra del Fuego. From the exuberant scenes of hunting, sex and religious ceremonial that predominate in the rock paintings, Luzia's life would have been very far from lacking in joys and excitement. Since some of the paintings show elaborate ceremonial head-dresses being worn, these would have had to be carefully prepared, and no doubt bodies painted or otherwise decorated. We need have little doubt that Luzia and her people had language (Darwin noted that the Fuegians spoke with hoarse, guttural clicking sounds, as if clearing the throat, very reminiscent of the Khoisan bushmen of Africa).[11] And the ceremonies to be seen in the paintings would probably have been accompanied by songs and chants. Overall, Luzia's life would have been much like that of Australian aboriginals right up to and beyond the time of white settlement. And as learned by not a few of those early white settlers who took the trouble to study it, in certain respects this life could be richer and more fulfilling than their own.

In facing Luzia, as so superbly facilitated by the magnificent reconstruction work of Richard Neave, are we seeing one of our fellow humans at an 'Adam and Eve' stage of our development? It would indeed seem so. But it would also seem that for her subsequent kindred life was to be as ill-fated as for their mythical biblical counterparts. For what would most certainly not be the last time in the human history of the Americas, any paradise that they may have enjoyed was about to be very painfully lost.

THE OLDEST TEXAN
*c.*8000 BC

When a team of archaeologists working with the Texas Department of Transportation excavated her bones in 1983, they nicknamed her 'Leanne', because they found her near Leander. The exact location was at Brushy Creek, twenty miles (32km) north of Austin, Texas, just off the route of a farm road extension that the Department planned to build. She lay ten feet (3m) below the present-day soil level, and as radiocarbon dating revealed, she had died some time between 7800 and 8000 BC, which put hers among the very oldest human bones ever found in North America.

That someone had once cared for her and mourned her passing there can be no doubt. Whoever buried her laid her out purposefully so that she lay on her right side, her knees drawn up in the classic foetal position, with her head resting on her right hand, the left beneath, as if she were asleep. Also in the grave were a rodent's bones, thought to have been provided as her last meal, together with a shark's tooth, a grinding stone and traces of a bison. Nearby were the remains of a Palaeoindian campsite that was probably where she had lived. The Texas anthropologists who studied her skull determined that she had died at around twenty-eight years of age, and they gave her the label 'Wilson-Leonard II female' after the Marjorie Ashcroft Wilson Archaeological Preserve at which hers was the second burial to be found.[1]

They then commissioned a facial reconstruction from the American specialist Professor Denis Lee, then head of the School of Art and Design at the University of Michigan, and a student of the Gatliff method. From Lee's fine work, we can see that Leanne bore significantly less 'African' and a great deal more 'American Indian' features than her predecessor Luzia. Along with the proximity of the Palaeoindian campsite, this leaves little doubt that she belonged wholly or partly to the incomers of Mongoloid origin who had followed the animal herds across the Bering land bridge. And once we can give Leanne such a 'Clovis'-type Palaeoindian label, then we can begin to see the many ways in which her lifestyle would have differed from Luzia's.

For instance, that the Clovis people were significantly more proficient as hunters than their 'aboriginal' predecessors is evident from the crafting of their spear-heads.

Larder for the earliest human arrivals in North America? American bison, among the several varieties of large grazing animal that 'Leanne' and her kind would have preyed upon. To bring down such large and potentially fearsome animals with mere stone weapons would have needed courage and substantial concerted effort.

Whereas the flint flakes associated with the pre-Clovis aboriginals are so nondescript that any human shaping of them remains open to dispute, the Clovis spear-points, fluted and double-sided, are utterly distinctive works of the art of stone-shaping. An American enthusiast, Bruce Bradley, has made convincing reconstructions of just how expertly such blades would have been shaped with a pressure flaker, mounted on wooden shafts and secured with string. Among the technological advances was careful channelling of the base of the blade so that it could be more securely fastened to its wooden shaft. This is thought to have been an invention exclusive to the American continent, since so far equivalents from this same period have not been found elsewhere.

Such was the Clovis spear's sophistication that it was undoubtedly lethal enough to bring down a mammoth or mastodon, as proven by the finding of Clovis points in association with such bones. Skill in flaking the blades, sometimes made from obsidian, gave them an edge sometimes keener than that of a modern-day steel scalpel. And this cutting edge could be put to a variety of uses besides tipping spears.

In this context our mention of the binding of the blade with string is not to be overlooked, for to Leanne's Clovis people this too represents a technological

Reconstruction of how a spear-point of the characteristic Clovis type was string-bound to a wooden shaft to create a very serviceable spear. The base of each spear-point was carefully grooved to accomodate either splints, or cleverly carpentered ends to the spear shaft, that helped hold the spear-point in place.

| 13,000 BC – Major Ice Age begins to weaken | 10,000 BC – Mammoth, bison, etc migrate from Siberia into North America, followed by Mongoloid hunters | 8000 BC – 'Leanne' lives as a hunter-gatherer in Texas |

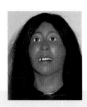

12,000 BC   **10,000 BC**   **8000 BC**

achievement just as important as their proficiency in working with flint, if not more so. Directly contemporary with Leanne bone needles have been found, one such example found in south-eastern Washington state, complete with neat eyehole,[2] again standing the closest comparison with any modern stainless steel version. From central European archaeology it is known that plant fibre products such as cordage, basketry, netting and even textiles were being produced some 25,000 years ago. So if Palaeoindian peoples of North America were working with needles it must mean that they too were already producing plaited fibres of various kinds to use in those needles, having presumably brought the necessary technological know-how with them when they crossed the Bering land bridge. Although the biodegradable nature of such material means that little has survived, there is still enough to show that among Leanne's contemporaries and near-contemporaries fibre artefacts were some twenty times as common as those made from stone.[3]

In New York state, for instance, the discovery at a Clovis-period site of an impression of a carefully made, diagonally twined fabric is one of a variety of indications that Leanne and her contemporaries wore clothes. In both California and Missouri archaeologists have found Clovis-period sandals, those in Missouri, in particular, showing just how intricate working in fibre had become by this time. As present-day Polynesians are happy to demonstrate, there are hundreds of artefacts, from house walls to food-dishes, hats or skirts, that can be made from weaving even the crudest fibres of the coconut palm. So there is no reason to believe that Leanne and her contemporaries were any less versatile working with the varieties of plant fibre at their disposal in what is today Texas.

There are some indications that Leanne may have dressed much more stylishly than is normally imagined even in Hollywood films such as *One Million Years BC* with its fur bikinis. Recent studies of prehistoric fashions made by the University of Illinois anthropology professor Olga Soffer have shown that as far back as 23,000 BC the prehistoric woman's wardrobe had developed considerably beyond the smelly animal hides of popular imagination. Before becoming an academic Soffer spent ten years in the fashion business. When she made detailed studies of the so-called 'Venus' figurines widely prevalent in prehistoric Europe, she found that although the statuettes often appeared naked, in actuality they indicated, sometimes in fine detail,

3000 BC – Beginnings of agriculture in Central America

6000 BC

4000 BC

2000 BC

1500 BC – First pottery appears in Central America

the wearing of clothing, jewellery and body art. In France in 23,000 BC fine string skirts were the height of fashion, while in the area of the Czech Republic the first known 'boob tubes' were being flaunted. So while the evidence for the earliest American equivalents in clothing is sketchy, to say the least, it favours a significant departure from Luzia's probable total nudity.

From the wealth of archaeological work that has been done on the Wilson-Leonard and other very early North American sites, it is also possible to glimpse other aspects of Leanne's everyday life. The mostly flat Texas landscape lacks any of the natural rock-shelters favoured by Luzia's people in South America. Instead the terrain's undoubted attraction, then as now, was its vast grasslands, providing an abundance of pasture for big grazing animals such as the mammoth, the mastodon, and the prehistoric horse and bison, and thereby a ready larder for any human group cunning enough to have developed the skills to bring such large animals down.

In addition, we know that Leanne would have enjoyed the comforts and uses of fire, since hearths are found at even the earliest Palaeoindian camp-sites, together with heaps of bones from the grazing animals that were butchered, cooked and eaten in the vicinity. The fact that Leanne's generation of Palaeoindians saw the total disappearance of the mammoth, mastodon, Pleistocene bison and horse, camel and sloth from North America says something about their skills as hunters, even if it says little about their common sense as food source conservators. Possibly the first instance of man causing a serious ecological upset, it would certainly not be the last.

Leanne no doubt drank fresh river water. As the Brushy Creek name implies, her camp was situated, like places of similar Palaeoindian settlement, close to a good water supply; the Colorado river was also nearby. We can be sure that she used no pottery, since this commodity had not been invented either in the Old or the New World in her time.[4] So we must guess that animal skins would have served when food and beverage containers were needed.

When in 1992 the US Congress passed the Native American Graves Protection and Repatriation Act, whereby any Native American remains sooner or later have to be 'repatriated' to their appropriate tribe, a high-quality cast of Leanne's skull had to be made so that it at least could be studied when the original became no longer accessible. With this in mind, in 1994 discussions took place between the Texas A & M University physical anthropologist Dr D. Gentry Steele and representatives of the Dow Corning Corporation, a Michigan company specialising in mould-making materials for medical and other scientific purposes. The following year Dow Corning specialists cast the skull and jawbone in silicone as negative moulds, then made positive moulds from these.

When it was found, Leanne's skull had been crushed to one third of its original size under the weight of overlying sediments and the cast replicated this. So Steele called

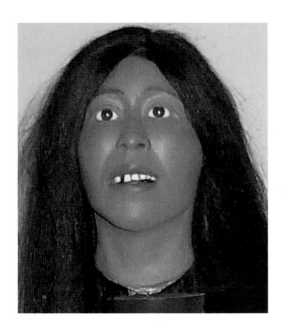

Reconstruction of Leanne's facial features, as created by Denis Lee from a cast of her 10,000-year-old skull found near Austin, Texas. There is some uncertainty whether even she fully corresponds to the Mongoloid type that subsequently became characteristic among native American peoples.

in the Oklahoma-based doyenne of 'American method' facial reconstructions, Betty Pat Gatliff. With the aid of a small rotary cutting tool used in dentistry, Gatliff carefully cut the cast into pieces, then fitted them together again to accord with her and Steele's estimates, derived from other early examples found in better condition, of the size that the skull had been in its original state. From this 'restored' skull Gatliff then made a preliminary reconstruction, soon followed by a second version created, again in association with Steele, by Professor Denis Lee, an ex-pupil of Gatliff's. It is Professor Lee's reconstruction that is featured here.

Professor Lee very kindly showed and explained an excellent copy of this reconstruction to me, which shows that Leanne had a relatively small face, with what anthropologists call 'a distinctive alveolar prognathism', in other words a rather prominent jaw. Curiously, this is a trait that is more common in Caucasians and Negroids than among Mongoloids, raising the question of whether Leanne had at least some genes of a pre-'Indian' population that had early on existed in North and South America, and with whom Clovis immigrants initially intermarried. Certainly the physiognomical differences between other early examples and the present-day Native American suggest this, which again raises questions concerning the origins of America's very first inhabitants that are now beginning to be taken seriously in a way that only a few years ago would have been considered unthinkable.

This is an issue which ultimately can only be resolved by DNA analysis, meaning that a fresh examination of the original bones is necessary. Thanks to the Native American Graves Protection and Repatriation Act, in many instances, not least the controversial Kennewick Man, this can now only be achieved with Native American co-operation and goodwill, something that is very far from assured. So the extent to which a full scientific study will ever be allowed is an open question.

Through Leanne, North America's prehistory has been dramatically re-fleshed. We find ourselves looking backwards in time to some of the very earliest human beings ever to have known the North American continent. But what of those living on the other side of the Atlantic, in Europe immediately after the Ice Age, in particular in what we now know as Britain?

4

CHEDDAR CAVEMAN
c.7150 BC

When, in December 1903, workmen came across his bones, there seemed little to be said of them other than that they belonged to an 'ancient Briton'. His skeleton came to light twenty yards inside Gough's Cave, part of the Cheddar Gorge and Cheddar Caves, during rock-blasting to create a better drainage system. After a local museum curator pronounced him 'a cave-dweller who lived between the Palaeolithic and Neolithic Ages', the Caves' entrepreneur owner, Richard Gough, lost little time in putting him on display in a glass case at the entrance.

Billed as 'Cheddar Man', there he stayed until 1980, when he was moved to the Natural History Museum in London. In 1998 it was decided that he should be examined by a team of Manchester University pathologists led by Robert Stoddart, to be followed up with a facial reconstruction by Richard Neave's Unit of Art in Medicine. A cast made of his fragmented skull was most conscientiously 're-faced' by Neave's departmental colleague Denise Smith, whereupon a set of features from 4000 years before Stonehenge gazed out upon a world that their original owner would have found far stranger than he could possibly have dreamt.[1]

Although Stoddart commented of those features that they resemble 'any modern inhabitant of a Somerset pub', the most reliable estimate of when Cheddar Man lived is around 7150 BC. Because of that dating, it is likely that he and his kind were hunter-gatherers, just like 'Luzia' and 'Leanne' before them, since early farming methods, though emerging further to the east, are not thought to have begun as yet in the English West Country.

In Cheddar Man's time the world's oceans had not yet risen to their modern-day levels, and Britain was not separated from the European continent. The topography around the Cheddar Gorge differed from that of the present day, both in its coastline and in its flora and fauna. After much of England had lain bleak and treeless throughout the Ice Age, global warming had brought heavy afforestation of birch, pine and hazel, which attracted large populations of deer, wild boar, wolves and bears. Cheddar Man and his companions would have pursued these creatures, armed

Human footprints of a family who lived c.5000 BC, preserved by freak circumstances on the shore of the Severn estuary near Newport, Wales. Cheddar Man roamed the other side of the Severn estuary some two millennia earlier.

with the now widely developed bow and flint-tipped arrows, his bow probably resembling a magnificent elm specimen from his time found in a Danish peat bog at Hölmgaard.

The Severn river, to the west, teemed with fish, including salmon and eel, and there is good reason to believe that our man and his fellows preyed on these as well. During the 1920s, in the Avelline Hole cave system not far from Cheddar, there were found a series of near-contemporary burials, and among the items accompanying the dead was a three-barbed harpoon made from a stag's antler. Still used by fishermen on the Severn to this day are elongated willow fish-traps called 'putcheons'. Similar examples have been found in Danish peat bogs that date back at least 6000 years, and therefore in all likelihood back to Cheddar Man's time also.

Common among the Avelline Hole burial finds were necklaces made of shells, probably gathered from the Severn's banks during fishing expeditions. The most direct evidence of this practice comes from sets of ancient footprints that came to light during an exceptionally low tide in 1986 on mud-flats near Newport, South Wales, only a little way up the Severn from the Cheddar Gorge. As

determined by Stephen Aldhouse-Green, now at the University of Wales College, Newport, these prints, of which there are more than a hundred, date back to about 7000 years ago, and were created by a whole family wandering barefoot on the mud-flats.[2] Their foot sizes range from those of small children to an adult male who, if he

13,000 BC – in Europe, era of
Lascaux cave paintings. Major
Ice Age begins to weaken

10,000 BC – Development of the bow and arrow.
Mammoth disappears from most of Europe. In
western Asia the earliest-known farming

13,000 BC   12,000 BC   11,000 BC   10,000 BC   9000 BC

lived in present-day Britain, would have taken an impressive size 12, normally worn by at least a six-footer. The Severn estuary's teeming bird population would probably have represented an additional food source for Cheddar Man and his family.

Cheddar Man was probably around five feet four inches (1.62m) tall.[3] No evidence survives for how he might have dressed his hair, so Denise Smith made two versions of him, one beardless, to convey his facial features with maximum clarity, the other bearded, his more probable day-by-day appearance.

As a hunter-gatherer, Cheddar Man lived a few millennia too early to enjoy bread. Europe's earliest known bread, two seriously overbaked lumps recently found only sixty miles from Cheddar at Yarnton, near Oxford, has been dated to between 3620 and 3350 BC, more than three millennia after Cheddar Man's time. Whatever he ate, and however he prepared his meals, his breath may not have been as bad as might be expected from an age so far removed from the invention of the toothbrush. Wads of birch resin have been found from around his time which are thought to have been chewed, much like chewing gum in our own time, as breath sweeteners.

According to anthropologists who have studied modern-day hunter-gatherers, they usually take only three or four hours to collect sufficient food for each day. The rest of their time they spend planning future food-gathering expeditions, making tools and accessories, devising or attending ceremonies, and otherwise organising their lives. So we can only guess that Cheddar Man may have occupied his leisure time similarly. But we can be virtually sure that dogs would have accompanied him constantly. The special treatment that these received in other West Country burials near-contemporary with him shows that even in Britain the inhabitants were already domesticating them. And although they no doubt assisted in hunting expeditions, they were being treated as much like pets in his time as in our own.

Living as he did before the age of writing, Cheddar Man had neither letters to write nor accounts to prepare. It is important to recognise, however, that he and his kindred are unlikely to have been entirely lacking in graphic and notational skills. No cave paintings have actually been found at Cheddar. But 3000 years earlier than Cheddar Man artists in France and Spain had established a fine tradition of painting the fauna around them. Equivalents of these may well simply have perished at Cheddar due to different climatic conditions. Also worthy of note is

The Cheddar Gorge as it looks today. Cheddar Man's 9000-year-old bones were found in Gough's Cave, one of the complex of ancient caves that perforate the Gorge's 430-foot-high limestone cliff-side.

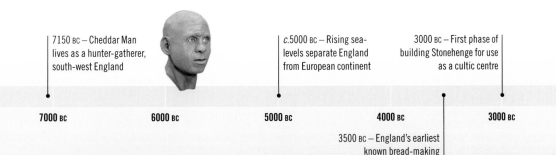

7150 BC – Cheddar Man lives as a hunter-gatherer, south-west England

c.5000 BC – Rising sea-levels separate England from European continent

3000 BC – First phase of building Stonehenge for use as a cultic centre

| 7000 BC | 6000 BC | 5000 BC | 4000 BC | 3000 BC | 2000 B |

3500 BC – England's earliest known bread-making

that pointed bone tools found in Cheddar Man's cave have engraved marks or notations similar to those on the so-called 'message sticks' used by Australian aboriginals up to and including the last century which could convey surprisingly sophisticated messages. So the marks may well have been considerably more meaningful and intelligible to those living around 7000 BC than they are to us today.

Unfortunately, because of the circumstances and early period of Cheddar Man's discovery, the exact arrangement of his bones was never properly recorded in the way that archaeologists would do today. So there can be no certainty that he received a formal burial, as distinct from having collapsed and died where he was found. However, since the burials in the nearby Aveline Hole cave certainly were carried out with ritual, this seems very likely in his case as well.

But of the manner of his death, something at least can be glimpsed. The evidence from Robert Stoddart and his fellow pathologists is that his demise was unmistakably associated with several serious, though not immediately lethal, blows to the head. One of these, landing directly between his eyes, caused a tiny piece of bone to become lodged inside his skull. From this there swelled up a grotesque-looking abscess that cannot but have given him a persistent, splitting headache. If he was not bad-tempered before, he is very likely to have been in the wake of this injury. More than likely the cause of his death was an infection arising from this abscess, a severe facial disfigurement that Denise Smith duly included in her reconstruction.

A quite unexpected angle of interest in Cheddar Man arose in 1996, when the regional TV producer Philip Priestley of HTV Bristol decided to make a programme on the archaeology of Cheddar and its environs.[4] As part of this project Priestley expended a high proportion of his production budget commissioning Dr Bryan Sykes of Oxford University's Institute of Molecular Medicine to take DNA samples from Cheddar Man's bones, with a view to checking how these compared with the modern-day population of Cheddar village. Sykes duly drilled one of Cheddar Man's molars for DNA, finding that this provided such a good sample that it could be scientifically sequenced.

This opened the way for local children and teachers to be invited to have their mouths swabbed to provide DNA samples for comparison with Cheddar Man's bones and those of others found in the caves. One of the schools participating in

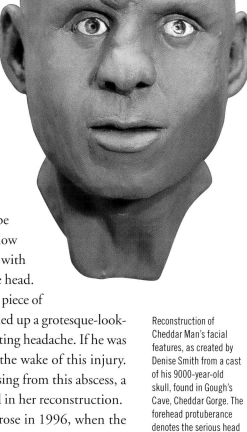

Reconstruction of Cheddar Man's facial features, as created by Denise Smith from a cast of his 9000-year-old skull, found in Gough's Cave, Cheddar Gorge. The forehead protuberance denotes the serious head injury that he sustained during life. This beardless version enables his likeness readily to be compared with that of his direct descendant Adrian Targett, shown opposite.

this project was Kings of Wessex School, Cheddar, and the result was quite astounding. As it turned out, the Kings of Wessex School history teacher, Adrian Targett, who had volunteered to take part only in order to make up the numbers, proved to be an extraordinarily close match to Cheddar Man. The difference between Targett's and Cheddar Man's mitochondrial DNA was just one base pair – that is, one letter of the genetic alphabet – out of 300, a change that over a period of 9000 years would be expected in any event by mutation. Since mitochondrial DNA is inherited down the maternal line, there could be absolutely no doubt that Adrian Targett is directly descended from Cheddar Man via his mother Hilda Gibbings. Genealogically, the furthest that this maternal line could be traced back was his great-great-great-grandmother, a baker's wife, Sarah Lute of Redcliffe, Bristol, who lived from 1807 to 1878. But if it were possible to track Sarah's line some 300 mothers further back, we would unerringly come to the ancient British woman who had been Cheddar Man's mother.

In fact Adrian Targett is far from unique as a descendant of poor, battered Cheddar Man. The Marquis of Bath, who asked to be checked out, was not a match, but his chauffeur was. And no doubt these are merely the first of many who might be discovered if the net were spread wider.

It is eerie in the extreme that Adrian Targett, who was born in Bristol, should today be living and working a mere few hundred yards from the last resting place of his direct ancestor from 9000 years ago. Equally eerie is Denise Smith's beardless version of Cheddar Man's face. When this is viewed side by side with Adrian Targett, it is by no means exact, but the familial likeness is quite apparent.

Cheddar schoolteacher Adrian Targett in Gough's Cave posing with a replica of the bones of his direct ancestor that were laid to rest in the same cave some 9,000 years earlier. DNA testing proved Targett and Cheddar Man to have been directly related via the maternal line.

5

The Hunter who Climbed too High *c.*3000 BC

He probably died without even a whimper. Quite possibly he was even asleep at the time, resting out a severe blizzard. The certainty is that he was a blue-eyed, dark-haired man, probably in his early forties, approximately five feet three inches (1.6m) tall, who took his last breath high up on an Alpine mountain path 10,530 feet (3,200m) above sea level. Equally certainly, snow and ice so quickly covered his body that no one of his time ever found it, and his very existence was forgotten for some 5000 years.

It was by this same path, merely yards from the Italian-Austrian border, that on 19 September 1991 a mountaineering couple from Nuremberg spotted the man's head and naked shoulders jutting out amidst ice and slush close to the Similaun glacier. Because an unusual thaw that year had brought to light several bodies of modern-day climbers lost in mountaineering accidents, he was initially mistaken for one of them, and the Austrian police duly implemented their normal recovery procedures.

But as various people, authorised and unauthorised, began rummaging around the clothing and belongings at the site, suspicions dawned that the dead man might be older, possibly even medieval. Accordingly, after five days the body was brought to the attention of the Innsbruck archaeologist Professor Konrad Spindler, who on taking one look at the accompanying copper-headed axe pronounced: 'Roughly 4000 years old – and if the dating is revised it will be even earlier.'

As Spindler recognised, here before him lay not a modern-day, nor indeed a medieval man, but a prehistoric one, complete with all his accoutrements, preserved far more perfectly, thanks to the ice, than any such find in modern times. It was a sensational discovery, acclaimed as such by the world's press, the Austrians among whom called the man 'Ötzi', after the Ötzal Alps region where he was found, while English speakers opted for the more readily pronounceable 'Iceman'. Then in June 1993 the US *National Geographic* magazine accorded Ötzi/Iceman the supreme accolade of a facial reconstruction specially commissioned from the Denver anthropological artist John Gurche.[1]

Ötzi/Iceman being prised from Alpine ice shortly after his discovery in September 1991. Found at an altitude of 10,530 feet, his body was initially mistaken for a modern-day mountaineer killed in a climbing accident – until the strange clothing and belongings showed him to date from several millennia earlier.

Exceptionally preserved though Ötzi was, the remoteness of the location and the fact that his antiquity was not at first recognised had led to some initial rough handling of his remains. The Austrian police had used a pneumatic chisel to prise his body from the ice, and this had gouged his left buttock. What had been thought to be an ordinary stick at the site, picked up, used and broken during the same digging operation, turned out in fact to have been part of Ötzi's hazel-wood and larchwood backpack, a unique contraption never before known from antiquity, and, as study revealed, remarkably similar in design to those still used today.

Even so, much of Ötzi and his belongings was astonishingly intact, extraordinarily well preserved by the near-perpetual Alpine ice, and as the remains were carefully conserved, examined, and reconstructed, a remarkably detailed picture began to be built up of how he had once been in life.

For instance, although his body was naked above the knees, in fact he had died fully clothed, his garments having been removed by the vicissitudes of the Alpine weather during his 5000-year slumber. A few feet from him lay the cone-shaped bearskin cap that had been on his head, its design not dissimilar to the bearskin busbies of the Guards regiments who protect Buckingham Palace. It was fitted with two leather chinstraps, and was found squashed flat, but otherwise intact. Nearby, though very fragmented, was what would have been a once rather splendid fur coat. This was made up of small squares of deerskin fur neatly sewn together using animal sinew thread, and must have been well used, since in places it bore home-spun repairs in grass thread.[2]

Reconstruction of Ötzi's face by American specialist John Gurche of the Denver Museum of Natural History. Despite the reconstruction's high degree of finish, Innsbruck archaeologist Professor Konrad Spindler is unconvinced that Gurche has achieved a reliable likeness.

10,000 BC – Development of the bow and arrow. Mammoth disappears from most of Europe. In western Asia the earliest-known farming

6000 BC – Development of copper metallurgy in western Asia

10,000 BC   9000 BC   8000 BC   7000 BC   6000

Around his waist Ötzi wore a leather body-belt carefully fitted with a pouch for his flint tools and fire-lighting equipment. This same belt also secured a scarf-like leather loin-cloth, a pair of 'Red Indian' style leggings, and the fibre scabbard of his flint dagger. On his feet he wore shoes of size 5 to 6 with oval cowhide soles and fur uppers, tied roughly round the ankle with grass cords, and stuffed with grass, presumably to provide insulation against the mountain cold. Like the coat, the shoes showed signs of repeated repairs.

Clearly intended for overall body protection was a thick knee-length cloak made from long grasses expertly plaited together. This would have been a far more practical garment than it might at first appear, light yet warm, waterproof as a thatched roof, and readily convertible into a sleeping-bag-cum-mattress for a night spent under the stars. Such garments are known to have been worn among Alpine peoples even as recently as the nineteenth century.

The seventy-odd objects comprising Ötzi's belongings proved as intriguing as his apparel. His axe featured a flanged copper head, indicating that the community from which he came had the ability to work copper. This had an important bearing on the date when he lived, since although metal-casting began in western Asia around 8000 BC, it only reached the eastern Alps around the fifth millennium BC, with flanges coming later. When Ötzi was radiocarbon-dated from samples sent to four European laboratories, the calculations ranged from 3365 to 3041 BC, confirming that Spindler had erred on the conservative side in estimating when he lived. Ötzi therefore straddled the era between prehistory and the first civilisations. While he was contemporary with the emergence of the latter, and his copper axe-head firmly takes him out of the Stone Age of Luzia, Leanne and Cheddar Man, in all other respects he was living the traditional life-style of the hunter-gatherer, which is why he has here been allotted to prehistory.

One source of particular joy for prehistorians was that his axe-head was still bound to its yew handle with leather thongs. It is the first prehistoric example ever to be found in Europe with the handle intact and these bindings still in place. Thousands of similarly ancient axe-heads have been found across the world, but exactly how they had been fastened to a wooden shaft had always been conjectural until the discovery of Ötzi.

4000 BC – In Mesopotamia, likely period for invention of the wheel and plough

3000 BC – Ötzi lives as a hunter-gatherer in the environs of northern Italy and Austria

2000 BC – Great stone circle erected at Stonehenge

5000 BC   4000 BC   3000 BC   2000 BC   1000 BC

1323 BC – Egyptian pharaoh Tutankhamun dies

Another of Ötzi's most interesting and important tools was his pressure flaker, designed to shape and sharpen stones into blades for implements, just as his Stone Age forbears had done for aeons before him. This was made from the point of the antler of a red deer, with a limewood handle specially crafted for it, as in the case of the axe. Also fitted with a handle, in this case of ashwood, was his tiny dagger, its flint blade just 1½ inches long, with the handle twice that.

Found next to the axe was a six-foot yew bow that had been carefully crafted with one rounded and one flat edge. When this was brought to room temperature it gave off a rancid smell, and tests for the presence of blood proteins proved positive. This indicated that it had probably been smeared with blood to waterproof it, since blood is water-repellent when it dries.

Ötzi's flint dagger with its ashwood handle still intact. Next to it was found its woven string scabbard (shown at left), the first of its kind ever discovered.

Clearly intended to be used with this bow were fourteen arrows carried in a deerskin quiver. Only two of these had proper double-sided flint arrowheads, and both were broken, but there were signs that Ötzi was making one good arrow from the two broken ones perhaps only hours before death overtook him. Certainly he had the equipment to bring all the arrows up to the same degree of finish, and their design and make-up is again indicative of some considerable technological knowledge. Their dogwood and viburnum wood shafts, thirty inches (76cm) long, were crafted in two pieces, those with the arrowheads having them affixed with pitch. They also had feathers closely trimmed into a spiral intended to give them spin when fired, the impression being that they were designed for accurate, straight-line travel over a long distance.

No less interesting was Ötzi's body. His teeth were found to be very worn, especially at the front, and he had a marked gap between his upper front teeth. Although at first sight he appeared bald and lacking any body hair except for a few wisps on his genitals, closer scrutiny disclosed a clump of dark wavy head hair among his upper clothing, and further thicker, curlier clusters beneath his chin. He seems to have been clean-shaven, and from hairs on the clothing it has been suggested that he had had a relatively recent haircut. A rectangular depression in his right earlobe indicates that he probably wore a stone in this as a kind of earring. Endoscopic images of his lungs, still well-preserved inside his body, showed them to have been blackened by smoke, probably breathed in from living in huts with smoky open fires.

In the case of Ötzi's genitals, although early press reports declared these missing, in fact they had simply been shrunken by the icy mummification, and his penis was found to be uncircumcised. Analysis of his mitochondrial DNA taken from bone fragments and tissue samples has indicated his close kinship to three or four people per hundred among present-day northern Europeans, rather than to any Mediterranean populations, suggesting that his roots lay north rather than south of the Alps. One Irishwoman studied by Dr Bryan Sykes of Oxford University (the same DNA specialist who conducted the analysis of Cheddar Man) in fact proved to be a direct descendant of Ötzi – though no doubt she is one of many who would come to light once everyone's DNA make-up ultimately becomes as familiar as our blood-groups are today.

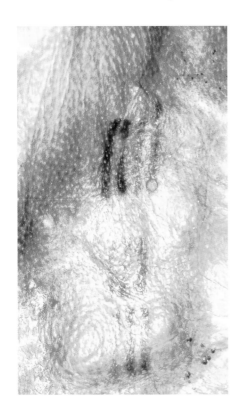

The earliest-known evidence of acupuncture? Tattoo-type marks on Ötzi's skin do not appear to have any decorative function, and from their locations they are now thought to derive from acupunctural treatment that Ötzi received for his back pains.

Clearly visible on Ötzi's legs and back are forty-seven tattoo-type marks, their form and locations atypical of what might normally be chosen for decorative purposes. Most, notably those on the back consist of groups of lines, while two take the form of crosses, one on the right knee, the other at the back of the left ankle. Acupuncturists have noted that nine of the fifteen groups on the back and left leg are close to, or directly on, the so-called 'urinary bladder channel' that runs along the back and down to the feet, and is classically used in acupuncture to treat arthrosis of the lumbar spine.[3] So when X-rays showed that Ötzi indeed suffered from arthritic degeneration in his lumbar spine, as well as in his hip, knee and ankle joints,[4] the possibility that he received treatment via a very early form of acupuncture had to be taken seriously.

This has been reinforced by five other tattoos at points associated with digestive functions. Numerous whip-worm eggs were found in Ötzi's colon, as well as a high proportion of charcoal (the latter administered even today for gastric upsets), confirming that he suffered from abdominal problems. So although acupuncture has long been regarded as an exclusively Chinese form of medicine, it is arguable that it originated more centrally, in western Asia or eastern Europe, then spread to the Alps by Ötzi's time, to die out subsequently in the West with the development of other medical approaches.

Bizarre conspiracy theories that Ötzi was just a hoax, an Egyptian mummy stolen from the British Museum (based on the purportedly missing genitals), have long been discounted. However, such is the extraordinary diversity of scientific knowledge that has accumulated, and continues to accumulate, around him that if anything it has exacerbated rather than diminished the mystery of who he was and how he came to die up in the mountains.

Thus when X-rays of Ötzi's chest showed that he had eight broken ribs, and these were said to have been at varied stages of healing at the time of his death, speculation arose about how he might have received these injuries. It was suggested that perhaps he became injured in some local dispute, causing him to flee for his life to the mountains.

Permanently snow-clad, the 10,530-foot-high site in the Alps, very close to the Austrian-Italian border, where an unusual thaw brought Ötzi's body to light after its having lain undisturbed for some 5000 years.

The current thinking, however, is that these breakages were not before his death at all, but were sustained when he was being crudely prised from the ice.

Another theory, suggesting a similar scenario, arose from English archery experts' observations that Ötzi's bow was broken, had never been finished (because it lacked any end notches to take a string), and was unstrung. In actuality, while the bow certainly was broken when it arrived in Innsbruck, this was only because of the initial clumsy attempts to free it from the ice. When the missing end came to light, it was obvious that it had been still intact at the time of Ötzi's death. Likewise, a study of twenty-four bows from the Stone Age has shown that one third of these lack notched ends, just like Ötzi's, and have similar tapering ends to which a string can be tied. As for the missing bow-string, there can be little doubt that it was a piece of sinew found carefully coiled up inside Ötzi's quiver, clearly his well-thought-out way of protecting it from the elements when it was not in use.

One particularly ingenious method used to try and unlock the mysteries Ötzi poses is the analysis of his fingernails by the Italian anthropologist Luigi Capasso. This revealed three transverse furrows crossing the back of the nail, which Capasso interprets as due to three prolonged episodes of some kind of stress or illness. Since fingernails grow at a steady rate of one-eighth of an inch (3mm) per month, these episodes must have been as recent as the last four months of his life, with the last one within two months of his death. What could this last episode have been?

In order to try to resolve such complexities, in 1998 the Romano-German Central Museum at Mainz, to which Ötzi's equipment had been taken, invited the

Australian microbiologist Dr Tom Loy[5] to look for trace elements on the surfaces of the tools that Ötzi was carrying. Accordingly, Loy, a world expert in such matters, undertook an examination that proved more than worthwhile. Studying the piece of flint that Ötzi had carried to use as a drill, Loy found that holes bored in the stiffener of Ötzi's quiver exactly matched it. This indicated that Ötzi must have made the quiver himself, using the tools that he carried in his tool-kit. Similarly, Loy found that scallop-shaped indentations on Ötzi's bow perfectly matched nicks and dents on the cutting edge of his axe. This showed that he must personally have finished the shaping of this bow, even if he may not have made it entirely himself.

As for the arrows, Loy found these particularly informative. On examining the shafts he immediately saw blood traces, and on testing for blood proteins he found a strong reaction until around twelve inches (30cm) from the point. So clearly these had once gone deep into the bodies of prey, indicating that on some earlier occasions Ötzi successfully shot the arrows into what must have been relatively large game animals. But similar research also revealed that more recently Ötzi's ability to hit his target had failed him. The presence of soil particles and the way that the arrows' shafts had broken indicated that they had uselessly impacted into the ground at high velocity, hence his need, high up in the Alps, to conduct repairs.

The picture of Ötzi that emerges from the study of such minutiae is not of a shepherd, as some have previously suggested. Nor is it of a refugee wounded by broken ribs who had fled to the hills to escape from a local skirmish. Instead, Loy is confident that Ötzi would have been 'a mature, highly skilled hunter'. As he points out:

> The tools in his kit were multipurpose, skilfully made and well maintained. Together they provided, with minimal weight, all the necessary tools for hunting, butchering and bringing back meat, skin, antlers or horn on his lightweight pack frame. His copper axe and bearskin hat were both utilitarian and displays of prestige. Copper implements were not common at that time, and in nearly all hunting societies the killing of bears… was a visible measure of hunting prowess… The skins of his clothing range from red deer to chamois and ibex, and perhaps domestic goat. These, combined with the powerful bow and light arrows designed to fly long distances, suggest that his hunting gear was not specialized for a forest setting, where a light arrow can easily be deflected by leaves and twigs, but for alpine hunting. Perhaps he was in the high pass hunting ibex, the only animal which retires to high rocky areas at night, while chamois and other animals move into the skirts of the lower forest.[6]

So maybe, after having taken more of a day than he could afford pursuing some particularly elusive quarry higher up into the Alps than was wise, Ötzi ended up with his arrows badly in need of refurbishment. Rather than return home empty-handed to do this, he decided to stay up at the high level and do the repairs there, in the hope that he might have better luck the next day.

If so, it was an undoubtedly fatal miscalculation. For as those who climb high mountains are all too aware, the weather has only to turn for the combination of high altitude and intense cold to take over – quickly translating a merely exhausted sleep into a hypothermic slumber from which the sleeper will never awake.

Today, after nearly 5000 years Ötzi has returned from his trip, and not just with one face, but with at least two. For despite the high degree of finish that Gurche gave to his facial reconstruction for *National Geographic*, even adding prosthetic eyes, real hair and convincingly weathered skin, the method that he used was the somewhat limited American one. As a result, Konrad Spindler, the archaeologist who first recognized Ötzi's prehistoricity (and for whom researching him has become a life's passion), proved less than impressed. He has declared that Gurche's reconstruction is nothing like how he would expect Ötzi to have looked in life from his day-to-day studies of the actual body, a body that Gurche never visited.[7]

So more recent reconstructions have been made, among these one by Professor Peter Vanezis of the University of Glasgow's Department of Forensic Medicine and Science, who uses a computer-based method. After scanning a replica of the skull made from CT scans, his system takes just thirty seconds to capture 20,000 surface coordinates. These it then converts into a 3-D model, which can be viewed from any angle, then given skin textures and key facial features from a library of such options, according to all the information known about the subject's race, hair colour, eye colour and so on. Since in Ötzi's case a wealth of such data is available because of the body's high degree of preservation, the potential for achieving a really accurate reconstruction of what he looked like is probably greater than for any other figure from prehistory. But whether it is Gurche or Vanezis who has best recaptured Ötzi's true features, or whether this awaits some future development of the method, remains an open question.

Overall Ötzi must be seen as something of an anachronism, roaming mountains practising the ancient skills of hunter-gathering in an era when people throughout Europe and the Near East were busily developing the arts of agriculture and keeping and breeding animal herds for meat. Whatever his reasons for wandering so high up in the Alps, today his home is a splendid new museum in Bolzano, northern Italy, where he enjoys the luxury of computer-controlled refrigeration. But with daily visits from tourists and parties of wide-eyed children, his rest must inevitably be rather less peaceful than in the icy stillness of the Similaun glacier that was his home for nearly 5000 years.

II

THE FIRST CIVILISATIONS

HISTORICAL INTRODUCTION:

From the earliest technologies to the era of the first money

It has long been supposed that since the end of the Ice Age the world's climate and geography have stayed fairly static, and that the first civilisations began in Egypt and Mesopotamia. Recent discoveries, however, tell a different story. Climatologists now believe that the melting of large tracts of ice left numerous large freshwater lakes across the Middle East, what is today Turkey and the areas to its east and north. One of these lakes lay in the depression now occupied by the salt-water Black Sea.[1] Although two cooler, drier periods – one around 9400 BC, the other around 6200 BC – shrank these lakes, the latter was but a blip on what was otherwise a particularly prolonged wet phase globally from 7500 BC to 3500 BC.[2] This enabled elephant, giraffe and antelope to flourish in what is now the Sahara desert. It created grasslands of what is now the Arabian desert, and dense forestation along the shores of the eastern Mediterranean.

With agriculture and animal husbandry both in their infancy, such marked climatic changes would inevitably have had their effects on the human populations, as indeed seems to have been the case. Perhaps because the drought just after the Ice Age drew people and their animals to congregate at oases, during the eighth and seventh millennia BC there appeared the earliest proper town settlements, and with them specialist technologies. One example was Jericho, sited by an exceptionally productive spring north of what is now the Dead Sea. Another was at Çatal Hüyük, on a plain in the middle of Turkey,[3] in which the dwellings were honeycomb-like rectangles entered via ladders through holes in the flat roofs. Çatal Hüyük's inhabitants practised weaving, leatherwork, basket-making, pottery-making, carpentry, stone- and bone-carving, jewellery-making and cosmetics manufacture. The world's earliest known textile, found at Çayönü, Turkey, dates from this same period, likewise the method of furnace-heating copper ore to the necessary temperature (1981°F, 1080°C) to create an ingot of pure metal. Religion was well developed, the Çatal Hüyük inhabitants possessing proper shrines with decorations indicative of a bull and mother-goddess cult. The bodies of their dead were left for vultures to pick clean, after which they gathered up the defleshed bones and buried them beneath the family clay bed.

But possibly because of the second particularly cool, dry period, Çatal Hüyük became abandoned in about 6200 BC. Although we do not know where its inhabitants went, one strong possibility is that they and other peoples moved to the milder climate and more reliable water supply provided by the 'Black Sea' freshwater lake, unwitting of the cataclysm that was shortly to befall this region.

The prolonged wet phase overall and the continuing Ice Age melt had been causing sea-levels to rise steadily, and around 5600 BC the Mediterranean Sea burst with great violence through the land bridge joining Bulgaria to Turkey. This not only created the Bosporus strait, it rapidly transformed the relatively small freshwater lake beyond into the vast saltwater Black Sea that we know today.[4] At much the same time the Atlantic Ocean broke through the bridge of land joining England to France, thereby creating the English Channel,[5] while much of the American coastline disappeared underwater as the Bering Strait was created, separating it from Asia.

In the Black Sea region there can be no doubt that the effect of the inrush of seawater – with the force of 200 Niagaras – upon peoples and animals settled by the freshwater lake would have cataclysmic results, arguably becoming seared into the survivors' folk-memories as the World Flood myth. And certainly soon after 5600 BC several apparently displaced peoples began appearing in a variety of locations spreading out from the Black Sea, some it seems deliberately seeking out places far enough inland to be free of flood danger. Amongst these were the Vinca, who introduced neat villages to Hungary, the LBK (*Linienbandkeramik*, or Linear Pottery Farmers), who spread out across Europe as far as Paris, and the Danilo-Hvar, who settled in what is now Yugoslavia. Not long after there appeared in Mesopotamia the long-skulled al-Ubaid people, precursors of the Sumerian civilisation, speaking a Hungarian-related language, and quite definitely bearing memories of a Flood.[6]

Other survivors may have travelled to Egypt, introducing its earliest-known pottery-making, together with domesticated cereals and animals, since these first appeared there at much this time. Yet others, again with long skulls, long noses, and a tendency to fair hair – distinctively Caucasian features – appear to have migrated to the then lakeside surroundings of the Tarim Basin north of Tibet, to become a strange enclave of Indo-Europeans, the Tocharians, in a milieu that was otherwise genetically Mongoloid.[7]

What is certain is that much of what we call civilisation thereupon took off with much greater impetus. As we earlier noted, there had definitely been some pottery and some metallurgy before the Flood. But these and other technologies, together with associated trading activities, now developed apace. Exactly who invented the potter's wheel, and where and when, is far from clear, but the first wheel-turned pottery appeared in the Near East at around this time, with Egypt's potters being particularly prolific. Evidence for the world's earliest-known wine-making has been found in the form of retsina-like residues on a piece of pot of *c.*5400 BC excavated at Hajji Firuz Tepe, in modern Iran near Lake Urmia.[8] Instead of the old practice of making garments out of animal skins, the new fashion now was to create clothes from spun flax. This involved soaking fronds of cut flax in water until they fermented, drying them in the sun so that the inner fibres became easily removable for spinning into thread, then weaving this thread on small purpose-built wooden frames to create cloth. In metallurgy, by 4500 BC at Varna, on the Black Sea's Bulgarian coast, there had grown up a flourishing centre for hammering gold and copper.[9] The whole era is often called the 'Chalcolithic' or 'Copper' age because it epitomises this phase of human development; Iceman Ötzi's copper axe is a late expression of this.

Some time around 3700 BC a new era dawned when some unrecorded metallurgist discovered that mixing ten per cent of tin with the copper created the much stronger metal alloy, bronze. Although this brought about its own logistical problems, since tin sources were few and far between – only Egypt's eastern desert in the Mediterranean world, otherwise Cornwall and Afghanistan – such was the impetus that bronze relentlessly progressed to become the world's most widely used metal throughout much of the next two millennia. The whole era has thereby become termed that of the Early, Middle and Late Bronze Ages,[10] though from the global point of view such labels are best avoided, since all around the world there were peoples who did not advance out of the Stone Age – a few indeed remain to this day.

But whatever metallurgical label may be given to the age, particularly spectacular were its advances in creating buildings of brick, wood and stone which developed at much the same time. In Mesopotamia there appeared temples of highly sophisticated design, the walls of some being superbly decorated with the newly invented art form we know as mosaic. Mesopotamian burials from the period involved the quite spectacular interment of whole palace households and their appurtenances, as we will learn from face number 6.

Likewise, again for funerary purposes, in Egypt around the mid-third millennium BC there rose the pyramids, built with the most meticulous planning, carefully aligned to accord with astronomical observations, and constructed of up to two million stone blocks. Although some of these blocks weighed as much as fifteen tons, all were cut square to fine margins of accuracy and manoeuvred into position, indicating engineering thinking and calculation of an impressive order even for today. Such was the prevailing penchant for shifting huge blocks of stone that even in far-off Britain, where a quite different culture prevailed, the building of Stonehenge had already begun.

Ancient Egyptian craftsmen displaying their skills. At top left a goldsmith weighs gold; at top right woodworkers create signs for a shrine, while below right a sculptor puts the finishing touches to a sphinx. From the 18th Dynasty tomb of Nebamun and Ipuky at Thebes.

Both in Egypt and in Mesopotamia as early as the third millennium BC more everyday furniture items such as chairs and beds were being made to standards of design and craftsmanship that would not look out of place in a modern-day furniture showroom. Although these may mostly have belonged to royalty rather than to ordinary citizens, nevertheless they represented enduring developments of functional items. Alongside such advances, artists were depicting the human form and creatures from the natural world to a high degree of realism.

Meanwhile there had appeared in Sumerian Mesopotamia the first writing. Initially this was in the form of picture characters, as in Egypt, which followed suit soon after. But even the very symbols used convey the markedly more sophisticated character of life as it had developed by this time. We now see the wheel, only recently invented, being used on two- and four-wheeled carts drawn by the now fully domesticated horse, a form of transport that would not be superseded until last century. We see signs for other recently domesticated animals such as cattle, goats and pigs. We can see that fish was a popular food commodity. We see signs for various food and drink containers, for seed-ploughs, for the socketed axe, for the dagger, for the bow and arrow, for boats, for musical instruments such as the harp or lyre.

Apparent from the paintings and reliefs with which Egyptians adorned the walls of their tombs are not only much the same furniture and equipment items, but also clear evidence that plant domestication had developed into advanced agricultural techniques. To such ends landscapes were altered for drainage and irrigation purposes, the hoe was refined and the ox-drawn plough near-perfected. Wheat, barley, dates, figs, olives and grapes were all being purposefully grown as food products, while bread-making in specially designed ovens had developed into a craft. As shown by tomb inscriptions, bread and beer – both products of intelligent observation and exploitation of natural fermentation processes – were the afterlife's two most popular commodities. During the third millennium BC there also appeared in Egypt true horticulture in the form of the world's first exotic ornamental gardens, properly planned to include fish-pools, flower-beds with roses, jasmine and myrtle, orchards of fig trees and date palms, and trellis to support grapevines. And almost simultaneously the Mesopotamians appear to have introduced and developed ornamental gardening to much the same levels.

The next two millennia saw the emergence of relatively few new technologies, but in a very real sense refinements of those already established. Egyptian boat-building, for instance, having adopted the single rectangular sail at least as early as the third millennium BC, merely produced variants on the same theme. Conforming to widespread practice, the boat was steered by a large paddle operated by a helmsman at the stern, and the keel was not introduced until probably as late as the New Kingdom (1550-1070 BC). Writing became less pictographic, and developed in form; writing materials proliferated. Thus the Mesopotamians opted to use special instruments to incise so-called cuneiform or wedge-shaped marks on tablets of wet clay which could then be preserved by baking. The Egyptians preferred to make their marks in specially prepared dark liquid – ink – written with a pen on papyrus leaves cleverly woven together and processed as the first 'paper'.

But both the Egyptian and Mesopotamian writing systems, like that of the Chinese, who developed theirs around 1500 BC, were hampered by too many and too cumbersome signs for the words they wanted to express, virtually necessitating that the craft remained confined to professional scribes. Although a swifter style of hieroglyphic, hieratic script, became developed, the really big advance came about 1700 BC, not from the Egyptians but from the biblical Canaanites. The prime seafaring merchants of their time, later known as the Phoenicians, they seem to have been the developers of the first alphabetic script, from which there would subsequently spring both the Hebrew and the Greek alphabets, later followed by the Roman alphabet in which you are reading this book.

There are indications that the transition from hunter-gathering to farming was not wholly beneficial in health terms, height, body size and longevity actually declining,[11] and various new diseases such as diphtheria,[12] rickets and leprosy[13] appearing. But working in bronze enabled the creation of a surprising variety of surgical instruments that can be seen depicted on the walls of ancient Egyptian temples, their shapes still to be found on modern-day operating-tables.

The discovery of glass probably happened by accident when someone noticed how certain sands fused when melted, leading to experiments from which it was discovered that materials used in soap-making helped the process. But around the middle of the second millennium BC, both in Egypt and Mesopotamia the first proper glass vessels began to appear, initially as luxury items, often in beautiful colours, using every recognised step of the process short of glass-blowing, which would follow in the Roman era.

The simple frames on which the first weaving had been done now developed into full looms capable of creating much longer and wider lengths of cloth. The Anatolians of Çatal Hüyük were almost certainly using vegetable dyes for fabrics as far back as the seventh millennium BC, but by around 2000 BC the Canaanitic port of Tyre had become a major centre for dyeing garments royal purple using the murex shellfish. Although Egyptian garments tended towards the simple, of plain colour, far more elaborate were those of the so-called Minoan peoples of Crete, as we will learn from our face number 7. Throughout the first half of the second millennium BC the Minoans made advances in building seagoing boats that enabled them to colonise neighbouring islands, and gave them trading ascendancy in the eastern Mediterranean. Even comparatively ordinary Minoan citizens were enabled to live in fine two-storey homes with efficient plumbing and tastefully frescoed walls. However, some time around 1500 BC Minoan civilisation appears to have been very seriously disrupted by a massive volcanic eruption that overwhelmed one of its colonial islands, Thera (Santorini). This had serious side-effects, among them, not long after, the fall of the Minoans to invasion by Mycenaean Greeks.

Meanwhile the Egyptians around 1700 BC were invaded by the 'Hyksos', now increasingly recognised as the Canaanite peoples of the Bible. They overwhelmed Egypt's north using horse-drawn chariots as mobile fighting platforms in much the manner of the modern tank. It took the Egyptians 200 years to win back the lost territory, and only then by developing the two-wheeled light chariot as a tactically superior horse-drawn fighting vehicle. They then embarked on the golden age of the New Kingdom, the Eighteenth to Twentieth Dynasties, during which they were led by great pharaohs such as Tuthmosis III, Seti I and Ramesses II.

But the entire eastern Mediterranean, including Egypt, received another rude shock around 1200 BC when some as yet imperfectly understood circumstance sparked off a mass migration from Anatolia of so-called Sea Peoples. The Twentieth Dynasty pharaoh Ramesses III managed to hold off an actual invasion of Egypt itself, though much of its former empire was lost, and it is from the reign of one of this Ramesses' successors that our face number 8 represents what was still a high point of Egyptian civilisation.

The incoming Sea Peoples brought with them a burgeoning metallurgy, iron-smelting, showing that they had mastered the achieving of the necessary temperature

(2800°F, 1530°C). And since iron deposits were far more plentiful than copper, and the finished metal much stronger for weaponry and agricultural implements, iron quickly became the dominant metal, giving its name to the Iron Age.[14]

This was one of the factors which caused Egypt to lose much of its former technological ascendancy when by around 900 BC it was the Mesopotamia-based Assyrians who began to emerge as the Near East's new strongmen. They brought an unsurpassed ruthlessness and cruelty to empire-building, advancing the arts of war to new fearsomeness by using siege engines, giant catapults and battering-rams to break down even the best-defended walled cities. It was their policy to uproot and take into slavery the peoples they overcame, and their successors, the Babylonians, did much the same before being in their turn overwhelmed by the rather more beneficent Persian Empire.

Amid all this Near Eastern activity, it must not be overlooked that China had developed sophisticated pottery and metallurgy. Meanwhile, between China and the Near East, scattered across the vast treeless territories of the Asian steppes roamed nomadic peoples who may not have had fine buildings or advanced agricultural methods, but whose lifestyle was hardly impoverished. Having domesticated the horse as their mode of transport, they virtually lived in the saddle from childhood, and on death their horses were sacrificed and buried with them. Often labelled 'Scythians', they consisted of numerous mobile groups whom the great Greek historian Herodotus called 'the most uncivilised nations in the world'. Yet they mummified their dead with a skill easily rivalling that of the Egyptians, and their stylishness and artistry in metalwork, woodwork and fabrics were as great as anywhere in the world. These peoples will be represented by our face number 9. Equally not to be forgotten are the Celtic peoples spread across western Europe, whose surviving metalwork was of similar excellence and whose woodworking skills might also have been extolled had Europe's climate allowed the results to survive.

The whole civilised world had so far managed to do without that now universal commodity, money. Although it was the kings of Asia Minor in the seventh century BC who first introduced the practice of stamping insignia on lumps of metal so that they could be used as officially approved tokens for trading in labour and goods, it was the Greeks who developed the minting and circulation of coinage for the purpose of commerce, much as we know it today. They also made a fine art of the coins themselves, some of these being artistic masterpieces in their own right.

But coinage was by no means all that we would come to owe to the Greeks. They adopted and advanced the surgical instruments that the Egyptians had developed before them, and we shall see that our face number 10 was a direct beneficiary of this surgery. In addition, thanks to the 'learning by observation' methods of Greek physicians such as Hippocrates, the principles of modern medicine became so surely established that the entire body of medical knowledge advanced comparatively little from then until a century and a half before our own time. Thus Hippocrates' code of practice for doctors – the so-called Hippocratic oath – is so fundamentally right that it remains the basis of medical ethics to this day.

Hand in hand with Greek medicine went the maintenance of a healthy body by sporting activities, and, not least in the recreational facilities they developed, the Greeks set standards that it would take two millennia to equal. The Greek gymnasium – with the single fundamental exception that it was an all-male establishment – could offer a range of facilities hardly excelled even today, while for artists, observation of the athletes exercising provided a life-class better than in any art school, accounting for the Greeks' pre-eminence in representational art. As not often realised, Greek marble sculpture was originally painted in realistic colours, so that instead of the white stone that we see today, the statues would have looked almost breathtakingly lifelike. As for ceramics, even the best potters of today would have difficulty surpassing the sophisticated vessel designs and decoration techniques that their Greek forebears perfected two and a half millennia ago.

Furthermore, in the wake of all the earlier power-jostling between Assyria, Babylon and Persia, it was in fact the Greeks who, welding their own quarrelsome peoples into single nationhood, were most successful under Alexander the Great, son of Philip II of Macedon whom we will meet as face number 10. Before Alexander was thirty-three his conquests stretched from Egypt in the south to India in the east, and he had created the largest empire the world had yet seen.

In the event, however, Alexander died young, of disease rather than in battle, whereupon his empire became divided up between his generals. From these divisions there would eventually emerge, still heavily tinged by its Greek origins, the ancient world's first and only seriously lasting superpower, that of Rome.

Common to all the first civilisations was, of course, the expenditure of vast effort to create temples, ranging from Stonehenge in Britain to Karnak in Egypt to the Canaanitic temple of Solomon to the Parthenon at Athens. And common to almost all was an accompanying pantheon of gods who, although their names differed from one culture to another, usually had clear equivalents. Thus Mesopotamia's great fertility goddess Ishtar (a deity inextricably linked with the domestication of animals), for instance, was known as Astarte to the Canaanites, Hathor to the Egyptians, Artemis to the Greeks and Kybele to the people of Asia Minor. In such a milieu priests, priestesses and their ilk had to be highly important functionaries, and it is therefore no surprise that we will find them strongly represented among the faces of the first civilisations that we are about to meet.

SUMER'S FERTILITY MISTRESS
c.2500 BC

From the inscription on a delicate seal that was found next to her shoulder, we know that her name was Puabi.[1] Thanks to the invention of writing only a little before her time, she is the first of our faces to whom we can give the name that they bore in life. When she died, in the ancient Sumerian city of Ur in lower Mesopotamia – today southern Iraq – she was aged around forty, and clearly a woman of considerable importance. Those who buried her laid her out with the greatest care, in finery crowned with a most spectacular head-dress crafted in gold, lapis lazuli and carnelian, complemented by great crescent-shaped gold earrings. And when in the late 1920s her grave was discovered by the British archaeologist Sir Leonard Woolley, the archaeologist's wife Katharine made a reconstruction of her face using the best available methods of the time. As Woolley grandiloquently though ill-advisedly described it: 'The whole reconstructed head presents us with the most accurate picture we are likely ever to possess of what she looked like in her lifetime.'[2]

What makes Puabi of Ur of exceptional interest is not so much the material extravagance with which she was buried, but the less quantifiable squandering of human and indeed animal lives that accompanied the burial. In the course of Woolley's excavations of Ur's so-called Royal Cemetery he came across Puabi's tomb, which he numbered RT (Royal Tomb) 800, immediately adjoining a similarly 'rich' grave, RT 789, which he thought belonged to her husband, though the body had disappeared in antiquity. Puabi herself was lying on a wooden bier, a gold cup by her hand, inside a rectangular chamber that had been generously supplied with grave goods and offerings. As Woolley summarised: 'Another gold bowl, vessels of silver and copper, stone bowls and clay jars for food, the head of a cow in silver, two silver tables for offerings, silver lamps, and a number of large cockle-shells containing green paint... presumably used as a cosmetic'.[3] Though such items were clearly intended for Puabi's afterlife, it was their other accompaniments that chilled the blood.

For crouched at her head and feet were the skeletons of two young women, presumably her most senior ladies-in-waiting. A third attendant lay a short distance

Reconstruction of the face of 'Fertility Mistress' Puabi, as created in the late 1920s by Katharine Woolley, whose husband Leonard was responsible for excavating Ur. Though the head bears the spectacular head-dress with which Puabi went to her grave, Woolley modelled the features on the skull of one of Puabi's attendants, using methods that have long since been superseded.

away. Immediately outside the tomb-chamber proper there was a spacious antechamber in which lay the remains of another woman, probably a wardrobe mistress, next to a large wooden chest that had probably contained Puabi's collection of clothes. In a passageway lay huddled the bodies of five soldiers, presumably her personal bodyguard. In the centre of the antechamber were the remains of a sledge on runners, together with the bones of the two oxen which had drawn this, and four more male skeletons, evidently the animals' grooms. Further back were the bodies of ten young women, all adorned with splendid head-dresses, while at their head lay a harpist, sex undetermined, his or her fingers still positioned where the strings would have been on what remained of a magnificent harp.

Clearly a most elaborate, moving but ultimately grisly funeral ceremony had taken place in Puabi's grave 4500 years ago, the astonishing feature being that all these people along with their accoutrements had seemingly voluntarily joined this woman in death, without the slightest sign of struggle. In trying to deduce what had happened Woolley attributed crucial significance to the small cups that were found beside most of the bodies. These, he surmised, contained a drugged or poisoned potion which each member of this colourful company had drunk at a prescribed moment, probably after a ceremony with hymns sung by the young women found with the harpist. As suggested by Dr P.R.S. Moorey of the Ashmolean Museum, Oxford, a Sumerian hymn to the goddess Inanna may well bring us very close to this ceremony:

Above: Similar to those found in Puabi's tomb, just some of the 74 attendants accompanying another high-ranking Sumerian to the grave. Plan of the disposition of skeletons found in the great 'Death Pit', another of the 'Royal Tombs' excavated by Sir Leonard Woolley.

> Oh lady the [harp of] mourning is placed on the ground
> One had verily beached your ship of mourning on a hostile shore.
> At [the sound of] my sacred song they are ready to die.[4]

It is possible that each of Puabi's grave companions, after having drunk the potions in their cups, peacefully settled themselves for death, following which someone from the land of the living entered the tomb to perform a last tidying-up. This is inferred not least from the fact that the bodies of the two oxen collapsed over rather than

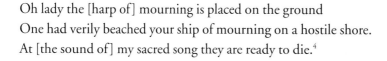

4000 BC – In Mesopotamia, likely period for invention of the wheel and plough

3700 BC Earliest known bronze-making in Near East

3100 BC – Earliest fully-recognised picture writing

5000 BC   4500 BC   4000 BC   3500 BC

under those of their grooms. The supposition, therefore, is that the animals were killed only at this final stage.

In fact, by ancient Sumerian standards Puabi's grave was by no means exceptional in the number of servants who joined their dead master or mistress in this way. Another in the same cemetery, which Woolley called the 'Death Pit', held as many as seventy-four attendants. Yet also quite apparent is that Sumerian society, by normal yardsticks, was far from bloodthirsty, but instead highly civilised. A superb picture of its lifestyle is provided by lively scenes created in shell and lapis lazuli on the so-called 'Royal Standard of Ur', found by Woolley in one of the Royal Cemetery's oldest tombs, and now in the British Museum.

Below: Detail of the famous 'Royal Standard of Ur', depicting in its two lower registers asses, sheep, goats, oxen and fish being brought to the 'court' of seated dignitaries seen in the upper register. Just out of the picture are a singer and harpist apparently entertaining the court.

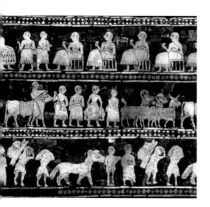

The Standard, thought to have been the sounding board of a musical instrument, features side-panels dubbed 'War' and 'Peace', and following Sumerian convention, the three rows of scenes in each panel are intended to be read bottom row first. On the 'War' side we see heavy four-wheeled chariots, fitted out with spear quivers and drawn by teams of onagers (tamed wild asses), being driven over the naked bodies of a defeated enemy. Cloaked, helmeted infantry armed with short spears then capture and lead off surviving enemy soldiers, and in the final, top row these prisoners are interrogated by a leader or king, who is represented as a head taller than everyone else. On the 'Peace' side kilted civilians bring asses, sheep, goats, oxen and fish as offerings to a seated individual, presumably the same 'king', behind whom a damaged but similarly seated figure may have been his 'queen'. This 'royal' pair are about to quaff beverages in the company of six kilted male individuals who sit facing them, presumably their court, while behind stands an entertainer strumming melodies on a bull-headed harp, alongside him a woman (distinguished by her long hair), probably a professional singer.

Quite obvious from these scenes, which essentially complement the Royal Tomb evidence, is that in marked contrast to the earlier 'hunter-gatherers', the Sumerian world that Puabi knew was one in which the domestication of animals had been achieved for some while, as had the invention of harnessing equipment such as bridles, rein rings (represented both on the Standard and by an actual example found

2500 BC – Puabi lives at Ur, Mespotamia. Pyramids at Gizeh, Egypt, begun	2000 BC – First palaces in Minoan Crete	1550 BC – Beginning of Egypt's New Kingdom	
2500 BC	**2000 BC**	**1500 BC**	**1000 BC**

in Puabi's tomb), and much else. There was a standardised civilian costume of sheep-skin kilts. Soldiers were issued with standardised weaponry and uniforms including copper helmets of a kind found in some of the graves, and long cloaks, which were almost certainly of felt, as still worn by traditional Turkish shepherds. Wheeled vehicles had clearly been developed, the essential principles of which are still embodied in present-day automobiles. The chair had come into existence as a finely crafted item of furniture, together with the bed, the latter represented by the bier on which Puabi was laid in death. Musical instruments of considerable sophistication had been created, such as the bull-headed lyre depicted on the Standard, and actual specimens found in Puabi's and neighbouring graves. There were even board games: again actual specimens were uncovered in the same excavations.

People were clearly employed in specialist professions – as soldiers, grooms, charioteers, musicians, metalworkers, makers of fine art objects. There must have been boatmen, merchants and diplomats, since many of the materials the Sumerians used, such as copper and precious stones, had to be obtained and transported from afar, sometimes from overseas territories. There were also architects, since the roof of Puabi's tomb was designed with a properly constructed brick barrel vaulting and apse-type ends. Likewise her theoretical consort's tomb featured a brick-arched door-way, while columns supported other near-contemporary buildings. In Woolley's words, 'All the basic forms of architecture used today were familiar to the people of Ur in the early part of the third millennium before Christ.'[5]

A society that could afford to employ so many of its populace in such a variety of non-food-producing occupations must have had farmers – a 'profession' that itself had only relatively recently come into existence – producing a generous surplus. And in Puabi's time the fertile valleys of the Tigris and Euphrates could certainly do this, with wheat and barley, grazing animals, fish and wild fowl all plentiful. Distributing such a food supply required the additional burden of administrative officials and their documentation. It is therefore no accident that, synchronous with all the other developments, it is in Sumer that we find the earliest evidence of writing surviving in any abundance. This consists of clay tablets enumerating a wealth of commodities being supplied to or delivered by officials, including wheat and barley, dairy products, bread and beer, and above all sheep. Such a writing system and its accompanying numeration (using a number system based on 60) had not arisen out of nothing; many of its pictographs – signs for such universals as 'star', 'god', 'water', 'earth' and so on – had long been represented in Mesopotamian and Iranian painted pottery. But with the emergence of the scribe as yet another profession, it rapidly expanded and became standardised, so that what had been up to thirty-two different signs for the word *udu,* sheep, were within a century reduced to two.

As we noted earlier, next to Puabi's shoulder was found a finely crafted cylinder seal bearing her name, followed by the word *nin*, variously translated 'lady' or 'queen', thereby, thanks specifically to the development of writing, enabling us very satisfyingly to put a real name to her face. And although it would be quite wrong to dismiss those whose 'faces' we have previously met, whose names we cannot know, as uncivilised, nevertheless there is something reassuringly civilised about being able to read her name and title across more than 4000 years, much as we can today read somebody's name-tag at a party or conference.

Yet even so, given the extraordinary mass suicide that accompanied Lady Puabi's demise, how much can we really know about her and her brand of civilisation? And just how accurate was Katharine Woolley's reconstruction of her face and head-dress?

As Leonard Woolley, to his great credit, readily admitted in his excavation report, the skull that his wife used for the reconstruction and display of Puabi's head-dress was not actually Puabi's, since it had been found too badly crushed and with pieces missing. Instead Katharine Woolley worked from another female skull of the same period and the 'same physical type'. It is important not to be too critical of this, for in general Woolley trail-blazed the retrieval and conservation of delicate artefacts that previous archaeologists would have lost. Even so it is a very great pity, for the Woolleys' medical consultant Professor Sir Arthur Keith – now notorious as the man thought most responsible for the faking of the Piltdown skull – did manage to examine the true Puabi skull, fragmentary though it was. This indicates that in the hands of a Neave a true reconstruction might have been possible (and indeed still might be).

Keith made some most interesting observations concerning the true Puabi. He determined that her cranium was of an exceptional capacity – some 97 cubic inches (1600c.cm), at least 15 cubic inches (250c.cm) above the female norm, and with an unusually high vault, some five inches (12.9cm) above the line represented by the lower margins of the eye sockets and the upper margins of the openings for the ears. Bearing in mind that the Sumerian people's origins are still mysterious, DNA analysis, had it been available at the time, might have opened up some fascinating insights on Puabi's genetic and ancestral background.

What about the clothes that Puabi wore? Given the inevitable perishing of fabrics, we can only infer the appearance of her base garments from the bare-shouldered, ankle-length dresses that Sumerian women are depicted wearing in contemporary art. But even without these the surviving overlying decoration presents a vivid picture. In Woolley's words:

> The upper part of the body was entirely hidden by a mass of beads of gold, silver, lapis lazuli, carnelian, agate and chalcedony, long strings of which, hanging from a collar, had formed a cloak reaching to the waist… against the right arm were

three long gold pins with lapis heads and three amulets in the form of fish, two of gold and one of lapis, and a fourth in the form of two seated gazelles, also of gold.[6]

The crowning glory, however, was the head-dress. A number of the grave's female attendants wore superb head-dresses based on lapis and carnelian bead headbands ornamented with leafy pendants, topped with flowers inlaid with lapis, gold and shell set on a three-pronged silver comb, complemented by chunky lapis and gold necklaces and great crescent-moon-shaped earrings. But Puabi's version was undoubtedly the most magnificent, consisting of a wide, heavy gold hair-ribbon; then an overlying wreath of lapis lazuli cylinder beads and carnelian rings, with hanging gold rings; then a series of overlying wreaths of beech and willow leaves fashioned in gold ornamented with carnelian, punctuated by gold rosettes. From the back of her head there arose a seven-pointed gold comb with seven gold rosettes. Huge crescent-shaped gold earrings dangled from her ears, while around her neck hung a delicate necklace of small gold and lapis beads supporting a circular gold rosette set with carnelian.

But as if this was not enough, there was a second, no less magnificent head-dress at her side. As described by Woolley:

> Onto a diadem made apparently of a strip of soft white leather had been sewn thousands of minute lapis lazuli beads, and against this background of solid blue was set a row of exquisitely fashioned gold animals, stags, gazelles, bulls and goats, with between them clusters of pomegranates, three fruits hanging together shielded by their leaves, and branches of some other tree with golden stems and fruit or pods of gold and carnelian, while gold rosettes were sewn on at intervals, and from the lower border of the diadem hung palmettes of twisted gold wire.[7]

Leonard and Katharine Woolley conducted their 1920s Ur excavations in association with the University of Pennsylvania Museum of Archaeology and Anthropology, and it was only when this second diadem of Puabi's was being put on display recently for an exhibition at the museum that Dr Naomi Miller, a staff archaeobotanist, happened to spot a detail never previously noticed, that the unidentified 'fruits' mentioned by Woolley had been mounted upside down. When she flipped them and allowed them to hang as pendants, her expert eye quickly recognised them as the male and female branches of the date palm,[8] a discovery with some very important consequences for our understanding of just who Puabi was.

For in all the Middle Eastern domestication of plants and animals that had been brought to such a pitch in Puabi's time, one of the more important plants to be cultivated was the date palm. When these palms grow in the wild the proportion of male and female trees is about half and half, with the females of course bearing the actual fruits. So when Mesopotamian societies such as the Sumerians cultivated date palms, they planted many female trees and just a few male ones, hand-pollinating the females from the males to obtain the most abundant crop. Although we do not know who was appointed to perform this vital 'sex act' on the plants' behalf, there can be no doubt that it would have been involved with religious rites, as was everything to do with fertility among ancient peoples. According to the Sumerian religion, mistress of this very process (specifically referred to as 'the one who makes the dates be full of abundance') was the goddess Inanna, the goddess of animal and human fertility in general, whose 'sacred song' quoted earlier might have been the possible cue for the death ritual performed for Puabi's funeral.

In this regard, now assuming rather greater significance is the fact that, although Woolley assumed the graves he found at Ur to have been royal graves, and straightforwardly supposed Puabi to have been a naturally deceased queen, wife of the 'king' whose plundered grave immediately adjoined hers, no Puabi occurs among the surviving lists of Ur's kings and queens. Equally puzzlingly, the rite that was accorded to her, a comparatively rare one, was certainly not accorded to all the members of Sumerian royalty. As tentatively suggested by Dr Moorey, those individuals who, like Puabi, were buried along with such great ancillary human sacrifice may have had a special religious significance. Although Moorey has declined to speculate further, conceivably the rite was associated with the spring fertility festival known to the Sumerians as the *akitu,* during which a Sacred Marriage occurred, with the temple high priestess in some way taking the part of the Fertility Goddess. Certainly a funeral as expensive in human life and jewelled finery as Puabi's could not or would not ever have been held annually. But might there have been certain special 'jubilee' festivals in which a high priestess such as Puabi was sent into the underworld arrayed and attended by a complete 'court' as if she were the Fertility Goddess herself? In such circumstances, our Puabi might actually have walked alive into her grave, just like her entire retinue, hence the cup which Woolley dutifully noted was found alongside her body also.

Whatever the answer, and uncertain and flawed though some details remain, in Katharine Woolley's reconstruction of Puabi we have sparked back into life a most intriguing and, as we now understand, highly sexed woman from civilisation's dawn years, a woman for whom a whole household of men and women were prepared to die in the sure and certain belief that they would serve her again in an afterlife.

7

THE PRIESTESS WITH BLOOD ON HER HANDS *c.*1650 BC

This woman's end was a sudden and violent one, and we can read the circumstances in extraordinary detail. The setting was the idyllic and highly civilised island of Crete, high on a hilltop looking northwards towards the palace of Knossos and the blue Mediterranean. With at least three others she was in the side room of a colourfully decorated temple, taking part in what must have been an emotion-charged religious ceremony. Even after thousands of years we can glimpse her attending a brightly painted altar, see a jar ornamented with the figure of a bull, catch the gleam of a strange-looking knife, hear the swish of her long, tiered skirt. Early though her 'Minoan' civilisation was, it was one with style.

But in seconds, all was over. Suddenly overhead masonry began tumbling, striking her with such force that she fell forward, legs splayed, never to move again. Her male companion had time only to look upwards, instinctively raising his arms to protect himself, before landing on his back as fatally overcome as she. Just feet away the person carrying the bull-decorated jar was similarly stricken, the jar smashing into more than a hundred pieces. Shortly afterwards the entire temple was engulfed in flames, the subsequent ruin apparently evoking such awed superstition that no one, either at the time or for centuries to come, ever dared rake its ashes.

Quite extraordinary therefore is that we can deduce all this across more than 3600 years, virtually without even using a jot of imagination. Thanks to Richard Neave's magic touch, we can contemplate our dead Minoan woman's face[1] as she would have looked in life, before fate so calamitously overtook her.

Yet of this lady and the occurrence that killed her the world remained completely unaware until 1979 when the Greek husband-and-wife archaeologists Yannis and Efi Sakellarakis began digging a hillside site called Anemospilia, near the present-day Cretan village of Archanes.[2] During exploratory surveying Efi had found quantities of ancient pottery, along with a piece of stone carved as a stylised bull's horn. She recognised this as a type that decorated religious buildings during the Minoan civilisation, made famous by Sir Arthur Evans's Knossos excavations. Suspecting that

Reconstruction of the Minoan priestess's facial features, as created by Richard Neave from a cast of her 3600-year-old skull found amidst the ruins of a hillside shrine at Archanes, Crete. The hairstyling, although conjectural, is based on known fashions among Minoan priestesses, as depicted on the stone sarcophagus shown overleaf.

the Anemospilia site might have been a temple from the same period, she and Yannis were thrilled to see emerging from the earth a distinctively tripartite building structure that duly confirmed this.[3]

Then the team came across the excavation's first set of bones, those of the person who had died while carrying the bull-decorated jar. Although this individual, perhaps an attendant, had been so badly crushed by falling masonry that neither age nor sex could be determined, the bones alone were an exciting find, as the only Minoans previously found were individuals who had received formal burial. The remains were found in a corridor area filled with offering jars that led to an ash-filled central room thought to have contained the temple's statue of a god, of whom all that remained were feet of clay. So it seemed that whoever this person was, he or she was in the act of taking the jar to the statue, never to complete the journey.

But it was the contents of the side-room to the temple's west, which the jar-carrier appeared just to have left, that really intrigued the archaeologists. By the west wall there lay the skeleton of a powerfully built man, six feet (1.82m) tall and middle-aged, who had died on his back, his hands raised to protect his face in a classic rigor mortis pose that pathologists call the 'boxer' position. On the little finger of his left hand was a ring with an oval bezel made of silver coated with iron, this latter a very rare and precious commodity in what was then still the Bronze Age. Attached to his wrist was a delicate agate seal depicting a man seemingly punting a slender boat. Since such objects had previously been found only in tombs thought to be royal, there could be no doubt that he was a Minoan of importance. Face down in the corner of the room just to the north of him lay our Minoan lady.

To musical accompaniment, Minoan priestesses offer up a bull as a sacrificial victim, part of the decoration of a stone sarcophagus preserved in Iraklion Museum, Crete. The young man whose bones were found on the altar at Anemospilia may well have been offered up in much the same way.

Most curious of all, however, and ultimately to reveal what was happening in the temple during its last moments, was a set of bones on what seemed to be an altar table next to where the tall man had fallen. The occasional Minoan painting depicts a bull being sacrificed trussed on an altar of this kind,[4] and the Sakellarakises' first assumption was that the bones must have come from some similar large animal. Then from the dust emerged a heavy bronze knife blade, engraved with a monster's face and still razor sharp, on further bones which were unmistakably human. More definitive analysis revealed that they were of a youth of about eighteen years old. He had been about five feet five inches (1.66m) tall, and he lay with his legs drawn up in a foetal position, exactly as if he had been trussed up like a sacrificial animal.

6000 BC – Earliest
settlement at
Knossos, Crete

A new significance suddenly dawned for the shattered, bull-decorated jar found in the corridor, the only object not in its logical place throughout the whole temple. Given that the location was a temple and that a rite was in progress, our Minoan lady and her tall companion with the ring had to have been some kind of priestess and priest. Probably alarmed by a spate of earthquake shocks – to which Crete is particularly prone – they or the people they represented had felt prompted to offer the young man's blood, and with it his life, as an appeasement to the god they believed responsible for such happenings.

But before the attendant carrying the blood-filled jar could reach the statue in the central chamber, a truly massive earthquake struck with devastating suddenness, so severely, as archaeology elsewhere has indicated, that it toppled not only this particular temple but numerous other major public buildings throughout Crete. As the temple's stone and wood roof collapsed on to the occupants, and (as is thought) oil from lighted lamps spilled on to the flammable furnishings and fittings,[5] the whole structure caught fire and disintegrated into a heap of rubble, the bodies of the three sacrifice 'celebrants', together with their victim, remaining undisturbed[6] until the arrival of the Sakellarakises.

From expert appraisal of her bones, our priestess, if that is indeed what she was, has been calculated as in her early to mid-twenties when she died, and a fraction over five feet (1.52m) tall.[7] Her teeth were on the whole healthy – she had lost only one of them at the time of her death – though tartar build-up would have meant she had bad breath. Scientific analysis of her bone-marrow indicates that she had been suffering (ironically in the circumstances) from congenital anaemia, a deficiency of red cells in the blood. This would have caused her to be pale-skinned, with a tendency to over-tiredness and spells of dizziness. Despite the fire her skull was relatively intact, and as expert study revealed, its vault was unusually thick, probably due to the anaemia. Another observation was that her skull's side bones were affected by osteoporosis, or brittleness, a condition apparently fairly prevalent among Minoans, even ones as young as she, possibly occasioned by a 'civilised' rather than hunter-gatherer type of diet.

Despite these deficiencies, Neave's striking facial reconstruction reveals a by no means unattractive face, the high forehead and turned-up nose bearing a marked, and therefore convincing, resemblance to Minoan women as depicted in the

2500 BC – Pyramids at Gizeh, Egypt, begun

2000 BC – First palaces in Minoan Crete

c.1450 BC – Minoan civilisation mysteriously collapses, Crete becoming taken over by Mycenaeans from mainland Greece

3000 BC

2000 BC

1000 BC

1,650 BC – Minoan priestess officiates in temple at Arkhanes, Crete

1290–1224 BC – Pharaoh Ramesses II on the throne of Egypt

brilliantly coloured frescoes at which this civilisation excelled, even when they decorated comparatively ordinary homes. The Greek archaeologist Professor Christos Doumas is currently unearthing numbers of such frescoes in a whole street of humble houses that were preserved Pompeii-style when a massive volcanic eruption overwhelmed a Minoan port on the island of Thera (Santorini), sixty miles (100km) north of Crete, only a hundred years after the earthquake which toppled the Archanes temple.[8] And these frescoes, along with female statuettes found at Knossos and elsewhere on Crete, provide important indications of the sort of attire that our priestess would have worn, since all too few clues survived from the temple itself.

For her hairstyle, for instance, Richard Neave's rendition of a snake-like forelock on her upper forehead, on which he was guided by Efi Sakellarakis, is firmly rooted in the depiction of the women in the Minoan frescoes. In an example from the West House on Thera, specifically interpreted as depicting a priestess making an offering, a fully realistic-looking snake can be seen forming a head-dress.

Minoan 'topless' female fashion? Statuette of a Minoan 'snake goddess', one of the many examples of a bare-breasted, but otherwise surprisingly Victorian fashion that seems to have been popular among the women of Minoan Crete.

However, the Thera frescoes also convey other even more spectacular features of Minoan women's attire, and adornment in general. Their skirts were long and multi-coloured, sometimes quite anachronistically Victorian-looking, with several tiers of flounces. They rouged their cheeks. They clearly loved jewellery, sporting giant earrings, rows of delicate necklaces, and colourful bracelets and anklets in designs that would look at home on stalls in any modern-day holiday resort. Most remarkable of all, despite or because of their exquisitely made bodices, they fully exposed their breasts, one of the few 'civilised' cultures in which women went about their normal life bare-breasted (and Minoan women were no servile underlings). It is more than likely that our priestess would have been thus dressed as she helped collect the blood of the youth at whose sacrifice she had officiated, and whose death her own followed with such untimely swiftness.

Puabi had been a Sumerian of the so-called Early Bronze Age (3200-2000 BC). Our Minoan priestess belonged to the Middle Bronze Age (2000-1500 BC), and she lived about a century earlier than the period of the Thera frescoes, nonetheless at a high stage of cultural development. The numerous pots in her temple had been thrown on the potter's wheel, fashioned to a variety of elegant shapes, fired in purpose-built kilns and painted with tasteful designs. Her high-fashion clothes would have been woven on a loom, dyed and made up as elaborately as any garments of today. She would have enjoyed exotic goods brought back to Crete by the proficient traders among her people. As we noted, the Minoans had exceptionally high living standards, with multi-storey houses, paved streets, toilets and cleverly engineered drainage systems, and she no doubt would have benefited from all this.

Yet although, not least on the strength of Neave's vivid reconstruction, it might seem easy to believe that we know a great deal about the Minoans, in fact they

Staircase section of the Palace at Knossos, indicative of the remarkably civilised way of life that the Anemospilia priestess would have known.

remain a people of considerable mystery to archaeologists.[9] It is unclear where they had come from before they arrived on Crete. Because their Linear A writing script has never been deciphered, no one even knows for sure what language they spoke. Of their social structure, if they had royalty in the fullest sense of the term (and that is undetermined), the only king whom anyone seems to have heard of is Minos, according to Greek legend a heartless tyrant who demanded of the Athenians the lives of seven youths and seven maidens as an annual offering to the mysterious bull-man monster, the Minotaur. Modern thinking has usually dismissed this as merely an old legend, and few scholars had cared to consider that a people as ostensibly civilised as the Minoans could have indulged in anything like human sacrifice – until the Sakellarikises' grim discovery at Archanes.

Barbaric and uncivilised though human sacrifice might seem to us, it is important not to judge our priestess and priest too harshly – or even to assume that they were necessarily a professional priestess and priest at all. Contemporary with, and culturally similar to, the Minoans were the Canaanites, of biblical fame. Among these and related peoples it was expected that whenever dire circumstances threatened, their kings and queens, above anyone else in the community, should sacrifice their eldest son or daughter to whichever god was adjudged in need of appeasement. Egyptian reliefs show this being practised when Canaanite towns were about to be stormed by an enemy, and a similar example can be found in the biblical story of King Mesha of Moab, as recounted in 2 Kings 3: 27.

So could our priestess and priest in actuality have been a local king and queen, with the hapless, trussed-up young man no ordinary victim, but none other than a much loved 'royal' son (perhaps the woman's stepson, given their ages)? In which case the emotion in that side-room of the Anemospilia temple must surely have been much more charged than we have dared to contemplate.

This question is not one of those idle historical ones to which we can never know the answer. The bones of those who died at the Archanes temple have been preserved – that is how Neave came to be able to make his reconstruction not only of the priestess but also of her tall companion – and if they were subjected to DNA analysis (assuming that it proved practical), this ought to determine whether they were related to each other, and if so, how closely.[10] We might find the 'attendant' carrying the bull-decorated jar to be of rather more interest than has previously been acknowledged. So might we also begin to learn rather more of Minoan origins and language.

Priest of Amun
*c.*1100 BC

When he died he was about five feet six inches (1.68m) tall and in his mid-forties. The elaborate mummification procedures that the ancient Egyptian morticians applied to his corpse have blurred any definitive forensic determination of the cause of his death. Because he was rediscovered before the era of scientific archaeology, even the location where he was buried is not known with any accuracy. But in this instance the complex of buildings that were his domain in life still stand, after more than three millennia. And despite their partially ruined state they still command nearly as much awe among present-day visitors to upper Egypt as they would have done in his time.

For his titles, recorded on his well-preserved sarcophagus housed in Leeds City Museum, tell us he was a *waab*, or priest of the largest religious building ever constructed, the temple of the god Amun at Karnak, adjacent to ancient Thebes on the Nile's eastern bank, just to the north of the modern city of Luxor. His titles included 'Scribe of Accounts of the Cattle of the Estate of Amun', Incense-bearer and Scribe in the Shrine of Montu, and a Scribe of the Oblations made to all the gods of Upper and Lower Egypt.[1] Thanks to a fine reconstruction by Richard Neave we can see his face as he would have looked in life, its accuracy being particularly assured given that, as a priest, he would have shaved his head completely. And for the second time among our faces we also know his name: as recorded on his sarcophagus, it is 'Esamun'.[2] Although this was first erroneously transcribed as Natsef-Amun, and still tends to be perpetuated in this form, we will here use the name by which his fellow-Egyptians knew him in life.

The sarcophagus containing Esamun's mummy was discovered around 1823 by an entrepreneurial young Italian antiquities-hunter, Giuseppe Passalacqua. It was almost certainly one of two fine examples which he found at a place he called 'Gournor', a complex of tombs of priests and priestesses in the vicinity of the mortuary temple of Queen Hatshepsut on the western, or 'land of the dead' bank of the Nile, not far from the Valley of the Kings. Passalacqua sent the sarcophagus to

The face of Esamun, (often alternatively referred to as Natsef-Amun), as reconstructed by Manchester University medical artist Richard Neave. Esamun was a priest of the temple of Amun during the reign of the Twentieth Dynasty pharaoh Ramesses XI.

Trieste, and after changing hands several times it was purchased by the Leeds Literary and Philosophical Society, via which it arrived at the Leeds City Museum in northern England.

The changes of ownership were only the start of Esamun's disturbances. In 1828, only shortly after the acquisition by the Leeds Society, the antiquities enthusiasts of the time unwound the many layers of wrappings, removed his mummified internal organs, amputated his hands, and sawed away the back of his skull, all in the name of scientific enquiry. During World War II the Leeds Museum received a direct hit from a German bomb, which blew to smithereens the showcase containing his sarcophagus and destroyed virtually every mummy except his. He was X-rayed in 1931, then again for dental studies in 1964, culminating, from 1989 onwards, in some particularly exhaustive probings by the Manchester Egyptian Mummy Research Project, including a full autopsy by the pathologist Dr Eddie Tapp, and a state-of-the-art CT scan.

Despite or because of all these studies, combined with the knowledge of ancient Egyptian life and times accumulated by Egyptologists, we know a surprising amount of detail about Esamun. A leather ornament that the nineteenth-century Leeds Society investigators found inside his wrappings bears the cartouches, or name boxes, of the Twentieth Dynasty pharaoh Ramesses XI, whose reign is dated *c.*1113-1085 BC.[3] From this we can be sure that Esamun lived around 1100 BC, a time when the Twentieth Dynasty pharaohs were based in the north, in Lower Egypt, while in Upper Egypt, where Thebes and the Karnak temple were located, an army general called Herihor had seized power and made himself High Priest of Amun, and so Esamun's overall boss.

Egyptological sources make it clear that the god Amun, considered Egypt's principal deity at the time, attracted a lot of wealth to the Karnak temple. The god's statue itself reposed in a gem-studded gold shrine inside a small rectangular chamber,

The world that Esamun knew - just a few of the 134 columns of the famous Hypostyle Hall of the temple of Amun at Karnak. In Esamun's time these columns would have been richly decorated and at their most magnificent, having been erected little more than a century before.

2500 BC – Pyramids at Gizeh, Egypt, begun. Earliest version of the Karnak temple may date from this time

c.1550 BC – Beginning of Egypt's New Kingdom

1323 BC – Egyptian pharaoh Tutankhamun dies

1100 BC – Egyptian pri Esamun lives at Temple of Amun, Karr

2500 BC   2000 BC   1500 BC

1290 -1224 BC – Pharaoh Ramesses II on the throne of Egypt

Egyptian priest (seen at left) performing a religious rite. Most were required to shave their heads, in the manner of present-day Buddhist monks, and Esamun's head was similarly shaven when found.

and successive pharaohs vied with their predecessors to make some new addition or alteration to the complex of buildings. There thus grew up the extraordinary agglomeration of pylons (gates), courtyards and halls through which the visitor wanders today in no little bewilderment and awe. In Esamun's time the temple was still largely in its prime; its most magnificent feature, the Hypostyle Hall, 54,000 feet square, with 134 columns, each twelve feet (3.65m) wide, up to seventy feet (21m) high and topped with carved lotus buds and papyrus heads, had been completed little more than a century before. Because any conquests of foreign countries were made under Amun's direction and in his name, all booty from such conquests was duly brought to the temple, its treasuries becoming ever richer and

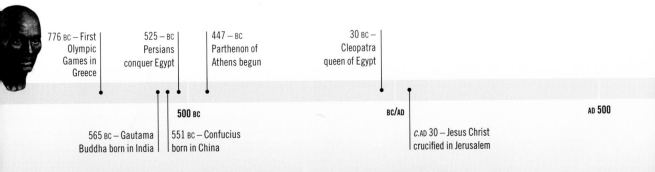

776 BC – First Olympic Games in Greece

525 – BC Persians conquer Egypt

447 – BC Parthenon of Athens begun

30 BC – Cleopatra queen of Egypt

500 BC

BC/AD

AD 500

565 BC – Gautama Buddha born in India

551 BC – Confucius born in China

C.AD 30 – Jesus Christ crucified in Jerusalem

more powerful. It is no surprise, therefore, to find that the Twentieth Dynasty temple was recorded as controlling a vast administrative estate, from the Nile delta in the north to Nubia in the south. Its administrators, scribes, functionaries and general labourers comprised at least seven per cent of the entire Egyptian population, in addition to which, at one tally, it controlled 81,000 slaves, 421,000 cattle, 433 gardens, 46 building yards and 83 ships.

As a result of all this, the life of Esamun and his fellow-priests would have been very comfortable, in a well-ordered society. Their main duties were to process with incense-burners to the sanctuary, sing hymns and perform various salutations before the god's shrine, take out his statue, undress it, wash and cense it, make up its eyebrows with cosmetics, and place offerings of food and drink before it. After withdrawing, backwards, in order to leave the god to enjoy these offerings they would later return the statue to its shrine. Apart from certain festivals when they carried the statue outside the temple, bearing it on their shoulders enclosed within a sacred barque or 'ark', they did not have to suffer intrusions from the general public, and they had no pastoral duties. As a 'Scribe of the Oblations made to all the gods of Upper and Lower Egypt', Esamun would most probably have participated in the ceremony of presenting the food and drink to the god's statue. And because the god ate and drank these things in spirit only, at the end of the day he and his fellow-priests would have been able to divide everything among themselves as part of their salary.

How priests such as Esamun were dressed we know well enough both from Egyptian art and from authorities such as the Greek Herodotus, who although he lived in the fifth century BC was able to observe customs that had changed little in millennia. According to Herodotus the priests 'wear linen only, and shoes made from the papyrus plant, these materials… being the only ones allowed them'.[4] A relief on the walls of the Amun temple depicting a typical priestly procession at festival time shows them wearing long, stiffly laundered linen kilts. The Egyptians had become exceptionally proficient in weaving linen, using huge looms that could produce finest-quality fabrics five feet (1.52m) in width and 180 feet (55m) in length. Even more vivid is a Ramesside wall-painting in the tomb of the priest Userhet at Thebes, showing priests officiating at a funeral. Esamun's apparel would have been much the same.

Another view of Richard Neave's reconstruction of Esamun, showing the distinctively Negroid cast of features. Ancient Egyptian society tended to be multi-racial, with Nubians from the south among its population mix.

From both works of art we can also see the priests to be bald-headed, corresponding to Herodotus: 'The priests shave their bodies all over every day to guard against the presence of lice, or anything else equally unpleasant', their concern apparently being for ritual purity. When Esamun's mummy was unwrapped in 1828 those present duly observed his head, eyebrows and beard to have been closely shaved, there being merely a few short stubbly hairs under his chin.[5] In the interests of the same purity, according to Herodotus, the priests bathed 'twice a day and twice every night', and observed 'innumerable other ceremonies besides'. They did this in the rectangular sacred lake that still forms part of the temple complex. Indicative of Esamun's fastidiousness about hygiene and personal appearance, his fingernails were well manicured, even to the extent of being coloured with henna.

Herodotus reported that circumcision was generally practised among the Egyptians, again 'for cleanliness's sake', but in Esamun's case this cannot be determined because no penis was found, having probably become too desiccated during mummification to survive. However, histological examination of what is likely to have been his scrotum revealed the presence of filaria worms, a parasite notorious for colonising and blocking the body's lymphatic channels and creating gross oedematous swellings to the affected areas. As Egyptians often worked in flooded conditions, or, as in Esamun's case, repeatedly bathed in a lake, such parasitic diseases were and indeed still are common, the worms penetrating the skin and sometimes growing to three feet long inside the body. When Esamun was mummified the desiccation involved would necessarily have reduced or destroyed any scrotal swelling, and there is no certainty that this is what killed him. But if he were indeed a fastidious man, he would undoubtedly have been deeply embarrassed by such an 'unclean' and disfiguring condition, which no amount of washing in the sacred lake would have alleviated.

Other symptoms of declining health can be seen to have accumulated for Esamun during his final months and days. Although, thanks to a sugar-free diet, his teeth showed no signs of decay, and, unlike the Minoan lady, he probably routinely cleaned them with twigs as part of his ablutions,[6] they were seriously worn in a manner that is commonly observed in the mummies of middle-aged ancient Egyptians.

The reason was almost certainly Egyptian bread. Thanks to the sunny climate, irrigation from the Nile, and the Egyptians' well-developed cultivation method, the emmer-type wheat then universally used for bread-making grew in abundance in Egypt – the Greeks called the Egyptians *artophagoi* or 'eaters of bread', because of the unusually large amount they consumed.

Because the dead were commonly supplied with loaves of bread to sustain them in the afterlife, enough examples have been found for detailed scientific study. All too commonly found among the dough are particles of sand, which Egyptian bakers seem to have been unable to prevent from getting into the product during the various stages of bread-making. There can be no doubt, therefore, that Egyptian bread, even that which was served to royalty, was unusually gritty. And although the crowns of human teeth have a sapphire-hard coating of enamel, repeated chewing on such grit inevitably takes its toll.

As a result, Esamun, like many of his fellow ancient Egyptians, including the pharaohs, had his front teeth worn to half the normal crown height, so that the enamel had all gone, exposing the sensitive dentine layer and making them look more like small pegs than teeth. As for his back teeth, he had lost several, and those that remained were flat and without cusps.

Despite such discomforts, however, it is unlikely to have been the state of his teeth that killed Esamun. This inevitably raises the question: what did? Although this is unclear from the pathological examination, one curiosity about him, paralleled only by one other example among the many thousands of mummies preserved in museums around the world, is that, even mummified, he was left with his mouth open and his tongue protruding. Among many cultures around the world – and the Egyptian was no exception – if a person died with the mouth open it was routinely closed by a bandage around the head. But in Esamun's case his morticians seem to have been unable to do this.

Although the protruding tongue provides a clue, it offers no certain answers. Whenever anyone dies by hanging or strangulation, protrusion of the tongue is usually seen. However, Esamun's neck has no visible ligature marks, nor was the hyoid bone at the base of his throat broken, as normally happens in such cases. Cancer of the tongue could cause severe swelling, but histological examination of Esamun's revealed no sign of this. Instead, the likeliest explanation is another oedematous fluid build-up that then shrank, exactly as in his scrotum, during the process of mummification. Conceivably a bee or wasp sting might have been responsible, triggering a fluid build-up in an allergic reaction that would have led to death by choking. But whatever killed Esamun ultimately remains speculative.

To make his facial reconstruction of Esamun, Richard Neave had the not inconsiderable difficulty that the priest's skull was still covered with desiccated flesh. This not only gave a totally distorted idea of how he would have looked in life, it also hindered Neave's normal procedure of working with a totally fleshless skull. To overcome this Esamun's mummy was scanned using computer tomography, giving X-ray information in 3-D. This was then passed to the Department of Medical Physics and Bio-Engineering at University College Hospital, London, where the data thus obtained were translated into a 3-D image viewable on a computer screen. From this a milling machine carved a faithful replica of the skull on to a block of polystyrene, enabling Neave to work from the cast of a skull as usual.

Esamun's sycamore wood outer coffin, as preserved in Leeds Museum. In common with many other Egyptian sarcophagi there was no attempt to represent the deceased's living likeness.

As Neave methodically built up Esamun's features to the appearance that they would have had in life, there emerged a surprising but unmistakable Negroid cast to them, much as in the case of Luzia. There can be no doubt that Esamun would have had such features, though how and why such a person should have attained relatively high office in the hierarchy of so traditionally Egyptian an establishment as the Karnak temple is by no means clear. The rule of the army general Herihor, who made himself high priest at Karnak in Esamun's day, included Nubia, the population of which was more markedly African than in Egypt proper. So it is conceivable that Esamun was a Nubian of known loyalty whom Herihor brought in as an aide in the administration of temple affairs. But given that it is Herihor's rival, Pharaoh Ramesses XI, whose name appears on Esamun's leather 'label', this must remain nothing more than a guess.

All that we can be sure of is that in death Esamun, the Karnak priest with the Negroid features, received the fullest and most traditional of Egyptian funerary honours. An incision was made in his abdomen, and his stomach, intestines, liver and lungs were removed. His brain was drawn out via a hook inserted up his nose. His arms were laid on his inner thighs. Then his cadaver was subjected to the seventy-day process of drying out, aided by natron salts, that would ensure its long-term survival. All this was in accordance with procedures that were still being carried out when Herodotus visited Egypt more than five centuries later. After being coated with unguents and wrapped in bandages, he was laid in two coffin sarcophagi, an inner and outer, like a Russian doll.

While those who buried him, as was customary, created in relief a human face and hands for both the inner and outer sarcophagi, again following the custom of the time they made no attempt to make either effigy a realistic likeness. That was a procedure which would have to wait for 3000 years – and the resurrectory art of Richard Neave.

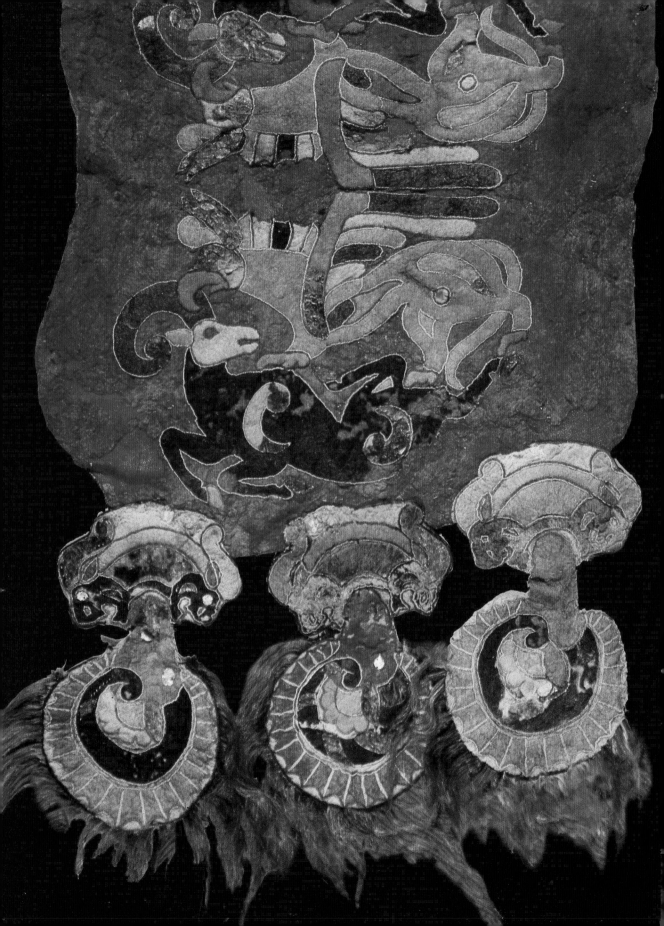

Horse-Queen of the Icy Steppes *c.*500 BC

9

By modern standards she was still only a young woman, about twenty-five years old, and five feet six inches (1.67m) tall, when she died on the 7500-foot (2300m) Ukok plateau in southern Siberia some time around 500 BC.[1] But her richly ornamented felt head-dress added over two feet to her height, requiring her log coffin to be made eight feet (2.4m) long. From this and the fact that six fine horses were specially sacrificed to accompany her to the afterlife, we can be sure she was an individual of power and influence. We do not know her name, nor what had killed her so young. Even her nationality is variously described as 'Scythian', 'Pazyryk' and 'Ukok'. But that she kept an eye on her appearance is evident from the wood-framed silver mirror that she carried with her to the grave. The survival of her clothing gives us a good idea of what she wore in life. And thanks to the preservation of her hair, and a fine reconstruction from her skull made by the Russian anthropologist Tatyana Baluyeva, we also know what she looked like – well enough for her almost certainly to recognise herself.

Left: Felt and leather saddle-cover from a Pazyryk burial, with decoration typifying the lively, stylised 'Scythian' art prevalent among the semi-nomadic peoples to which the 'horse-queen' belonged.

Below: Typical terrain of southern Siberia as frequented by the horse-queen and her tribe.

'Scythian' is a general term loosely applied to the various ancient horse-loving peoples, many of them semi-nomadic, who lived as largely autonomous tribes scattered across the vast, treeless grasslands extending eastwards from north of the Black and Caspian Seas to China. The Greek historian Herodotus, a near-contemporary of our 'horse-queen', wrote of the Scythians as 'a people without fortified towns, living… in wagons which they take with them wherever they go, accustomed, one and all, to fight on horseback with bows and arrows, and dependent for their food, not upon agriculture, but upon their cattle'.[2] In some tribes women warriors, adept with the bow and javelin, apparently fought on horseback alongside the men. With his characteristic eye for detail Herodotus described the mummification methods that they used for royalty, how the stomach was 'slit open, cleaned out and filled with various aromatic substances… then sewn up again and the whole body coated over with wax'.[3] He also related how, when the royal body was laid in its great rectangular pit tomb, it was customary for up to fifty servants and fifty horses to be slaughtered, mummified in the same way as their master or mistress, then buried alongside.

All of this, despite Herodotus' reputation as a historian, might have seemed so much folk-tale. Then in the late 1920s the Russian archaeologist Sergei Rudenko, exploring the Ust Ulagan valley in southern Siberia's Altai mountains, came across a number of kurgans or mound-covered pit-graves dating mostly from the fifth to third

centuries BC.[4] When Rudenko opened them up he found they contained the bodies of men and horses remarkably preserved by mummification methods strikingly similar to those described by Herodotus. Water had seeped into the pit-graves during the region's few warmer months, the only time that the ground was soft enough to be dug into. It had then frozen hard (and stayed frozen because of the kurgan's insulating properties), thereby preserving even better the graves' contents.

Despite looting by gold-seeking Turks who invaded the region from the third century BC onwards, the skin and tissues as well as the garments were often surprisingly intact. One male was found to have intricate tattoos on his skin, and the horses' felt and leather saddle-covers often still bore the distinctive, highly stylised animal motifs with which they had been decorated.

But nearly half a century of stagnation in Russian archaeology followed the Second World War, and it was 1990 before Rudenko's pioneering work was taken up again by Natalya Polosmak of the Russian Institute of Archaeology and Ethnography at Novosibirsk. On the recommendation of a colleague she visited the archaeologically

The face of the horse-queen as she would have looked in life, reconstructed by Russian anthropologist Tatyana Baluyeva. Her features have a classically Mongoloid cast to them. To the right of the bust is a sketch showing part of the elaborate plume head-dress that the horse-queen wore in death. Her coffin needed to be made longer to accommodate this.

1323 BC – Egyptian pharaoh Tutankhamun dies

c.500 BC – Horse Queen lives in southern Siberia

333 BC – Alexander the Great conquers Persia

1500 BC

1000 BC

500 BC

776 BC First Olympic Games in Greece

565 BC Gautama Buddha born in India

447 BC Parthenon of Athens begun

unexplored Ukok plateau, a hundred miles (160km) south of the Ust Ulagan valley, where in her very first season she came across an ice-locked kurgan containing the skeletons of a forty-year-old man and a sixteen-year-old girl. Each had been provided with battle-axes, knives and bows, and buried with them were ten horses.

Although this grave, like those opened up by Rudenko, had been looted in antiquity, in July 1993 Polosmak had a breakthrough. Excavating a ruined-looking kurgan just ten yards from Russia's border with China, she came across a shallow coffin containing the body of a man who had been buried with three horses. This too had been looted, but she suspected that a more important burial probably lay below this. Polosmak dug down further and to her delight came across the unbroken roof of what could only be a very substantial tomb-chamber. This meant that whatever lay beneath was almost certainly unlooted.

Careful removal of the chamber's roof revealed a dauntingly solid block of ice, which slowly began to melt in the daytime sun, enabling portions to be steadily cut away until dark shapes came into view. Then, with the aid of buckets of hot water, little by little there began to emerge grave goods, among these a coffin lid, and two short-legged birchwood salvers bearing joints of meat. Immediately outside the chamber, against its north wall, lay the bodies of six horses, each with neat holes in their foreheads from the axe used to despatch them. These were caparisoned with colourful felt saddlecloths and superbly ornamented trappings; even the iron bridle bits were joined to gilded, carved wood fastenings. From analysis of their stomach contents the Swiss specialist Mathias Seifert determined that they had been munching on grass, twigs and pine needles only shortly before their deaths, and that the season was springtime.

Inevitably the prime focus of attention was the contents of the tomb's eight-foot-long coffin, expertly hollowed out from a single larchwood log, and decorated with deer motifs in appliqué leather. Inside, lying on her side with hands crossed over her pelvis, the face simply a skull, but some flesh elsewhere surprisingly intact, was our 'horse-queen'.

And quite a woman she proved to be. Although her immediate wrapping was a much-decayed blanket of marten fur, beneath this she was elegantly dressed in a

*c.*AD 30 – Jesus Christ
crucified in Jerusalem

622 – The Hegira, or flight of
Mohammed to Medina, starting
point of the Muslim calendar

1096 – First
Crusade
launched

yellow kaftan-style silk top with maroon piping, possibly made in China, and a full-length woollen skirt decorated with horizontal white and maroon stripes. On her head was a tall, heavy, complicated contraption. It was partly a wig, partly her own hair, and difficult to undo, so that she may well have needed some special support for it at night. Its accompanying plume head-dress was of felt on a wooden frame, decorated with eight golden cats. Like Ötzi the Iceman she was tattooed, though this seems to have been purely for ritual or decorative purposes rather than for health reasons. On her well-preserved

The horse-queen's grave as photographed moments before the opening of the coffin. Archaeologist Natalya Polosmak with her dog watches from above.

flesh a lively stag was etched in a style strikingly similar to the art of the Scythians, known from the fabrics and metalwork preserved in the Hermitage, St Petersburg. A creature more difficult to identify was tattooed on her wrist. Facially, as revealed by Tatyana Baluyeva's reconstruction, she had classically Mongoloid features.

We know something of the foods she ate, and even something of how she ate them. On one of the two tables among the grave furniture there was a small joint of mutton from the fatty, tail end of a sheep that Kazakhs call *kurdyuk*, with on the second table a joint of horsemeat. The smell that these gave off as Polosmak and her helpers melted the ice around them made it quite apparent that they had begun to rot before the kurgan's insulation properties had locked them in permanent deep-freeze. A bronze knife was stuck into the piece of horsemeat. Our horse-queen probably ate her meat much as Mongolians do to this day, by holding a chunk in the teeth and using the knife to saw away the excess. Wild onions and garlic would have added flavour to meats of this kind, which are thought to have been served boiled.

In one corner of the burial chamber a wooden vessel decorated with cats on its handle, and supplied with a wooden stirrer, contained a dairy product thought to have been some kind of yoghurt. Such products as cottage cheese and a fermented mare's milk called *koumiss* are still popular among the horse-riding peoples who frequent the Ukok plateau to this day.

Our horse-queen's semi-nomadic life was most probably spent on horseback during the summers, living in portable huts or tents called yurts, roving the local grasslands to find the richest pastures for the tribe's flocks of sheep. Then each October she and her people would return to Ukok, where the plateau's scouring winds keep the grass relatively free of snow and where the worst of the winter could be spent in the comfort of more permanent cabins built from the same timber as that used for her burial. Colourful fabrics similar to those used as saddle-covers no doubt decorated the walls, and felts carpeted the floors.

The geography of the Ukok region makes it clear that in order to inter our horse-queen, the burial party had to travel fifteen miles (24km) to the nearest forest in order to find logs for the tomb's sides, and to select a stout tree for the coffin. They then had to drag the wood back to the burial site, perhaps using horses. A huge pit had to be dug deep into the soil, a task that would have been impossible in the winter, when the ground was deep-frozen. After a big enough rectangle had been excavated, it had to be lined with the logs, each trimmed to the required shape, then the floor was covered with felt to make it comfortable for the afterlife.

According to Herodotus, even when ordinary people died, the Scythian custom was for the corpse to be taken around the neighbourhood in a cart for forty days, during which banquets would be held and the corpse served with food, just like the living.[5] No doubt similar feasting, but on a grander scale, preceded the roofing-over of our horse-queen's tomb and the final mounding of earth on top to create a traditional kurgan. It remained a funeral custom in the Altai region even up to the beginning of the twentieth century for a harnessed horse to be sacrificed and buried with the deceased,[6] a tradition clearly harking back to the practice already well established in our horse-queen's time.

The discovery in 1993 aroused world-wide interest. There was no question of her being allowed to remain in Ukok, in the grave that her people had so painstakingly made for her.

The horse-queen's freshly enshrouded body seen awaiting transfer to Novosibirsk. From there it was taken to Moscow where conservation procedures were implemented.

On 2 August of that year a helicopter arrived to take her to Novosibirsk. From there, because of the need for specialist preservation procedures, she was taken to Moscow's Biological Structures Research Institute, one of whose earlier clients destined to be immortalised had been a certain Vladimir Ilyich Lenin.

No doubt there is more to be learned from our horse-queen's remains, not least from comparison of her DNA with that of today's inhabitants of the Ukok plateau. But, stung by losing her to Moscow, the government of the Altai Republic has banned any further archaeological excavation of kurgans for the time being. So if out on the icy steppes there are other 'horse-queens' whose kurgans are yet to be discovered, they at least can slumber on undisturbed for a while yet.

10

THE FATHER OF ALEXANDER
336 BC

A sturdy, bearded forty-six-year-old, between five feet six and five feet eight inches (1.67-1.72m) tall, he died in a year that posterity would come to know as 336 BC. He was confidently standing in his capital's theatre, enjoying enthusiastic applause from crowds who had gathered there to celebrate his daughter Cleopatra's marriage, when suddenly one of his own bodyguard, Pausanias, sprang menacingly forward. Before he could even begin to protect himself, the assassin had plunged a knife into him, and he fell dying to the floor. History knows him as Philip II of Macedon, the king who in two decades had transformed the backward northern Greek state of Macedon or Macedonia into a vigorous military and trading power that had eclipsed Athens and was poised to do the same to the might of Persia. It also knows him as father of Alexander the Great. However, it is thanks only to the art of Richard Neave[1] that we can put a face to him, a face that, as Neave's expertise reveals, even in life bore some fearsome scars from Philip's struggles to achieve his nation's ascendancy.

According to classical historians, Alexander was only eighteen years old when he so unexpectedly succeeded to the throne. He apparently dealt swiftly with the assassins, then 'took every possible care of his father's burial' at Macedon's capital, Aigai. But where exactly was Aigai? Until thirty years ago most scholars assumed it to be Edessa in what is today northern Greece. They expressed considerable disbelief when in 1968 Professor Nicholas Hammond of Bristol University put forward the argument that it was the town now known as Vergina, forty miles (64km) to Edessa's south-east. Yet it fell to one of the disbelievers, the veteran Greek archaeologist Professor Manolis Andronicos, to prove Hammond right nine years later.

In October 1977, in the course of excavating a huge mound at Vergina, Andronicos came upon ancient burials of evidently royal status. One tomb had been plundered in antiquity, but another was intact, consisting of two chambers, each containing marble sarcophagi. Inside the smaller sarcophagus was a gold casket containing a woman's bones that had been partially burnt, as if on a funeral pyre,

The face of King Philip II of Macedon, as reconstructed by Richard Neave. Neave's recreation of the king's disfigured right eye derives from particularly meticulous research, and the styling of the beard is based on the ivory reproduced on p.107.

then wrapped in what remained of a cloth of purple and gold. These were clearly the trappings of royalty, but it was the casket found inside the larger sarcophagus that was to prove revelatory.

This was of solid gold, weighing over 24 lbs (11kg), and its lid was embossed with a sixteen-point star, the symbol of the Macedonian kings. Inside, again wrapped in cloth of purple and gold, were a skull and other bones that had undergone partial burning. There was also a delicate wreath of oak leaves and acorns. Although neither the casket nor the tomb bore any identifying inscription, pathological examination of the bones indicated that the occupant was a man aged between thirty-five and fifty-five at the time of his death. Accompanying pottery suggested that he lived during the second half of the fourth century BC. Since Alexander the Great, who died in 323 BC, is known to have been buried at Alexandria in Egypt, the likelihood had to be that the bones were either those of Alexander's father Philip II, or of Alexander's successor and half-brother Philip III Arrhidaeus, who met a similarly violent fate in 317 BC.

Although even at a very early stage Andronicos's suspicions favoured Philip II, he was careful never to claim this publicly while he looked for any opportunity that might properly clinch the identification. Accordingly, when in 1978 Dr John Prag of the Manchester Museum suggested that Richard Neave might make a facial reconstruction from the skull, Andronicos needed little persuasion. In September 1981 Neave flew to Thessaloniki, Greece, where, in the city's museum, he carefully moulded casts of the skull bones and took them back to Manchester to make a proper reconstruction. Although there was some concern that the burning might have shrunk and distorted the bones, painstaking research by Bristol University's Dr Jonathan Musgrave showed any shrinkage to be as little as ten per cent, and serious distortion highly unlikely.

Even so, certain peculiarities and asymmetries prompted Neave to seek advice from specialists in congenital malformations and major facial injuries. One oddity was an underdevelopment of the left side of the head, which he was advised would have been barely noticeable in adult life and would not have affected mental development. Another, far more dramatic, was an injury to the bones of the right eye-socket and displacement of the right cheekbone. According to the medical

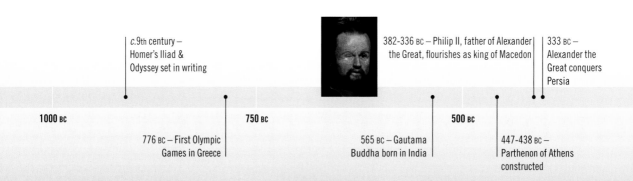

c.9th century –
Homer's Iliad &
Odyssey set in writing

382-336 BC – Philip II, father of Alexander the Great, flourishes as king of Macedon

333 BC –
Alexander the
Great conquers
Persia

1000 BC

750 BC

500 BC

776 BC – First Olympic
Games in Greece

565 BC – Gautama
Buddha born in India

447-438 BC –
Parthenon of Athens
constructed

The magnificent gold casket in which King Philip's cremated bones were found in 1977. The starburst on the lid is a symbol of the royal dynasty of ancient Macedon.

experts Neave consulted, a number of years before his death the skull's owner had suffered a serious facial wound that had healed, indicated by the degree the bone had knitted back together. A projectile striking the eye from above had inflicted this, almost certainly causing it to be blinded.

For Neave, for Prag, and not least for Andronicos, this represented most important corroboration that the bones were genuinely those of Philip II. As recorded by the first-century BC historian Didymus Chalcenterus, Philip had 'had his right eye cut out when he was struck by an arrow while inspecting the siege engines and the protective sheds at the siege of Methone'.[2] This occurred in 354 BC, eighteen years before his death. Another slightly later commentator described the comparative levity with which Philip treated this injury at the time:

146 BC – Romans
conquer Macedonia

*c.*AD 30 – Jesus Christ
crucified in Jerusalem

BC/AD   AD 250   AD 500

44 BC – Julius   30 BC – Death of
Caesar assassinated   Cleopatra, queen of Egypt

Left: Ruins from the classical period at Vergina, Greece. Only within the last generation has this been reliably identified as the site of ancient Aigai, Macedon's capital in King Philip's time.

The wound did not make him slower in war, or angrier with his enemies, so much so that a few days later he granted them peace at their request, and was not only restrained but also mild to the vanquished.[3]

From such information Neave learnt enough to build up in clay over the plaster skull not only the general shape of Philip's face, but also the disfigurement he had suffered. The plan was for this model, once fully finished in clay, to be fired, cast and translated into wax to be shown in the most lifelike form possible at a classical archaeology congress being held in Athens in 1983.

But for fine details of Philip's appearance, it was important to take advantage of any additional clues available. For Philip's hair and beard, nothing of which had survived the cremation, help came in the form of a miniature ivory head of a bearded man found in his tomb, originally attached, with several others, to a funerary couch long since rotted away. From clues such as a nick to the ivory's right eyebrow, suggestive of Philip's facial injury, the likelihood had to be that this represented Philip himself, and it therefore provided a useful reference for the TV make-up artist Ruth Quinn, who was brought in to make all the final touches.

For the hair and skin colour Mrs Quinn chose the dark hair and tanned appearance common among Mediterranean peoples. For the beard length she carefully followed the tomb ivory. A marble head of Philip in Copenhagen also proved helpful.

This left by far the most difficult task: how to render the historically crucial eye-wound. On the initial model shown at Athens in 1983, Mrs Quinn made it look inflamed, drawing upon her first-hand observation of a terrible axe-wound suffered by a Canadian lumberjack that had been left untreated for several weeks and had healed naturally. However, subsequent to the Athens congress Dr Christopher Ehrardt of Otago University, New Zealand, pointed out a classical reference that Prag and Neave had overlooked. This recorded that the Greek doctor Kritoboulos had 'achieved great renown for having extracted the arrow from the eye of King Philip, and for having treated the loss of eyeball without causing disfigurement to the face'.[4] Kritoboulos is thought to have deployed a surgical instrument specially developed for removing arrows, and if he was similarly skilled in post-operative care he may well have spared Philip much pain and a disfigurement that might have

Above: Ivory miniature found in Philip's tomb, thought to be a contemporary portrait of the king. This and contemporary coin portraits guided the styling of the beard and hair tfeatured in the reconstruction reproduced on p.102.

been altogether more serious. Neave's reconstruction was therefore modified in order to take this new information into account.

Three pairs of greaves (armour to protect the leg below the knees, worn by foot soldiers) were found in the tomb chamber. These are unlikely to have belonged to Philip, since kings of Macedon fought on horseback, before the invention of the stirrup. They are more likely to have been war trophies. More plausible as having belonged to Philip is a helmet found in the tomb. Although we cannot be sure he was wearing it when injured, it is in a style that would have failed to protect him at the very point where the arrow appears to have struck his eye. Here contemporary fashion was against him, for had he worn the Corinthian-style helmet that was the vogue during the previous century his field of vision would have been more limited, but at least he would have been better protected.

Thanks to the great advances in civilisation achieved by Macedon's Athenian neighbours at their apogee little more than a century before his lifetime, Philip was able to enjoy a lifestyle that would be considered comfortable today, and included many elements that we take for granted. For instance, the fine classical styling of his tomb reflected a standard of excellence in architecture that, even two millennia later, during the time of the American Revolution, was being emulated rather than outshone. As evident from murals in the tomb, painting had reached standards of naturalism that would not be achieved again until the Italian Renaissance. Proficiency in metalworking was such that coinage, invented only three centuries before, had become widespread and attained high technical and artistic quality. Some of Philip's coins, well up to today's standards, featured his equestrian image on their reverse.

Of the woman who was buried in the other sarcophagus found in Philip's tomb, her identity is not obvious, since the Macedonians were polygamous and Philip had made six or seven marriages for political reasons. Historically it is known that shortly before his death he repudiated Alexander's mother Olympias, a Molossian, in favour of a high-born young Macedonian called Cleopatra. Dr Prag and his colleagues favour this identity[5] for the woman buried with Philip, forensically determined as around twenty-five when she died, though from a golden quiver and other accoutrements buried with her another possibility is that she was either a Getic princess, daughter of King Cothelas, or a Scythian princess, daughter of King Atheas. Both the Getic peoples and the Scythians were renowned archers. Herodotus, in the section of his *Histories* detailing the Scythian funerary rites so pertinent to our 'horse-queen', described it as customary for a Scythian king's wife to join her husband in death, sometimes being strangled for this purpose.[6] Something similar certainly seems to have happened to the woman buried with Philip, one possibility being that her cremation was on the very same funeral pyre.

III

FACES FROM THE ROMAN ERA

HISTORICAL INTRODUCTION

Rome from the republic's birth to the empire's fall

I f the Greeks succeeded in creating a lifestyle that most of us would find congenial today, the Romans went on to succeed in spreading it with some degree of permanence across much of the known world. They also managed to change every culture that they came across, though in the process they themselves often absorbed something from each encounter.

In the sixth century BC, when Greece was enjoying the age of Pericles, Rome was but a minor city-state, becoming a republic for the first time in 510 BC. A few decades later the Romans defeated and absorbed the neighbouring Latins and Volscians, and most notably the Etruscans of Tuscany, a people whose advances in art, architecture, town-planning, metallurgy and much else had a great deal in common with the Greeks, but whose language was quite different. Our face number 11 was a well-born Etruscan woman living under Roman rule.

Although for some three centuries the Phoenicians of Carthage checked the Romans from taking over the western Mediterranean, the Roman victory at the battle of Zama in 202 BC proved a turning point. Soon the Roman military machine was systematically overcoming the Gauls of what is now France, and the native tribes of Spain. Then it was the turn of the Greeks, the Macedonians, and the Illyrians (in the area until recently known as Yugoslavia). Although Celts in far-off Britain, such as our face number 12, survived for a while longer without Roman intrusion, even for them it was only a matter of time.

In the first century BC a series of very able Roman generals vied with each other for political mastery. From these struggles Julius Caesar emerged supreme, in the process bringing much of Africa, including Cleopatra's Egypt, under Roman sway. Gifted as an orator, writer and administrator as well as a soldier, Caesar furthered social policies that made him acceptable to a consensus of the republican Senate as king in all but name. But this attracted sufficient enmity for him to become victim of history's most famous assassination, in 44 BC. It thereupon fell to his young great-nephew Octavian, then a nineteen-year-old student in Greece, to bring to fruition what may justly be termed the world's first real superpower, the Roman Empire.

To win his spurs Octavian had to fight a series of battles, among them that of Actium against Antony and Cleopatra in 31 BC. On his victory he emerged with a control of the Roman Empire that gave him a despot's total authority – though to avoid his uncle's fate, he was careful always to maintain the outward form of the old republic, and to use his power wisely for the greatest social benefit.

In 2 BC, Octavian, having assumed the title Augustus twenty-five years before, was dubbed 'Pater patriae', 'Father of the fatherland', a title which acknowledged that he more than anyone had brought the empire to its apogee. Thanks to Roman biography, one of the many arts that he fostered, Augustus is one of the earliest figures in history whom we are able to see as a flesh-and-blood human being, much as we can our reconstructed faces. This is the description of him in old age that the biographer Suetonius has provided:

> His left eye had only partial vision. His teeth were small, few and decayed; his hair yellowish and rather curly; his eyebrows met above the nose; he had ears of normal size, a Roman nose, and a complexion between intermediate and fair. Julius Marathus… makes his height five feet seven inches [1.7m]… He had a weakness in his left hip, thigh and leg, which occasionally gave him the suspicion of a limp… In winter he wore no fewer than four tunics and a heavy woollen gown above his undershirt; and below that a woollen chest protector; also underpants and woollen gaiters… In summer he… always wore a broad-brimmed hat to protect himself against glare.[1]

Yet despite such human frailty Augustus lived to the age of seventy-seven, and the stamp that he imposed both on his native city and on the world that he controlled from it was definitive. In the case of Rome itself he claimed without exaggeration to have 'found it brick and transformed it into marble', reflecting his erection of a new forum, theatre and various temples, arches and porticoes. Far greater, however, were his achievements on behalf of its lowlier inhabitants and their dwellings. When he came to power many of Rome's million-strong population lived in shoddily built high-rise tenements prone to fires and structural collapse. Robbery and lawlessness were rife. Although sewers ran beneath the streets, only the wealthy were connected to them, and epidemics killed slum-dwellers by the thousand, as is evident from mass graves uncovered by archaeologists.

For administrative purposes, Augustus divided the city into districts, empowered to hold local elections to choose officials to run them. He introduced building regulations to curb shoddy standards of housing construction, set up a police force to deal with civic crime and created a fire brigade. He arranged for a civic body to control the river and the city's water supply. He instituted a body to regulate the corn requirements, so that rations could be provided for the needy. With these measures he ensured that Rome was clean, well-ordered, with a good water supply, and had the control structure to stay that way.

It is important to appreciate that Augustus did not create these things out of a vacuum. Following Greek and Etruscan precedents his predecessors in the republic had already brought the city's more well-heeled citizens to advanced living standards. But what he achieved was what Romans in general most excelled at: bringing good order, something which stretched well beyond their own city and time.

Reflective of this good order was the means of communication via a simple but effective alphabet. With the exception of the letters 'j', 'u' and 'w' (which were added later) we owe directly to the Romans the very lettering[2] used nowadays for the text of most European and American newspapers and magazines – both the letters themselves and their shapes. Read the inscription at the base of Trajan's column in Rome, carved in AD 114, and you will be looking at letter shapes that are essentially identical to the capital letters of the commonly used Times Roman typeface. We also owe them much else that we take for granted, such as our calendrical system, which has undergone only one major modification since the days of Julius Caesar.

An expression of Roman order, already well established, was the coinage system, which acted as a backbone to the entire economy. With coins of too high a quality to counterfeit easily, it meant that trading transactions could be conducted with total confidence and assurance hundreds of miles apart. Behind Rome's legions came merchants, and with those merchants a wealth of goods and services that enhanced many lifestyles. Roman ships plied the Mediterranean transporting all manner of commodities, one of the men who manned those ships being our face number 13. We take for granted the shop as part of modern life. Yet it may come as a surprise to learn that such merchant establishments were just as much the norm under the Roman aegis 2000 years ago. The Romans may not have been the world's first shopkeepers, but thanks to coinage they certainly gave a powerful boost to shopping as an everyday activity.

Another example of Roman order was the land distribution system, under which land was apportioned, not in lots of random or convenient shape, but in exactly measured squares, the outlines of which still show up in aerial photography. Likewise, Roman military camps were laid out to the same exacting standards, and again their regimented outlines are instantly recognisable from the air.

A major achievement was the road system. Starting with their home territory and continuing wherever they made a conquest, the Romans built good roads so that

Typifying the impressiveness and durability of Roman engineering, the Roman aqueduct over the river Gard (or Gardon). This was constructed in the time of Augustus to convey a reliable water supply over a thirty-mile distance to the city of Nemausus, now Nîmes, in southern France.

communications could be quick and easy, and control thereby facilitated. In Italy the Via Appia, which extended all the way from Rome to modern Brindisi, would be considered a remarkable engineering feat even today. In Britain, which the Romans invaded in the mid-first century AD, a few decades after Augustus' death, their roads remain the country's straightest, such as the old Fosse Way from Exeter to Lincoln. Instead of routing a road via whatever natural contours might involve least effort, the Romans went to enormous lengths to build viaducts across chasms or to dig tunnels through solid rock. Enabling them to achieve such high engineering and construction standards were teams of professional surveyors who worked much like their present-day counterparts, marking out lines at right angles to each other by taking sights from a central point using a surveying instrument called the groma, predecessor of the theodolite.

The foundation of the first proper hospitals, or valetudinaria, as they were called, was another expression of Roman order. These were first set up in Rome for army surgeons to treat soldiers who had been sent back home because of disease or injury. As the empire spread its frontiers, they began to be established as army hospitals at key provincial locations; several examples have been excavated. Greeks, because of their medical expertise, were widely employed as physicians. Greeks throughout the empire were mostly encouraged to remain in places that they had colonised before the Romans; hence many stayed on under Roman patronage in the former Greek colony of Egypt.

Part and parcel of this apparent magnanimity is that, immensely practical and pragmatic though the Romans were in mundane matters such as plumbing and drainage systems, they also had their superstitious streak, from the lowliest peasant to Augustus himself. When they engaged in a war of conquest they liked to believe they had divine sanction to do so. They wanted to feel that they were doing it for genuinely worthy reasons, and that it was their duty to govern with fairness those they vanquished. The Roman poet Virgil, whom Augustus patronised along with other literary luminaries such as Horace and Livy, expressed the ethos of the Roman imperial ideal:

> Roman take heed, with empire rule the world!
> These be thy arts – to set the law of peace,
> To spare the vanquished and to quell the proud.[3]

In doing what was right and just, clearly the upholding of law itself had to be the key. And all too rarely appreciated is that the principles of Roman law were so sound that they form the foundation of the legal systems used to this day. As early as 451 BC the Romans formulated a civil law of twelve tables governing the way one individual was expected to behave towards another, tables which became handed down from one generation to the next. Good decisions made in earlier cases grew into a legal precedent system so well grounded that, even when Rome fell into the hands of mad and bad emperors such as Caligula and Nero, it served to keep the fabric of state together. It is no accident that our very words 'judge', 'justice', 'judicial' and 'jury' are all based on the word *ius*, law. And, at least under Augustus, high moral standards were set. Women, certainly the higher-born ones, could have plenty of power and influence. Marriages producing children were regarded as the ideal. Prostitution was tolerated – a city such as Pompeii had establishments that openly plied their trade. But adultery, certainly in the early empire, was proscribed, so that when Augustus' own married daughter Julia misbehaved sexually she was banished to an island.

Time and again, if we look to institutions or processes that we suppose to be modern, the Romans already had them. Although we might suppose the glass bottle to be modern, in fact glass-blowing appeared in the Syro-Palestinian province of the Roman Empire some time around the middle of the first century BC,[4] and within a few decades had been developed to the perfection of the Portland Vase. As we shall see, our face number 14 was buried with the finest Roman glass, even in the far-off province of Britain.

The Romans had advertising, for there were many election notices and brothel advertisements to be seen in and around Pompeii. For their military communications they used a system of semaphore from one observation post to another. They encoded their state secrets. Indeed, with the exception of printing, in the tide of human progress there was very little up to two centuries ago that the Romans had not already developed – one of the few factors distinguishing modern society from theirs being industrialisation. And the Romans even came close to this, for they had water-mills, windlasses and the like, for which they used gear-type wheels of exactly the same principle as those that would drive the Industrial Revolution. But they were hampered by having to make such machinery of wood, having failed to advance their metallurgy to the necessary degree. Furthermore, any incentive to industrialise was blunted by the near-inexhaustible labour force of slaves they had at their disposal to carry out menial and repetitive tasks at the snap of a finger.

An aspect of the Roman way of life inherited from the Greeks and Etruscans which contributed both to their downfall, and in a perverse way to their reformation, was the passion for using human lives as arena entertainment. Among the most spectacular of the Roman Empire's surviving ruins are those of its amphitheatres, the most famous being the 70,000-seat monster in Rome now known as the Colosseum. In such stadia (and virtually every large Roman town had one), the local impresarios vied with each other to present scenes of spectacle and violence. Popular events were animal hunts, with tigers, panthers, giraffes, ostriches, zebras – all captured, shipped to the amphitheatre and released to be hunted and killed, a practice which probably led to the extinction of several entire species from the Mediterranean environs.

But the greatest thrill offered by arena entertainment was the shedding of human blood. A Roman mosaic from Zliten in North Africa depicts a man being pushed forward in a small wheeled cart, bound to a stake and helpless to prevent himself from being torn to pieces by a leopard no doubt specially starved to enhance its viciousness. Although victims of these atrocities were often convicted robbers and murderers, under the more bestial of the emperors they might be women whose only crime was espousal of the strange religion founded by Yeshua, Jesus Christus as the Romans dubbed him, crucified in the Roman province of Judaea. During the reign of the first-century emperor Domitian the early Christian bishop Clement described how women Christians were tied to the horns of a wild bull and gored to death as a cynical re-enactment of the classical myth of Dirce. In Carthage during the early third century two young mothers, Perpetua and her slave-girl Felicitas, were thrust naked into an arena enlivened by a free-roaming leopard, bear, boar and wild cow.

To the consternation of arena promoters, on occasion audiences reacted with pity and sympathy towards those being offered up for public entertainment. Indeed, Christian values inexorably spread from slaves upwards to the high-born as offering a code of greater value than the Roman civil law. So when in the early fourth century the would-be emperor Constantine took the decision to lead his army with the Christian monogram Chi-Rho as its battle-standard, he not only won the battle, but a mastery of the whole empire to equal that of Augustus.

Today religion tends to be so undervalued in our society that it is all too rarely realised what an extraordinary turning point that was. If Constantine had decided otherwise there might never have been church spires the length and breadth of Europe and North America. There might never have been a Sistine Chapel ceiling, and our art and literature would have been much the poorer. But Christianisation was far from an unqualified blessing for the Roman world, certainly in the short term. Along with his embrace of Christianity, Constantine shifted the empire's capital from Rome east to Constantinople. That, together with other changing factors, led to a weakening of its overall defence structure.

Up to the end of the fourth century AD, Germanic tribes known as the Ostrogoths and Visigoths had been fairly peacefully settled in valleys around the Black Sea. Then, around AD 370, fierce Huns from the east sent them westwards to refuge within the empire's borders. Once displaced they proved both restive and, as skilled horse-people, fully capable of taking on Roman armies softened by a long peace. In 410 this led to the capture of Rome by Alaric the Visigoth, followed by two further sacks within the next fifty years, the worst being by the Vandals in 455. With the withdrawal of permanently stationed legions, Roman control of Britain was lost.

11

A Tuscan Matriarch
*c.*150 BC

Though the formal name by which archaeologists know her is Seianti Hanunia Tlesnasa, her fellow Etruscans probably called her Hanunia, the feminine form of 'Hanu', a popular given name amongst the Seiante clan into which she was born.[1] She was a short, plump, well-to-do, but in later life painfully disabled woman who died at the age of around fifty-five in the environs of what is today the little Tuscan hill-town of Chiusi, some ninety miles (150km) south of Florence. At the time of her death, around the middle of the second century BC, Chiusi was called Clusium, immortalised in Macaulay's *Lays of Ancient Rome* as the seat of the Etruscan king Lars Porsena, whose army the valiant Horatius ('Captain of the Gate'), almost single-handedly, prevented from capturing Rome. Half a millennium before Hanunia's time Clusium had been one of the twelve sovereign cities of a thriving Etruria. But in 472 BC the Greeks took it over following a naval victory in the bay of Naples, and by 280 BC it had become subject to the Romans. Even so it seems to have been allowed reasonable autonomy. From the style of her burial our Hanunia had clearly enjoyed prosperity from her marriage into the Tlesnasa clan, and had been a woman of some substance.

The Etruscans buried their more well-heeled dead in considerable style in whole cities of chamber tombs that were often magnificently decorated with frescoes depicting their daily life. And it was in one such chamber tomb, albeit undecorated, that Hanunia's sarcophagus was discovered in 1886 at Poggio Cantarello, a little over two miles (5km) west of Chiusi. The tomb was unlooted and a number of silver objects were still hanging on its walls, but both these and the painted terracottta sarcophagus containing Hanunia's remains were acquired by the British Museum in the same year. Though the silverware disappeared when the Museum's collections were moved for safety during World War II, inventories show them to have consisted of toilet accessories such as a scent-vase, a toilet box and a mirror, the reported thinness of the silver suggesting they may have been purpose-made as grave goods rather than intended for daily use.

Etruscan 'city of the dead'. Aerial view of the vast Etruscan necropolis at Cerveteri, Italy, laid out as a city, with the tombs like houses. This typified the attention that the Etruscans devoted to their burial of their more illustrious citizens, such as Hanunia.

But thanks to the inscription of Hanunia's full name in typically Etruscan right-to-left lettering on the base of the sarcophagus, we know that she and her husband enjoyed a high status in Etruscan society. And it was a society that in its heyday was forerunner to much of the excellence of Roman culture. The Etruscans were highly skilled in commerce, architecture, town planning, metallurgy, local government and art, and they passed many of these skills on. Roman roads, for instance, probably had their origins in the well-built roads that the Etruscans constructed to link their towns. And, revealing artistic prowess, and showing us what Hanunia looked like, the lid of her sarcophagus is particularly illuminating. In typical Etruscan manner, her appearance in life has been modelled life-size in terracotta, with considerable artistic and clay-firing skill.

Above: Seianti Hanunia Tlesnasa's sarcophagus, with on its lid her sculptured likeness lifesize in painted terracotta, as preserved in the British Museum, London. Hanunia's full Etruscan name is inscribed along the edge of the lid, and her bones and some grave-goods were found intact inside the sarcophagus.

This clay sculpture is there to be seen by any visitor to the British Museum's ground-floor classical section. It portrays Hanunia reclining on a plump cushion, the length of her body made comfortable by a striped mattress. She is clad in a full-length classical tunic or chiton, plain white except for a red edging band. It is fastened at the shoulders with rudimentary buttons (a device known to the Greeks and Etruscans, then forgotten until the late Middle Ages), and held in at the waist with a gold cord belt. An ornamental diadem on her head supports a long veil, and her centre-parted brown hair is clearly well tended. She wears a gold necklace, and her other jewellery includes stylish earrings and a thick rope bracelet.

Remarkably, it is possible to check something of the accuracy of this portrait thanks to the preservation of Hanunia's skeleton, essentially intact, albeit de-mineralised, in the sarcophagus proper beneath the sculptured lid. In 1989 Professor Marshall Becker of Pennsylvania's West Chester University examined this skeleton as part of a wide-ranging anthropological study of Etruscan skeletal remains. From the eroded state of her pelvis, and also from the state of her teeth, Becker supposed her to have been around eighty when she died.[2]

However, thanks to a technique developed by Dr David Whittaker of the University of Wales Dental School for determining age from teeth, this estimate has

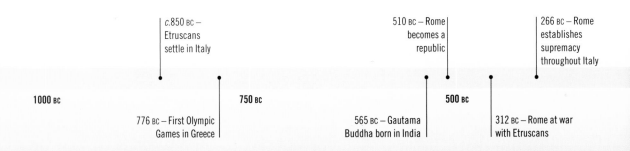

*c.*850 BC – Etruscans settle in Italy

510 BC – Rome becomes a republic

266 BC – Rome establishes supremacy throughout Italy

1000 BC

750 BC

500 BC

776 BC – First Olympic Games in Greece

565 BC – Gautama Buddha born in India

312 BC – Rome at war with Etruscans

been rather drastically revised downwards to around fifty. Furthermore, studies of the robustness of the upper bones of Hanunia's legs show her to have been very athletic in youth, developing powerful muscles for hip and leg movement. This was almost certainly because she indulged in the Etruscan love of horse-riding, perpetuated to this day in the traditional Palio horse-race held annually in Siena (once an Etruscan town). Like the Ukok horse-queen and Philip of Macedon before her, as well as the modern Palio competitors, Hanunia would have ridden bareback, without stirrups or saddle, simply gripping the horse's body with her thighs. Strong muscular development at shoulders and chest can similarly be attributed to the considerable strength acquired from controlling the reins.

But it is very likely that, in the course of this riding – and from the state of her muscle development, it must have happened some time after she was sixteen – she suffered a serious accident that was the true reason for the pelvic erosion observed by Becker. The likeliest scenario is that her horse fell heavily on its right side, trapping her right leg so badly that her femur was pushed into her right hip-bone. The accident damaged her pelvis's sacrum and ilium bones, causing internal bleeding and the early onset of arthritis in the damaged areas. Although she recovered, and the medical opinion is that she may even have taken up riding again for a few years more, her spine took on a compensatory curve to the left. Ultimately the pain in her right hip would have seriously impaired any kind of movement on this side.

This was far from the sum total of Hanunia's afflictions. Probably during the same riding accident, the right side of her face suffered a severe blow, perhaps responsible, several years before her death, for the loss of all the lower molars from both sides of her face. Because her right upper teeth had nothing on which to bite, tartar built up massively, inevitably causing difficulty in chewing, and making any movement to the right side of her lower jaw intensely painful. Poor oral hygiene would not have helped, causing dental caries and plaque build-up. Although Etruscan dentistry was state-of-the-art for the time, even advanced enough to be able to provide false teeth, in Hanunia's case the pain in the jaw would have precluded these as an option. Most probably she opted for foods such as milk puddings that would have saved her painful chewing. Indeed, extensive calcification of her bones indicates that she did have a high proportion of milk in her diet.

Below: The face of Hanunia, as reconstructed by Richard Neave. Forensic evidence shows her youthful vigour to have been curtailed by a serious accident, probably sustained while horse-riding.

150 BC – Etruscan matriarch lives near Chiusi, Tuscany

AD 410 – Goths under Alaric sack Rome

BC/AD

AD 250

AD 500

44 BC – Julius Caesar assassinated

30 BC – Death of Cleopatra, queen of Egypt

As a once vigorous woman, Hanunia must have taken it hard that she could no longer comfortably eat the foods in which the region abounded. Etruscan cuisine seems to have offered much the same delights as its present-day Tuscan successor, with good wine from the vineyards, good bread from the abundant wheatfields, plus excellent local meats and fish. Etruscans greatly enjoyed their banquets, as is evident from the lively scenes with which they decorated their tombs. To the scandal of the Greeks, for whom such occasions were all-male affairs, it was normal for Etruscan wives to dine alongside their husbands during such festivities. It was also quite normal for male and female diners alike to be attended by young men who went totally naked, male nudity, as in the case of the Greeks, causing no social offence. Exactly who these young men were, whether they were slaves or simply younger members of the family who were expected to wait on their elders, is unknown, as is much else concerning the lowlier individuals, rural and urban, who enabled aristocratic families such as that of Hanunia and her husband to enjoy their rarefied lifestyle.

An enforced lack of exercise and a preponderance of calcium-rich foods almost certainly led to Hanunia, in her later years, becoming puffy-faced and overweight. This element to her appearance was duly hinted at by the artist who created the effigy on her sarcophagus with a discreet plumpness. As gauged by Richard Neave, this tomb-sculpture was probably an attempt at a genuine portrait, and a successful one at that, the similarities of the eyes, mouth and nose to Neave's own medical reconstruction being very striking, particularly in the overall proportions. In fact it was typical of the artists who created Etruscan tomb sculptures to adopt a warts-and-all approach to depicting their subjects, frank depiction of wrinkles, facial disfigurements and pot-bellies being not at all uncommon. From such knowledge Neave could confidently give Hanunia the same hairstyle, head-dress and head-covering that her tomb sculptor had conveyed. However, because the sculpture shows Hanunia rather more youthful-looking than she would have been at the time of her death, allowance has to be made for its creation some years beforehand.

Given the lengths to which the Eruscans went to create elaborate cemeteries for their dead, we may guess that Hanunia had strong religious beliefs. The Etruscan gods, although with Etruscan and/or more Latin names, were much the same as those of the Greeks, for example 'Tin' – Zeus; 'Menerva' – Athene; 'Apulu' – Apollo.[3] They were particularly noted as astrologers and soothsayers. Although we have no idea whether Hanunia could read and write, it is more than likely that she could, since high-born Etruscan women in general are known to have been literate. Her full name was inscribed on the lid of her sarcophagus, and we know this to be but one of some 13,000 surviving examples of Etruscan writing.

Frustratingly, for the most part these are brief inscriptions; genuine lengthy texts that might tell us about the Etruscans are rare indeed. One of the longest surviving exceptions is a strip of linen, the *Liber Linteu,* today preserved in the National Museum, Zagreb, Croatia, which survived solely because it was transported all the way to Egypt to end its days as part of the wrappings of an ancient Egyptian mummy. But although it bears around 1200 words, it is thought to be no more than a calendar of the various annual Etruscan religious festivals by which Hanunia's life would have been ordered, together with some of the prayers and rituals performed at them. From artistic depictions of such linen 'books' in Etruscan tombs, it appears that linen was a popular material for writing, perhaps as prolifically used among the Etruscans as papyrus was among the Egyptians, but it has simply not survived because of a different climate and greater perishability.

In fact, although Etruscan inscriptions are readily legible – their twenty-six-letter alphabet was borrowed from the Phoenicians and the Greeks – actually deciphering any long inscription is more difficult as scholars have as yet assembled a vocabulary of only 500 words for the language itself.[4] There are thirty Etruscan-Latin bilingual epitaphs, and in 1964, at the former Etruscan port of Pyrgi, three gold tablets were discovered with parallel texts in Etruscan and Phoenician, describing the dedication of a sanctuary to the goddess Uni, the Astarte of the Phoenicians. From what can be gleaned from such sources, the Etruscans are thought to have called themselves 'Rasna'. They usually wrote from right to left, in the manner of Hebrews and Phoenicians. Among their words that can be transliterated with some certainty are *puia*, wife, and *apa*, father, the latter reminiscent of the Aramaic *abba* with the same meaning. From such findings it is clear that the Etruscans spoke a language differing significantly from the Latin and its variants spoken by the peoples with whom they shared the Italian peninsula, though exactly what that language was is far from fully determined. Some early historians thought they had long been native to Etruria. But Herodotus says that they were relatively new arrivals, having a few centuries back migrated from Asia Minor in order to escape famine. The fact that they spoke a non-Latin language suggests Herodotus' opinion is more likely, though it cannot be considered certain.

Ultimately DNA tests may shed important new light on Hanunia's ancestry, and thereby the Etruscan language. It is already known that many present-day Tuscans have much the same genes as the ancient Etruscans, so clearly the charm of the Tuscan countryside has kept much of its population static for millennia. While Hanunia slumbers in her British Museum showcase, far from the Etruria she knew and from the tomb originally made for her, it is anyone's guess how long it will be before some living person directly descended from her can be properly traced.

Etruscan husbands and wives feasting, attended by naked 'waiters', detail from a scene depicted on the walls of the Tomb of the Leopards. As a high-born Etruscan, Hanunia would undoubtedly have attended and perhaps hosted such feats as part of her regular lifestyle.

A Severnside Farmer
c.150 bc

A thousand miles north-west of Hanunia's Etruria was an Iron Age village in which there lived and died a farmer who was almost certainly a close contemporary of hers, though their lifestyles were very different.

Today the English village of Bleadon, nestling in the West Country, a region known for its cider apples, has no visible ancient monuments of any significance. It does not rank among England's most historic places, and is generally dated back only to Saxon times. Yet in its close vicinity as early as 150 BC there farmed a sturdily built man who in later years suffered from toothache and arthritis.[1] In the conventional historical record this man, like almost all of his kind and time, has left no written trace of himself, so that we have no idea even of his name. Thanks to the expertise of Richard Neave and his Manchester Art in Medicine Unit, however, we have a very good idea of what he looked like. We know that he had a big nose, that his eyes were deep-set, that his lower jaw was larger and stronger than that of most people today.

To archaeologists our Severnside farmer has become known as Bleadon Man. He came to light in the late 1990s when an archaeological survey of the barnyard of Whitegates Farm, conducted as a routine preliminary to work on a new housing development, turned up several ancient burial pits clustered around the one that contained his well-preserved skeleton. He was laid out hunched up in a crouching position, one arm at his side, the other drawn up so that its fingers were under his

Left: The face of a Severnside farmer of the 2nd century BC, as reconstructed by Richard Neave and Caroline Wilkinson. The hair-styling is necessarily conjectural.

Right: Artist's reconstruction of the Bleadon landscape as it is thought to have looked during our farmer's lifetime. The small woodland clearing at the lower left of the picture represents the likely original appearance of the site where the farmer's and other bodies were found buried cemetery-style. To the right are Iron Age huts of the kind in which he and his kindred would have lived.

chin, while his legs were tightly flexed in the so-called 'foetal' burial posture often found among prehistoric peoples. Although his skull, hard up against one side of the pit, was cracked into more than a hundred pieces, Neave accurately and convincingly put it back together again, much as if he were repairing a broken jar.

While Neave, assisted by Caroline Wilkinson, was painstakingly working at refleshing this skull via a plaster cast, other specialists were equally painstakingly analysing the soils from within and around the grave, as well as core samples taken from lower-lying fields. Careful sieving of the soils through running water brought to light ancient, blackened seeds. Analysis by Vanessa Straker of Bristol University showed that the crops grown by our farmer and his fellows were two types of ancient wheat. There was emmer, prehistory's most staple cereal, which the bakers of ancient Egypt had used for Esamun's bread nearly a thousand years earlier. And there was spelt wheat, developed in the ancient world only three or four centuries previously.

A variety of the core samples, extracted by Richard McPhail of University College, London, and Matt Canti of English Heritage's Ancient Monuments Laboratory, showed that around our farmer's time some of the Bleadon area had only recently been cleared of woodland. Other parts of the terrain were salt marsh, which would have provided seasonal pasture for grazing animals. Sifting of the burial pits also produced a wealth of animal bones which, when identified by the Southampton University specialist Dale Sergeantson, revealed what livestock our farmer and his kinsfolk had reared.

Some bones were horse, of a similar breed to the Exmoor pony, others dog, and yet others cattle. These last were of a variety much smaller than cattle now, their nearest modern-day equivalent being the Dexters kept at the Cotswold Countryside Park. Although Dexters are quite small, standing no more than three feet (1m) high, experiments training them to pull replica prehistoric ploughs have proved that their diminutive size belies their strength. They are extremely powerful animals, and when yoked around the horns can easily plough over half an acre in one day. Butchery marks on the bones show that they were also eaten as meat – one bone appears to have been used in a stew or soup. And there can be little doubt that the cattle were milked as well.

But by far the most prevalent among the animal bone were those of small sheep, of a prehistoric variety today represented by the Soay, which survive in remote parts of

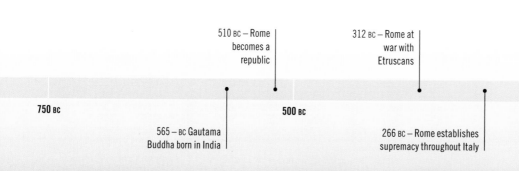

510 BC – Rome becomes a republic

312 BC – Rome at war with Etruscans

750 BC

500 BC

250 BC

565 – BC Gautama Buddha born in India

266 BC – Rome establishes supremacy throughout Italy

150 BC – Farmer lives near Bleadon in England's West Country

Soay sheep, modern-day representatives of the prehistoric variety that the Severnside farmer and his family are known to have reared.

Scotland. More closely resembling a goat than a sheep, the Soay was the second main sheep variety after the Moufflon to have been domesticated in ancient times, and both its ewes and rams have horns. Our Bleadon farmer's Soays were certainly eaten for their meat – the present-day animals' product is remarkably fat-free and much like venison. The Iron Age animals' bones were cracked so that even their highly nutritious marrow could be extracted.

There is every likelihood that the Bleadon Soays' wool was also well used by our farmer and his kindred, for whom little would have been wasted. Although such wool is 'short staple', or short in length, it lends itself well to being spun into yarn and woven into fabric on a simple loom. This was in fact the Soay breed's major advantage over the Moufflon, which could furnish only felt, the earliest form of cloth. From loom weights that have been found in Iron Age houses it is quite definite that England's Iron Age inhabitants, although they had not developed the large, sophisticated looms of Egypt, used upright wooden frames on which they hung the yarn's warp or vertical threads. The function of the weights was to keep the warp threads hanging straight while the weavers worked crossways weaving the weft. We may assume that our farmer's garments were made at home by this means; such work was traditionally done by the household's women, in addition to their other duties.

Of the particular house in which our farmer lived, no traces have yet come to light, but the location of his burial pit within Bleadon suggests that it lay relatively close by, probably in the centre of the present-day village. In fact a very plausible glimpse of its likely appearance can be gleaned from the fine reconstructions of Iron Age English houses at the Butser Ancient Farm near Petersfield, Hampshire.

What may be envisaged as our farmer's homestead is a cluster of cone-shaped thatched houses set within a fenced compound, in an arrangement resembling the kraals still to be seen in South Africa's Zululand. The compound probably included pens for the animals needing closest attention, as well as a haystack for winter fodder.

Butser's 'Great Roundhouse', based on an actual example excavated at Longbridge Deverel Cowdown in Wiltshire, is circular in ground-plan, some forty-five feet (15m) in diameter, and has double walls formed from wattle and daub supported by wooden posts. Its vast roof is made up of fifteen tonnes of thatch supported in a

43 AD – Romans under Claudius begin conquest of Britain

410 – Goths under Alaric sack Rome

BC/AD

AD 250

AD 500

44 BC – Julius Caesar assassinated

60 AD – Boudicca leads revolt against Roman rule in Britain

408 – Last Roman troops withdrawn from Britain

conical shape by wooden rafters and a hexagonal ring. Although our farmer's house at Bleadon may not have been quite as impressive, its design, and the materials used, would have been similar.

Inside, the cooking would have been done either in a beehive-shaped oven or on an open hearth, which also served as the central heating system. Smoke would have been filtered out through the thatch, enabling any foods or hides needing curing to be 'smoked' in the process. The establishment also no doubt had a quern or stone hand-mill that would have been used for grinding grain into flour.

So how was a date established? Pottery found at the site initially created confusion by suggesting that he lived in the Bronze Age. But dating of a small fragment of his thigh bone by Chris Ramsey of the Oxford University radiocarbon dating unit showed that he lived between 200 and 100 BC – i.e. around much the same time as the Etruscan Hanunia – a date supported by the finding of the spelt grains.

Modern-day reconstruction of an Iron Age thatched-roof house of the kind in which the Severnside farmer and his family would have lived.

He was a strongly built individual, used to a life of hard manual labour. Measurement of the length of his thigh bones determined that he stood about five feet six inches (1.68m) tall. His hip joints showed the signs of wear associated with arthritis, his age being roughly estimated as around fifty. His strong jaw, commonly found among people from this period, has been attributed to the heavy chewing that would have been required of the bread produced from the quern-ground flour. It would also have been well exercised by masticating meat from animals that had usually led rather longer and more active lives than their modern-day counterparts. His teeth were heavily worn, with his lower jaw sporting abscesses that must have caused him acute discomfort in later life. No doubt to his misfortune, his fellow ancient Britons did not have the Etruscans' reputation for dentistry.

Although there is no proof that our man was a farmer, several indications make it highly likely. As is evident from the soil analysis, the milieu in which his bones were unearthed was heavily agricultural. Very few fish bones were found in the vicinity. Isotope analysis of his thigh bone, which the Oxford laboratory conducted along with their radiocarbon dating work, revealed no sign of the ingestion of any marine-derived food. The strong inference, therefore, is that he almost exclusively ate the produce from his own patch of agricultural land rather than any fish from the River Severn, even though he lived less than two miles from the river's edge.

While some Iron Age British burials were provided with swords, shields, other well-crafted metal objects,[2] and even whole chariots, our farmer's grave was furnished with no weapons of war, nor any goods obtained via commerce. From all that we can tell, this was a man who simply grew his crops on the patch of land that he had charge of, and who strove to get the best results from breeding and grazing his livestock, subject to whatever vicissitudes the English climate might cause him.

It is arguable that he was fortunate to have such a solidly utilitarian means of livelihood, for as shown by another near-contemporary Celt, Lindow Man, also reconstructed by Neave, the early Britons' Celtic religion had a savage side every bit as bloodthirsty as that of our Minoan priestess's Crete. Discovered in a peat bog at Lindow Moss, Cheshire, in 1983, Lindow Man was an individual in his late twenties, five feet six inches (1.68m) tall, whose fingernails showed that he had never had to perform the heavy manual labour of our Severnside farmer.[3] Yet his life was brought to an end in the most unimaginably savage manner. He was struck on the back of the head with an axe. He was knifed in the neck to sever the jugular vein. He was garrotted with such savagery that his spinal column snapped. Then he was thrown into the peat bog, with no evidence that this was as a result of warfare.[4]

From the classically Celtic triple nature of the killing, and from a fragment of burnt oatmeal found in his stomach, the general understanding is that Lindow Man had been chosen by lot to be a sacrifice to the gods, in fulfilment of one of his Celtic religion's darker rites.[5] And from the number of similar 'bog' bodies that have been found in Britain and other countries of north-west Europe in recent centuries,[6] his fate was not an exceptional one. The young and the high-born were notably among the most common of the victims.

Given the startling findings regarding Cheddar Man, might our farmer still have descendants in the locality? The possibility of determining this came when a sample of his thigh bone, submitted to the Cambridge University blood specialist Dr Erica Hegelberg, proved to furnish some strands of his DNA, far from complete, but enough to provide some clues to his genetic make-up. On the strength of this, Hegelberg visited Bleadon to take blood samples from forty-eight villagers whose families, as evident from parish registers, could be reliably traced as residents back through several generations.

Of the forty-eight, the DNA sequences of five – Guy Gibbs, David Durston, Raymond Bailey, Margaret James and Doris Gould – proved to have marked similarities to that of our farmer. But the most revelatory moment came when Neave and Wilkinson's facial reconstruction was ceremoniously unveiled at a specially convened meeting in Bleadon's Coronation Hall. The assembled villagers instantly and unanimously recognised that our farmer's face bore a quite uncanny and unmistakable resemblance to that of a long-standing villager, Guy Gibbs. Indeed, apart from a cleft to the chin and slightly differing forehead lines – the latter always a conjectural detail – Gibbs might have posed for the reconstruction.

Guy Gibbs, one of five present-day villagers of Bleadon whose DNA was found to have marked similarities to that of the Severnside farmer who lived *c*.150 BC. In Guy Gibbs' case there was also a striking facial resemblance.

13

A Roman Sailor
c.7 BC

Just as our British West Country farmer was a man of the soil, so our Roman was a man of the sea: the Mediterranean Sea, so called because it seemed the centre of the known earth. If Italian archaeologists' calculations of his age and date are correct, when he was born Julius Caesar had not yet met his 'Ides of March'. By the time of his death the emperor Augustus ruled every Mediterranean shore except for modern Morocco and Algeria.

But not even the 'divine' Augustus could control storms, and when one of immense violence struck the Roman harbour at what is now Pisa, thought to have been in 7 BC, our sailor was caught unawares. As the merchant ship on which he served suddenly capsized, its cargo shifted and toppled on to him. Amidst the chaos, his foot appears to have been caught by a rope and was quite possibly torn off, since it was found separate from the rest of his body. Whatever the exact circumstances, he undoubtedly drowned, with alongside him a dog resembling a basset hound that would seem to have been his shipboard companion. Sailor and dog remained undisturbed for over 2000 years until recent archaeological excavations brought the ill-fated ship to light, together with fifteen other Roman ships dating between the third century BC and the fifth century AD.

One surprise is the location of the excavations, not underwater, but at San Rossore railway station, Pisa, several miles from the present coastline. This is because the old, lagoon-like Roman harbour, which lay at the confluence of the Arno and Auser rivers and was joined to the sea by a canal, long ago became silted up and was reclaimed as land. Under the direction of the Italian archaeologist Professor Stefano Bruni, both the human and canine skeletons were excavated during the summer of 1999. They were then passed to Professor Francesco Mallegni, a lecturer in anthropology at Pisa University's Department of Archaeological Sciences, who promptly put in hand a reconstruction of the sailor's facial features.[1] This was then displayed in a special exhibition of the Pisa ship finds at the Archaeological Museum of Florence from 20 February to 14 May 2000. The dog was similarly 'revivified' for the same purpose.

Roman cargo ship. Vessels plying the Mediterranean and beyond carrying foodstuffs and other commodities were a key expression of the unity, stability and quality of life that the Roman Empire provided in return for its citizens' loyalty. Although a multi-oared vessel is represented on the mosaic seen here, that on which our sailor died was powered solely by sails, steered via a single oar at the stern.

As in the case of the Severnside farmer, although we do not know this ill-fated Roman sailor's name, a surprising amount can be learnt about him. Anthropological calculations put his age at about forty, and his height at five feet six inches (1.68m). According to Professor Mallegni, he was 'vigorous and strong, with the powerful chest of a man used to hard work, such as carrying heavy loads, and dealing with sails and rigging'.[2] In this instance it was only his upper incisor teeth that were worn down to the roots, suggesting not the effects of gritty bread but rather that he may have used these teeth in his work, perhaps holding ropes with them while climbing rigging.

Above: No doubt once filled with a fine wine, one of the amphorae that the Roman sailor's vessel was carrying as cargo when it so fatally foundered.

His job on board ship was therefore probably as a deckhand, and as such he was likely to be a paid employee rather than one of the many slaves that the Romans used to crew their ships. His short-legged basset hound was probably trained to sniff out rats and so protect the ship's foodstuffs, his responsibilities including both the crew's rations and any edible cargo.

Classical sources tell us that Roman cargo ships could be very large, some nearly 200 feet (60m) long. Thanks to the modern-day development of scuba diving and underwater archaeology this has been confirmed by the hundreds of Roman wrecks that have been found around the Mediterranean. Among them, albeit rare, are ships of 400 and even 600 tonnes.[3] These and their kind plied the Mediterranean from end to end carrying cargoes such as grain from Egypt and Libya, marble from Greece and Asia Minor, spicy fish sauce from Sardinia, fine wines, olive oil, needed in great quantity for lighting and cooking, metal ingots, specialised construction materials, and much else. As surviving Roman administrative documents make clear, big

510 BC – Rome becomes a republic

750 BC   500 BC   250 BC

266 BC – Rome establishes supremacy throughout Italy

Below: The face of the Roman sailor, as reconstructed by Professor Francesco Mallegni. His teeth were found to be worn down to the roots, possibly from the practice of holding rope in his teeth while climbing rigging.

business interests lay behind such haulage, and all the transactions and insurances associated with it, much as they have done ever since.

A typical run-of-the-mill merchant ship would have a mainmast with a large single sail, a bowsprit carrying a smaller second sail, a large stern-fastened steering oar, and an elevated stern section with cabin. Besides the wealth of information gleaned from archaeology, clear depictions of these in their original pristine state can be seen in surviving Roman mosaics, frescoes and reliefs. Remarkably similar trading vessels can be seen to this day in many a traditional eastern harbour. Below deck there would be a hold for the storage of cargo providing ballast or needing protection from the elements, while other less perishable items would be kept above.

Although the vessel on which our deckhand served was far from one of the biggest of its kind, it was sturdily built. This was necessary since it was carrying a substantial number of *amphorae*, big pottery jars capable of containing up to eight gallons (39 litres) of wine or other fluids, made leak-proof with bitumen and the like. Sand found at the bottom of these *amphorae*, when analysed, proved to match that from the Gulf of Naples region, indicating that it was from there that our deckhand, his vessel and its cargo are likely to have hailed.

The Italian mainland surrounding the Gulf of Naples was called Campania in Roman times, and included flourishing ports such as Puteoli (present-day Pozzuoli), Herculaneum and Pompeii. In the first century BC the export of fine wines from this region was at its height. And because southern Gaul, later the Roman province of Gallia Narbonensis, had not yet developed its own wine-growing, and the land route to it was unsafe until Augustus' reign, many of Campania's wine exports were carried by sea.

It is very likely, therefore, that our sailor's home port was Pompeii, the fiery destruction of which still lay a

31 BC – Octavian, who will assume the title Augustus, wins control of Roman Empire

*c.*7 BC – Roman sailor drowns in coastal storm near Pisa

410 – Goths under Alaric sack Rome

BC/AD

AD 250

AD 500

44 BC – Julius Caesar assassinated

*c.*AD 30 – Jesus Christ crucified in Jerusalem

AD 79 – Colosseum, Rome, begun

century into the future, or one of its Gulf of Naples neighbours. Originally Etruscan, and then a 'free town' until it took the losing side in a rebellion, Pompeii was forcibly colonised by the Romans in 80 BC. But this enhanced its prosperity, with many houses enlarged to multi-storey, the water supply linked to the Roman aqueduct system, gymnasia, theatres and new market-places built, and the provision of many other civic amenities.

Although the thriving Pompeii that the Vesuvius eruption preserved for posterity dates from AD 79, we know that even in our sailor's time it would have been quite a buzzing place. The roads were well paved in the Roman manner. There was an excellent *macellum* or covered market for the sale of fresh foodstuffs. Eating out was well catered for – there were restaurants and fast-food outlets, or *thermopolia*, with hot meals 'ready to go'. For exercise there were public baths and gymnasia. For entertainment there were theatres and gladiatorial performances. If our sailor did not have a home or wife in Pompeii, his sexual urges could have been readily satisfied at one of the port's many brothels. Although we cannot be sure how many of these there were in our sailor's time, by AD 79 there were at least twenty, their purpose evident to modern-day visitors from the explicit frescoes painted on their walls.

So what more does the reconstruction by Professor Mallegni and his colleagues tell us about our sailor? The method that they used was the 'American' rather than the Neave 'Manchester School' one. Even so, the result that they have come up with is very distinctive, a strong face that looks immensely practical and hardened to a vigorous outdoor life. Dr Stefano De Caro, superintendent of the Naples Archaeological Museum, likens it to a facial type that, he says, is still often to be seen around the Naples coast and its adjoining islands of Ischia, Procida and Capri. Although we do not know the language that our sailor spoke, according to Professor Bruni his provenance from southern Italy makes it most likely to have been a rough dialect of Greek rather than Latin. This would have been a great advantage to a sailor, since Greek, not Latin, was the Roman world's *lingua franca*, and with it he could make himself understood virtually anywhere throughout the Mediterranean, from Alexandria to Marseilles.

Since our sailor came to light so recently, there is undoubtedly more research to be conducted on him. If, for instance, sufficient DNA could be obtained from his bones and a comparison made with that from a representative selection of long-established present-day Neapolitans, particularly those from the coast and islands, then some interesting similarities might well be found, much as in the case of our Severnside farmer. This would prove once again that despite history's many vicissitudes of war and mass displacements of persons, substantial elements of populations can and do remain where their fathers and forefathers lived long before them, even when the individual concerned is a roving Roman sailor.

A street walked by the sailor? Since sand from his ship's wine cargo matched that of the Gulf of Naples, Pompeii (as seen here) may have been the port from which his vessel had sailed prior to the calamity which overtook it off Pisa.

14

LONDINIUM PRIDE
*c.*AD 300

Instead of the itinerant and impoverished life of the sailor, her lifestyle was rather more static, though considerably more opulent. It was also chillier, since the climate she knew, certainly during her last year (or years), was that of the far-flung province the Romans called Britannia, now Britain. She was from a wealthy family and died in her twenties. She lived in the fourth century AD in Londinium, as the Romans called London. We do not know her name, and archaeologists are still struggling to piece together many topographical details of the Londinium that she knew. But thanks to the art of Richard Neave and Caroline Wilkinson of Manchester University, we can view her face-to-face as vividly as if she were once more alive before us.

In the spring of 1999 archaeologists called in to investigate a twelve-acre site at Spitalfields on the edge of the City of London, prior to the start-up of a major new office development, brought to light an important medieval burial ground. They found the remains of some 8600 men, women and children who had been buried adjoining the renowned medieval hospital of St Mary's Spital. But, to the archaeologists' surprise, just at the edge of this medieval site there came to light a Roman cemetery. And one of the most impressive-looking finds there was a stone sarcophagus with its lid still intact, the first such from Roman Britain to be found in three decades.[1] Very strong signals from a metal-detector indicated that it contained a large metal object. When its stone cover was slid back, a mud-caked lead coffin was revealed, its lid superbly ornamented with a cable pattern divided into diamonds and triangles, and filled with clusters of scallop-shells. As the soil surrounding the sarcophagus was being removed so that it could be lifted, several beautiful objects emerged. There was a long tubular glass phial, superbly crafted in a trailed style datable to the fourth century AD. This is thought to have contained an expensive perfumed oil. Other utensils were made from jet. Clearly, whoever had been laid in the coffin was an individual of considerable substance, initial speculation suggesting perhaps some Roman governor or his wife.

Garbed for protection against unknown microbes, two Museum of London archaeologists survey the Roman lady's bones and grave-goods, just after removal of her coffin lid. Although no identifying inscription has been found, the stone sarcophagus and inner lead coffin indicate that she has to have been an individual of considerable status and importance.

On 14 April 1999 seven archaeologists assembled at the Museum of London to open the coffin, each clad in spacesuit-like hoods, masks, gloves and overalls to protect them from high lead levels and any unknown microbial hazards.[2] As the lid was gently raised a skeleton of slender build was revealed, the skull inclined to one side, the left arm bent across the chest. To the more forensically knowledgeable among the archaeologists the width of the pelvic area strongly suggested that this was a female. The woman had been laid on her back, and although a layer of silt had built up around her to a depth of about an inch and a quarter (3cm), careful sifting revealed fragments of textiles and gold thread, as though from the fine garments she had worn. Behind her head were the remains of some kind of head-dress made from bay-leaves, perhaps a substitute for a laurel wreath. Frustratingly, the burial entirely lacked any surviving inscription by which to identify her.

What can we nevertheless glean of this woman, clearly high-born, of Roman Londinium? She stood an estimated five feet four inches (1.62m) tall, and the state of her bone development shows that she died in her twenties, though no cause of death has yet been established. Indeed, this may well not be determinable from the available evidence. While to die as young as this may seem unusual to us, it was not exceptional in an era in which only one in ten lived beyond forty-five. From the reasonably good condition of her teeth, and the state of her bones in general, she is thought to have enjoyed a healthy diet, with plenty of meat, vegetables and fruit. Cucumbers and peas, apples, pears, quinces, cherries and plums are known to have been plentiful commodities in Roman Britain, with olives and figs imported from the continent.

As subsequent, more specialist analysis determined, however, this young woman's teeth had more to tell than just her good dentition. One metal that the Romans mined and used extensively was lead. They wrapped their dead VIPs in sheets of it. They used it to line their plumbing and their public baths, such as the Great Bath at Aquae Sulis (today better known as Bath). They also used it for many drinking vessels, and particularly because of this the lead levels in Roman bones are often found to be dangerously high. During childhood, when the teeth are forming, the lead builds up in the enamel. Thereafter it will never disappear, even after the passage

510 BC – Rome
becomes a republic

31 BC – Octavian, who will
assume the title Augustus,
wins control of Roman Empire

500 BC

250 BC

44 BC – Julius
Caesar
assassinated

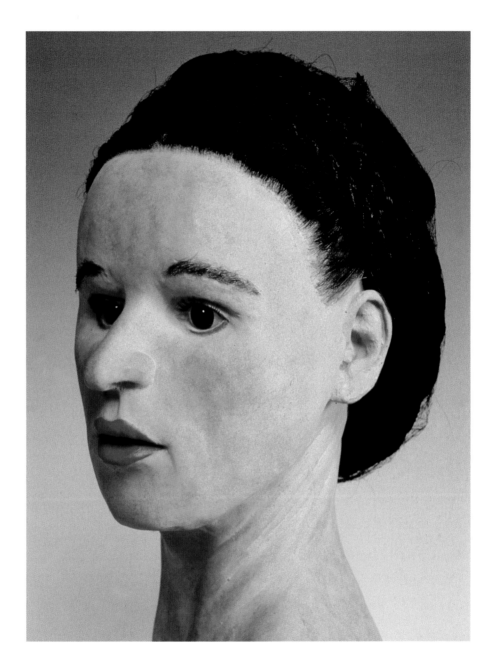

The face of the Roman lady, as reconstructed by Caroline Wilkinson. Trace elements of probably Spanish lead in her tooth enamel suggests she may have spent her early years in Spain before moving to Roman London.

AD 43 – Romans under Claudius begin conquest of Britain

64 – Nero sets fire to Rome, blaming Christians

*c.*400 – Roman lady lives prosperously in Londinium, Roman London

477 – Saxons gain foothold in southern Britain, shortly followed by Angles

AD 250

AD 500

60 AD – Boudicca leads revolt against Roman rule in Britain

312 – Constantine the Great, with Christian symbol as his battle-standard, wins battle of Milvian Bridge

408 – Last Roman troops withdrawn from Britain

410 – Goths under Alaric sack Rome

of millennia, as long as the teeth themselves survive. And since lead isotope ratios vary quite distinctively according to the geology of its various sources, it is possible to determine from the ratios in a deceased person's teeth the particular area in which he or she may have lived during childhood.

One potential source of misleading findings was her body's long interment in the lead coffin. However, analysis of the coffin's isotope ratios proved these to be typical of the ores of known Romano-British lead mines in the Mendips and the Pennines. In the case of the lead in her teeth, on the other hand, particularly the molars that would have formed when she was between eight and ten, the isotope ratios showed that the source was definitely not Britain. Instead, it must have come from the south, probably from south-western continental Europe, in particular the Iberian peninsula.[3] The strong inference, therefore, is that our Roman lady spent her childhood in Roman Spain or thereabouts. Then she married some senior official who was perhaps posted to Londinium.

The London our Roman Lady knew? A rare contemporary glimpse of the Roman city's long-lost entrance gates, seen behind the kneeling figure on this early 4th-century Roman medallion. 'LON' stands for Londinium, the city's Roman name.

One further indication of the lady's elevated status has come from further specialist analysis of the fragments of textiles found in her coffin. Some of these can be identified as silk that must have been transported all the way from China. The characteristics of the fine gold threads with which her garments were decorated indicate that they were woven in Syria.

Since we can be sure, from the very location of her burial, that this lady must have spent at least her last years in Roman Londinium, what picture can we build up of the city she knew? The Romans founded London in AD 50, seven years after the emperor Claudius' successful invasion of Britain in AD 43. But just a decade later Queen Boudicca of the Iceni tribe led a fierce Celtic revolt during which the newly established city was sacked and burnt. This was done with such devastating thoroughness that to this day archaeologists digging deep trenches repeatedly come across a thick fire layer that they can confidently attribute to Boudicca's handiwork. Such was the Roman character, however, that they determinedly fought back, whereupon the whole province soon settled into acceptance of the benefits of Roman rule, and the rebuilt Londinium went from strength to strength.[4]

By the fourth century, when our Roman lady was alive, and indeed well beforehand, Londinium had become thoroughly Romanised. Although Britain's population had grown to five million, thanks to the Romans' scientific agricultural

Further indication of the Roman lady's affluence, a superbly crafted glass phial and jet rod found alongside her sarcophagus.

methods three permanent legions of soldiers, together with substantial urban populations at centres such as Londinium and Eboracum (modern-day York), could be supported with relative ease. For defence purposes Londinium was fully walled, to a height of around twenty feet (6m), from present-day Blackfriars in the west to what is today the Tower, to the east. In accordance with Roman law the cemetery where our lady was laid was located just outside these walls, at the start of the great northward route of Ermine Street.

The Roman city's hub, its great forum with central market and meeting place, is known to have stood on high ground at what is today Cornhill. Its huge basilica, with town hall, municipal administration headquarters, law courts, shops and offices, sprawled nearby in the environs of what is today Leadenhall Court. There was an amphitheatre, only very recently discovered, for popular entertainment within a stone's throw of where London's medieval citizens built the still extant Guildhall.

From the end of the second century AD Roman Londinium is understood to have gone into decline as a metropolis. Even so, its wealthier citizens, among whom must certainly be counted our lady, would have lived in fine houses with mosaic floors, ducted so that heat from underfloor furnaces could percolate from below. When she entertained, she undoubtedly had fine glassware available to her, as is evident from the beautiful specimen found by her tomb. If she hankered for the olive oils, high-quality wines and fish sauces that she would have enjoyed in continental Europe, these and like commodities poured in to the city's bustling docks, one sixty-foot (18m) section of which has only relatively recently been found in the grounds of Guy's Hospital, on the south bank of the Thames.[5] Much if not all of the Roman money that our lady handled would have been minted nearby. Londinium had been granted its own mint from AD 288, and this continued spasmodically into the fourth century.

Regarding our lady's religion there is some uncertainty, scholars having reached no firm conclusion as to whether she was Christian or pagan. The fact that she was given a burial, as distinct from cremation, provides no sure clue. Romans in general practised both burial and cremation, with fashion veering from one to the other at different periods. The grave's orientation east to west, and her position with the left arm across the body, accord with known Roman Christian burials from elsewhere. But this may have been mere lip-service. According to Jenny Hall, the London Museum's specialist curator for the Roman period, our lady could well have been buried with rites from a mixture of religions in order 'to appease all the gods that were being worshipped at the time'.[6]

Certainly, Roman London catered for many faiths. There were temples to the traditional Roman gods. There was a shrine to Mithras, as is evident from the fine Roman head of him excavated in London in 1954. And following the Roman emperor Constantine the Great's Milvian Bridge victory of AD 312, which he attributed to the Christian god, Christianity became increasingly tolerated throughout the Roman Empire, becoming the official religion by the mid-fourth century AD. Some fine Romano-British villas of the period, such as that at Hinton St Mary, Dorset, show clear signs of Christian ownership.

What language did our lady speak? The likelihood is that even though she was probably resident in Spain during her childhood, she was from an upper-class Roman family, perhaps in the diplomatic service, used to moving from one part of the empire to another. The best guess, therefore, is that Latin would have been her first language, with Greek, as the empire's *lingua franca*, her second.

Given that our Roman lady has only recently been discovered, study of her remains continues apace, and no doubt fresh insights, perhaps regarding the clothing that she wore, will duly emerge. Such researches are being co-ordinated by the London Museum and its go-ahead, publicity-minded director Simon Thurley, and the speed with which findings have been made public has been exemplary. Strands of her DNA have already been isolated at Oxford University which tend to confirm that her origins lay in south-western Europe, though this and other aspects of the research are far from finalised.

As so often when ancient human remains are found in Britain, it fell to Manchester University's Unit of Art in Medicine to make the definitive facial reconstruction that the public at large is now beginning to expect. And this was done with commendable rapidity. The BBC TV series *Meet the Ancestors* specially commissioned Neave's unit, and it was his staff colleague Caroline Wilkinson who performed much of the task. In the classic Neave manner she first prepared a cast of the skull, then built up the muscle structure in clay, based on the known average facial tissue depths for white females in their twenties. In this instance, because of the needs of television, she cast the final version in wax, adding prosthetic brown eyes, and a wig in a hairstyle known from the fourth-century Roman period. Because this was a woman who would certainly have known the luxuries of cosmetics, the specialist Alison Levy provided final make-up touches.

The face that stares out at us is highly distinctive, and shows that our lady must have been quite a beauty. The fact that she received such a VIP burial indicates that the Roman Empire was still reasonably stable, and had not yet undergone the collapse of control that far-flung provinces such as Britain would suffer in the fifth century. If only our Roman beauty could be made to speak, what tales might she tell of the political intrigues of her time?

IV

THE PRE-MODERN AGE

HISTORICAL INTRODUCTION:

From plainchant to firepower

The decline and fall of the old Roman Empire undeniably spelled a Dark Age for western Europe, though it is important to recognise that this was a relatively localised phenomenon. In Constantinople and its environs Graeco-Roman culture and know-how were perpetuated in considerable splendour under the Byzantine emperors, and would continue, albeit with some disruption, until 1453. Further east, the Chinese, who had experienced their own classical civilisation's rise and fall under the Han Dynasty, entered perhaps the greatest phase of their history under the Tang and Sung emperors, who ruled between the seventh and thirteenth centuries AD. On the American continent, New World civilisations developed high standards of agriculture, urbanisation and stone architecture quite independent of, and therefore not synchronous with, their Old World counterparts. And even in western Europe, the Dark Ages were far less barbarous than they are sometimes painted.

Sweeping movements of peoples were the main cause of unsettlement. Frankish tribes who had previously been living just outside the empire's northern sector moved into northern France. From the east, Germanic Visigoths migrated into southern France and Spain; Ostrogoths, despite enlightened rulers such as Theodoric who behaved with much restraint toward the peoples they displaced, took over much of Italy. Vandals, after running amok through southern France into Spain, crossed into North Africa, eventually settling in the environs of Carthage. Huns reached as far as northern France, only to be defeated and driven back. From the provinces of the northern Netherlands known as Friesland, Saxon and Angle mercenaries, invited to help defend England's shores, opted to settle there, driving the native Celts west and north into Wales, Devon and Cornwall, and Ireland and Scotland. The map of Europe became transformed into a series of kingdoms, among which, while a semblance of the old Roman institutions often lingered, Germanic tribal leaders called the tune.

The main loss, undoubtedly, was civic law and order of the kind that Augustus had so painstakingly built up in Rome at the turn of the Christian era. Also lost – not least due to a marked decline in coinage standards – was the previous ease of local and international trading that only a world power as widespread as that of Rome could assure. Although many western European cities, including Roman London, had been waning well before the old empire's fall, now they declined markedly further, along with their road and drainage systems and the general infrastructure. A fragmentary Anglo-Saxon poem, *The Ruin*, poignantly conveys how powerfully this affected a typical Romano-British city, probably Aquae Sulis, now Bath:

> The castles have decayed; the work of giants is crumbling. Bright were the castle-dwellings, many the bath-houses… till fate the mighty overturned that. The wide walls fell… the woodwork of the roof is stripped of tiles; the place has sunk into ruin.[1]

Along with this, the loss of the Romans' scientific methods of animal husbandry likewise had its effects on farming. The average size of farm animals such as cows, pigs and sheep was actually reduced. Human life-expectancy also decreased; boys were considered adults at twelve, girls married in their early teens, and even those who reached what we would consider adulthood mostly died in their forties. Despite all the infiltrating peoples, England's population dwindled to probably little more than a million, compared to an estimated five million during the Roman period.

But not all was gloom and doom. For instance, literate as the Romans were, they had never really progressed beyond producing documents in long rolls or scrolls; when the great library of Graeco-Roman Alexandria was burnt in AD 640 it was said to have contained 500,000 scrolls, not books. But from Christianity's earliest beginnings the most convenient way of recording testimonies of Jesus' life was found to be by writing on both sides of papyrus sheets, bound together as a book.

So when the Roman Empire became officially Christian in the fourth century whole bibles began to be produced in this mode. Many of those to whom the empire fell – Franks, Angles and Saxons – were pagan, and Christian missionaries lost little time evangelising them, whereupon the newly converted proceeded to bring their own style to the creation of bible books. The resulting masterpieces included the beautiful bibles of Winchester, Kells and Lindisfarne, with more secular works being produced in much the same book format, all, of course, still laboriously hand-written, one at a time.

With the geographical boundaries all too loosely defined between the new kingdoms into which the old Roman Empire had split, there was unavoidable jostling for position. By around the middle of the seventh century a certain stability had been restored, only for the Mediterranean world then to be rocked by a new menace – from the Arabs. Fired by the new Islamic religion founded by the prophet Muhammad, these peoples burst out of the Arabian desert on horses and camels to sweep across virtually the entire north African coast from Egypt to what is now Morocco, and on into Spain. They also moved northwards to take over the Holy Land and Asia Minor. Although checked at the walls of Constantinople, still they managed to retain a vast territory, controlling an Islamic empire stretching from Spain to Afghanistan.

The contribution of these former desert-dwellers to world progress was very far from negative. Under the Abbasid dynasty, synchronous with some of Europe's darkest ages, there blossomed a golden era of Arab art and science with magnificent architecture, versatile craftsmanship, genuine strides in the fields of mathematics, astronomy and medicine, and extensive international trading. Córdoba in Spain grew into the largest town in Europe after Constantinople, its streets abuzz with the activities of bronze founders, gold- and silversmiths and ivory carvers, and brimming with a population estimated at between 500,000 and a million.

Meanwhile in northern Europe the strong new Holy Roman Empire became established under the rule of Charlemagne, a veritable giant of a man (said to have been seven feet, 2.13m, tall), who extended Frankish domains into present-day Italy, Spain and Germany. It was under Charlemagne's direction that the English scholar Alcuin standardised the Roman alphabetic lettering into the upper and lower case that we know today. It should be appreciated that throughout the old Roman Empire Latin continued to be the main language. But, influenced by the different localised cultures, it increasingly evolved into the specific forms that we know as Italian, French and Spanish, among others.

In the wake of the Arabs, two more predatory peoples were unleashed. Magyars occupied what is now Hungary and began harrying the borders of Italy, while from Scandinavia boatloads of land-hungry Norsemen or Vikings swept southwards around the coast of Spain to southern France and northern Italy, eastwards along river systems deep into Russia, and westwards ultimately as far as North America. These new marauders had fast, highly manoeuvrable vessels that were designed to be rowed or sailed, and they could raid some coastal town or river settlement and disappear before any army could be mustered to counter them. Particularly easy prey were Christian monasteries built on small British islands such as Iona and Lindisfarne; these establishments were often rich in gold and jewellery.

But because of a highly restrictive land inheritance system in their home countries, many of the Norsemen also had a serious intent to colonise. They steadily founded settlements in Iceland and Greenland, the Scottish islands, much of northern England, south Wales, southern Ireland, and Normandy and the Loire valley in

France. From among those who settled in what is now York, in northern England, comes our face number 15. Exactly as in the case of the earlier invaders, conversion to Christianity had a taming effect, and they became relatively peacefully assimilated.

Far from going against the tide of human progress, they even contributed to it, their clinker or framework-first method of shipbuilding becoming standard, and still widely used. It was also about this time that the stirrup, which had first appeared among the horse peoples of Asia just before the turn of the Christian era, found its way to western Europe. The great benefit of this ostensibly simple device was that it enabled the rider to avoid being unseated when he clashed with another rider. So when shortly after 1066 the Bayeux tapestry, 231 feet (70m) long, was woven to commemorate the warlord William of Normandy's successful invasion of Anglo-Saxon England, the embroiderers faithfully depicted the Norman knights using stirrups on the horses they brought with them across the English Channel. This development opened up a whole new era of horseback warfare that would last for nearly a thousand years.

As we have already noted, the Christianity that some of the Roman emperors tried so hard to snuff out had done much to stabilise post-Roman Europe. Even so, some of its aspects might well seem strange to us. In England and elsewhere during the so-called Dark Ages, the clergy did not have celibacy imposed on them. In many religious establishments men and women lived together and worshipped together. Cathedral canons were often married men. But following a period of degeneracy, from the tenth century on the Church began to assert many of its present-day rules, and to flex its political muscles rather more strongly. It was in the eleventh century that Christianity split into western and eastern denominations, the Western Church led by a pope in Rome, the Eastern by a patriarch in Constantinople. For Rome, even though geographically under less threat from Islam than its Eastern Orthodox opposite number, Islamic control of the Holy Land inevitably represented an affront that sooner or later needed to be addressed.

Until the eleventh century, Christians had mostly been allowed to visit and tend the Christian shrines within Arab territories. Under this tolerant atmosphere

A priceless window on the so-called 'Dark Age' world. A section of the Bayeux tapestry, showing tree-felling and boat-building in preparation for William of Normandy's successful invasion of Anglo-Saxon England. Carried on the invasion boats were horses that the Normans rode with stirrups, an invention that would play a key part in the horse-borne warfare of subsequent centuries.

European scholars visited Islamic Córdoba, Toledo and elsewhere to translate into Latin both the Arabs' own new learning and the works that they had been preserving and transmitting from the old Greek and Indian civilisations. Pope Sylvester II (*c*.940-1003), the most scientific and mathematically minded of all popes – he is credited with inventing the first mechanical clock – may well have studied such writings during his time in Spain. Particularly important among the Arab works were treatises by the ninth-century al-Khwarizmi, an Arab mathematician, via whom[2] we gained not only algebra but also the modern numbering system, including the hitherto inconceivable concept of zero. Arab medical textbooks were highly prized. The Arabs are also thought to have taught Europeans the art of stained glass, with which Christian cathedrals were beginning to be decorated.

But in the 1070s more fanatical Muslims of Turkish origin wrested the Holy Land from the very Arabs whose faith they shared. The Arabs won it back temporarily, but not before Pope Urban II had called for the First Crusade, plunging Europe into over three centuries of religiously motivated expeditions against Islam. As late as 1329 the dying wish of the owner of our face number 16, the Scottish king Robert the Bruce, was that his heart be cut from his body and carried on crusade against the Muslims, a wish duly honoured, though with tragic consequences for the bearer. Despite the romantic overtones that the Crusades have acquired in popular fiction, the truth is that they often involved unspeakable savagery on the part of both Christians and Muslims. The religious bitterness that they created lingers to this day, and the whole concept of the Crusades ultimately proved futile.

Influenced to some extent by these encounters, a new Europe emerged almost seamlessly out of the Dark Ages and into the Middle Ages. Those descendants of the old barbarian tribes who returned from their eastern adventures were inspired to compose travelogues, chronicles and poems. They acquired a taste for eastern fabrics such as muslin, eastern foodstuffs, seasonings and their accompanying recipes, all boosting international trade. They had learned to be concerned about hygiene. A burgeoning trend of founding universities and medical institutions accelerated the impetus to disseminate the Arab world's scientific knowledge. Arab medical treatises included those on the treatment of diseases such as smallpox and measles, and on the surgical treatment of wounds, the latter, apparently, to the particular benefit of our face number 17, a soldier in far-off England.

From 1234 dates were put on coinage. Although al-Khwarizmi's Arabic numbering system, taken for granted today, was not immediately used for this purpose, slowly its worth over the old Roman system became appreciated. Smart though the Romans had been, their expression of a number as MCCXXXIV was hardly conducive even to the simplest addition and subtraction. By expressing it the Arab way as '1234' everything from engineering to accountancy could be facilitated.

The period of transition from Dark Ages to Middle Ages has been known as a 'Little Optimum' because the climate in the years 950-1300 was significantly warmer than in the preceding or succeeding centuries. Southern Scotland enjoyed temperatures similar to those of southern England now, while the latter's climate was more like that we now associate with central France.[3] At the end of this period the spread of the ice cap south again would claim as one of its chief victims the colony that the Vikings had founded on Greenland. The green valleys in which they had originally settled became more and more icebound, as did the waterways, and when a German merchant ship made an all too rare visit in 1540 the crew found no one to greet them and the farmhouses and fish-sheds empty and eerily silent. There was no sign of any attack and all the inhabitants had been neatly buried bar one man. He was found lying face down in the open, and had clearly been the last survivor.

Meanwhile, as the desire grew to learn about the world in general, entrepreneurial merchants such as the Polos of Venice became motivated to travel all the way to China. Although it had fallen to nomadic Mongols, a rather more barbarous people than the native Chinese, it still appeared to them as a country of fabulous prosperity. Eventually there percolated back to the West Marco Polo's stories of some of the amazing products they had seen, including a black stone which could be burnt like wood, soon to be known as coal, and money in the form of printed paper.

Although many disbelieved Marco Polo's tales, there was a crying need for some better method of producing books than turning them out laboriously by hand with rows of scribes. So it was not long before printing, which the Chinese had pioneered in the eighth century, made its debut in the West, where the Romans' alphabetic system of writing might have been made for it. In 1456 Johannes Gutenberg of Mainz completed the first bible created from movable type by casting individual letters in metal, and arranging or 'composing' them in lines on wooden frames. And such was the impact of this new technology that within three decades London, Stockholm, Valencia, Budapest and other European cities all had their own printing presses, bringing into being with surprising rapidity the whole industry of printing that we take so much for granted today.

Another Chinese import, and one with no less momentous implications for the future, was the method of mixing saltpetre (potassium nitrate) with sulphur and charcoal to produce the highly explosive substance later known as gunpowder. Ironically, a pacific thirteenth-century English Franciscan friar, Roger Bacon, was one of the first to report on this to the West, but the substance proved so difficult to control that, throughout the Hundred Years War fought between England and France from 1337 to 1453, it was the millennia-old longbow that remained the most potent offensive weapon. Those who loaded and fired the earliest cannon were often in rather greater danger than those upon whom they fired.

By the end of the fifteenth century firearms technology had improved sufficiently for it to have a significant strategic value, alongside the high quality of metallurgy now developed for armour and for bladed weapons such as swords. And this was bad news indeed for one group of peoples geographically too far removed to keep abreast of such developments, the inhabitants of the New World.

During the late fifteenth century, advances in navigation and ship design, including the development of the mechanical watch, spurred eagerness to find a sea route for direct trading with the Far East, in particular the still fabled Cathay (China). It was hoped to find an easier route than via the Cape of Good Hope, and to minimise the huge middleman costs for goods transported overland across Asia. This adventurous climate fired mavericks such as Christopher Columbus and John Cabot to venture far out into the Atlantic in the hope of reaching Asia by sailing westwards, leading to the discovery, not initially recognised, that a very large and richly exploitable New World lay in between.

Ironically, neither Columbus nor Cabot realised that they had found a 'New World'. Nor did they themselves ever make contact with the great civilisations such as the Aztecs and Incas – like the North American 'Indians', descendants of the old Mongoloid migrants from Siberia – who controlled much of Central and western South America. Much like their Old World counterparts, these New World civilisations and their predecessors had developed farming, pottery and metallurgy of gold and copper. The Mayans, who had largely disappeared as a nation by the time of Columbus, had also developed a pictographic writing system.

But there were crucial ways in which even the most civilised peoples in the New World seriously lagged behind the Old. Not a single New World culture had domesticated haulage animals, the horse having died out until re-introduced by the Spanish. They had no ploughs. They had no wheels as transport aids. They had neither iron and steel nor gunpowder. Furthermore, just like many a European during the centuries before Christ, the Aztecs and the Incas indulged in human sacrifice, the former on a particularly large scale. And for the sixteenth-century European mind this categorised them as but pagan savages, ripe to be treated as such.

It was the Old World's advancement in steel-making and gunpowder that gave it a particular potency that proved overwhelming. In the wake of Columbus, entrepreneurs like Cortés and Pizarro, whom we will meet as our face number 18, deliberately sought out the Aztec and Inca empires. And in each case they were able to demonstrate how even a tiny force of Old World soldiery, equipped with steel swords, body armour and a modicum of artillery, could take on the largest of New World armies. Contemporaneously, thanks to forceful East European leaders such as Tsar Ivan IV, the tiny principality of Muscovy, a Viking settlement much less technologically advanced than those in western Europe, managed to check hordes of Mongol Tartars advancing from China, and to found the state of Russia. Ivan IV, more popularly known as Ivan the Terrible, is our face number 19.

However, not least because of the gold, silver and gem resources that the Aztec and Inca cultures revealed, it was the vast New World continent that represented the tempting prize for entrepreneurial-minded Europeans. Soon the tide of adventurers crossing the Atlantic became a flood, with the fiercely nationalistic countries of Spain, Portugal, England and even France vying for the greatest share of the spoils. It will be an ill-fated member of a French colonising expedition as late as 1686 whom we will meet as our face number 20.

But it was not only a flood of precious metals and stones that was transported back to the Old World (all too often attracting fierce piracy on the high seas). Accompanying this cargo were other New World products which, although they might have seemed more perishable, brought about major, lasting changes to European eating and living habits, some beneficial, others rather less so.

Thus Cortés first came across the Aztec emperor Montezuma drinking a brown liquid from a gold cup. The liquid was chocolate, hitherto unheard of in the Old World. The Aztecs had tomatoes, beans, and various gourds and squashes. They also enjoyed smoking another unknown commodity, tobacco. They used rubber, and played ball games with it. The Incas for their part had the potato, likewise completely unknown in Europe. Many of the peoples of the West Indies, Central America and northern South America civilised enough to wear clothing cultivated for it a fibre that we now know as cotton.

Besides such new commodities, the New World had terrain suitable for growing products that were hard to produce in the Old World, not least sugar. Although sugar was first used in India back in the mists of history, and was introduced by the Arabs to Egypt and southern Europe, in the Old World it remained a rare, luxury product, until Columbus had the foresight to carry sugar cane shoots with him on his second voyage to the 'Indies' in 1493. Within decades the Spanish were starting the first Caribbean sugar plantations. In 1751 sugar cane was also introduced to Louisiana on mainland North America. With slave labour to keep costs low, Old World teeth were about to meet their greatest challenge since ancient Egypt's bakers and their sandy bread, a challenge which gives many a dentist a good living to this day.

But these and many other developments fall within our own modern era, a period of innumerable technological advances. One of these was to be the invention of photography, the means by which faces would be so faithfully recorded that there would be no need for the reconstructions we have been relying on to see our ancestors. Let us now meet face to face some of those who lived during the last centuries before that time.

A Jorvik Viking
*c.*AD 1000

When he died, somewhere in the environs of modern-day York, he was between twenty-eight and thirty years of age, and about five feet six inches (1.68m) tall. He lived some five centuries after the Romans, undermined by internal weaknesses, had withdrawn their legions from Britannia. Following the province's infiltration by Angles, from whom it would gain the name 'England', his Viking forebears had arrived just over a century before his time, in AD 866 capturing the Angles' town of Eoforwic, formerly Roman Eboracum. Re-naming it 'Jorvik', they developed it into a major port and trading centre, which was still flourishing in his time even while politically and socially it was being absorbed back into a renascent England. We do not know his name – 'Eymund' is just the nickname that his archaeologist discoverers gave him. But thanks to computer technology and the skills of the York sculptor Lynn O'Dowd we can put a face to him, a face seen by thousands daily since it was given to an animated character in York's popular tourist attraction, the Jorvik Viking Centre.

If the word 'Viking' automatically conjures up the mental image of a fearsome warrior with a horned helmet, such expectation is doomed to disappointment. It is true that 'Viking', as very loosely applied to Danish, Swedish and Norse peoples, means 'pirate' in Norse. But as has long been recognised, the majority were not warriors at all, and occupied themselves relatively peaceably as farmers, fishermen, metalworkers, weavers and craftsmen. Most of those who occupied England – at the heyday of the 'Danelaw' controlling all except King Alfred's Wessex – were of Danish origin, and this was probably where our Eymund had his roots. The main mark that they left on English culture was the introduction into the language of Scandinavian words such as 'call', 'take', 'thin', 'law', 'ill', as well as place-names ending in '-by' ('village') such as Wetherby, Derby, Fernby and Sutterby. As for horned helmets, even those Vikings who were full-blooded warriors preferred cone-shaped, hornless helmets for any real fighting.[1] However, because they left very little pictorial trace, historians had a limited idea of what Eymund and his fellows looked like until relatively recently.

Quintessentially Viking, the famous Oseberg ship, used for a 9th-century Norse chieftain's burial, and incredibly well-preserved thanks to the properties of the blue clay in which it and other of the chieftain's accoutrements were buried.

The face of Eymund receiving finishing touches from York-based sculptor Lynn O'Dowd. O'Dowd worked from a three-dimensional foam reconstruction of Eymund's head milled following instructions provided by computer.

Although knowledge of England's 'Dark Age' Viking era had been very hazy, it was radically extended in the late 1970s following a decision by York City Council to allow the clearance of a large section of the historic Coppergate district to make way for a major redevelopment. Given the city's rich historical past, from Georgian all the way back to Roman times, this compelled some intensive archaeological investigations, implemented under the auspices of the York Archaeological Trust.

Hardly had the archaeologists started turning the soil before they began to come across finds that exceeded all expectations. From levels specifically identifiable to the Viking era there emerged, unusually well preserved by waterlogged conditions, some of the most complete wooden buildings of the period ever discovered, even the whole lower part of a tenth-century street.

As was clear from surviving artefacts left by the street's original occupants, many of the dwellings were the workshops of craftsmen, among them carpenters,

408 – Last Roman troops withdrawn from Britain

477 – Saxons gain foothold in southern Britain, shortly followed by Angles

622 – The Hegira, or flight of Mohammed to Medina, starting point of the Muslim calendar

787 – Earliest recorded Viking attacks on Britain

AD 400   AD 500   AD 600   AD 700

leather-workers, cup-makers (none too obviously, the district of Coppergate gets its name from these) and jewellery-makers. Although often initially unrecognisable, fragments of clothing came to light, including a sock, portions of silks brought from considerable distances, and well-crafted leather shoes. Ice-skates had been skilfully fashioned from bone.

Food remains showed that they kept domesticated animals such as goats, pigs, sheep and cattle, the latter revealing a marked diminution in size resulting from the abandonment of the Romans' scientific methods of livestock breeding. Fish seem to have featured prominently in the diet, with freshwater species such as bream, perch, pike, roach and rudd, as well as marine varieties such as herring, haddock, flatfish, cod, eels, salmon, and shellfish including oysters, all popular. Among the numerous domestic and industrial objects discovered were combs, pottery, coins, tools, fish-hooks, gaming pieces, spurs, and even the remains of musical instruments.

Clearly, a thriving and fascinatingly diverse community lived in York in Viking times. And rather than present the discoveries in the form of dry archaeological reports, the York Archaeological Trust, prompted by some entrepreneurial prodding from a Lancashire businessman, Ian Skipper, decided to reconstruct the street life-size exactly as it would have looked in the tenth century. Indeed, the aim was to recreate not only its sights, but even its sounds and smells.

Thus was born the Jorvik Viking Centre, now one of England's top tourist sites. A highlight for visitors is a Disneyland-style ride back through the centuries to the River Ouse waterfront as it would have looked at the time when Eymund lived. In the course of the ride they can reach out and virtually touch a street from a full millennium ago. Amidst the noise of metalsmiths hammering at their craft they can catch faint snatches of the Old Norse that Eymund and his kindred would have spoken on the streets. They can peer into the workshops with their thatched roofs and rush floors. They can savour the smells of the food market as well as catch the faint reek of the steaming dung-heaps. Not least, they can come face to face with no less than twenty-two life-size, animated Vikings complete with authentic costumes.

Initially the faces on these human replicas were simply based on the members of the team who had helped build the Jorvik Centre. However, when numerous

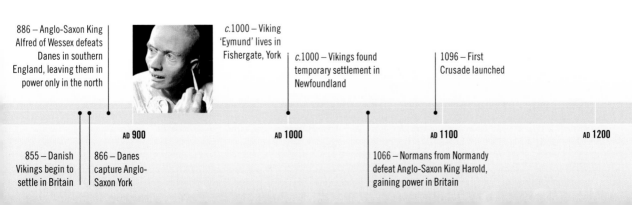

886 – Anglo-Saxon King Alfred of Wessex defeats Danes in southern England, leaving them in power only in the north

c.1000 – Viking 'Eymund' lives in Fishergate, York

c.1000 – Vikings found temporary settlement in Newfoundland

1096 – First Crusade launched

AD **900**   AD **1000**   AD **1100**   AD **1200**

855 – Danish Vikings begin to settle in Britain

866 – Danes capture Anglo-Saxon York

1066 – Normans from Normandy defeat Anglo-Saxon King Harold, gaining power in Britain

Revealed, the foundations of the Jorvik that Viking Eymund knew. A view of the York Archaeological Trust excavation work in progress during the 1980s, before the site was handed over for commercial redevelopment.

well-preserved skeletons came to light – not least from a Fishergate graveyard with sixty-eight burials belonging to a small church or chapel which had fallen out of use around the mid-eleventh century – in the late 1980s the York Archaeological Trust decided to go one better. Their plan was for each replica Viking to be fitted with a real face, reconstructed from the excavated remains. The first skeleton chosen was that of 'Eymund'. He was a man of slight to medium build, and because he was buried at Fishergate the inference was that he made his living by fish, whether as a merchant or as an actual fisherman.

In the event the method that was chosen for reconstructing Eymund was not Neave's. Instead it was the high-tech, computer-linked one that University College Hospital, London, had developed to forecast the results of facial surgery, a variant of which we saw was used for the Beijing hominid and for Esamun. At University College's Medical Physics department, Eymund's skull was scanned by low-power laser on a turntable. The data from this was combined with the known average facial tissue thicknesses at key points of the skull as determined for north-west European males. Then, with the aid of a modern face of the same type similarly scanned to act as a template, there emerged on the computer screen a 'morphed' likeness theoretically very close to that of the true Eymund as he had looked in life a thousand years ago. Via a linked milling machine this computer face was translated into three-dimensional form on a block of hard foam, and passed to Lynn O'Dowd for the addition of the necessary elements to make it realistic – prosthetic eyes, a hand-knotted wig, complexion details and so on.

With the final addition of a body dressed in garments reconstructed from the fragments discovered during the excavations, the result is as if Eymund were once more alive – indeed, given that he is full-length and animated, rather more so than any other reconstruction featured so far. As the York Archaeological Trust director Peter Addyman felt bound to comment when the reconstruction was first presented publicly in 1991:

> The figure is unnervingly real. It is quite staggering to meet an almost thousand-year-old face like this; probably the first time anyone has met the gaze of someone from the Viking age. This has been a real breakthrough.

The fact that Eymund can stare out at us as he does is indeed a remarkable achievement, given that the Romans' high standards of portraiture had long fallen away by the Viking era and we have no realistic portrait of even a single Viking from the time. One of the very few glimpses that we have of the Vikings' physical appearance derives from the Arab writer Ibn Fadlan, who observed a group of them burying one of their leaders on the banks of the Volga in present-day Russia:

Never have I seen people of more perfect physique. They are tall as date palms, have reddish hair and fair skins. They wear neither shirts nor coats with sleeves. The men wear cloaks with one end thrown over the shoulder, leaving a hand free. Every man carries an axe, a sword and a dagger, and is never seen without them.

Ibn Fadlan further remarked on an aspect impossible to reconstruct from any bones: 'Each man has [tattooed upon him] trees, figures and the like, from the fingernails to the toes.'

While we cannot be sure whether this was how Eymund looked, or exactly what clothes he wore – the Jorvik reconstruction provided him with two tunics, a cloak and trousers – it is quite definite that the clothes of his time were more brightly coloured than those generally portrayed in Hollywood movies set in the period. The use of natural vegetable dyes allowed bright reds, greens, blues and yellows. And we can be pretty sure that the garment fastenings he knew would have been clasps, thongs and brooches, since the Europe of his time had forgotten the button, and the invention of the button-hole lay another two centuries into the future.

Although Eymund's place of settlement was at Jorvik or York, in his day the geographical spread of Norsemen, Swedes and Danes was remarkably wide, with England close to the hub rather than at the rim as in the Roman Empire. As a group of peoples the Vikings had developed exceptionally sturdy and versatile ships, combining sail and oars and designed even to be moved across land on rollers. Their excellence has long been appreciated from late nineteenth-century discoveries such as the Oseberg and Gokstad vessels,[2] as well as no less than fourteen examples found more recently at Roskilde, Denmark.[3] Modern-day enthusiasts who build and sail life-size reconstructions of these vessels never fail to extol their seaworthiness.

With these craft the Vikings not only penetrated Asia by river, they also developed the confidence to venture further and further into the Atlantic, navigating the ocean, as has only recently become understood, by a simple portable sun compass based on the sun-dial principle. They may well also have benefited from the climate in the so-called Little Optimum Period, which created north Atlantic temperatures significantly warmer than today's. It is certain that they reached North America at Newfoundland, at a latitude now notorious for its icebergs. The archaeological discovery in the 1960s of Viking-style turf houses and a smithy dating from about AD 1000 at L'Anse aux Meadows on northern Newfoundland has confirmed that the story told in the Norse sagas of voyaging to, and temporarily settling in, what they called 'Vinland'[4] to the west of Greenland is no myth, but based on historical reality.[5] And although they had early on to abandon the Newfoundland settlement, and their colony on Greenland became extinct by the sixteenth century, Iceland, which the Norse first colonised in the ninth century, is peopled by their descendants to this day.

In the case of Eymund at the similarly colonised Jorvik, there is no evidence of disease on his skeleton. So we do not know the cause of his death, only that he died in his late twenties. It should once again be noted that what we would consider a very young age for death was rather less unusual by the standards of the eleventh century AD, when only half of those who survived the hazards of birth reached the age of twenty. In Eymund's time the population of England had shrunk to something of the order of a million. As a people, too, the Vikings had undergone a marked change. Although they were initially pagan, to the extent that in the seventh century they had all but wiped out the monastic settlements established by St Augustine, the late tenth century saw the wholesale conversion to Christianity of Viking communities as far afield as Russia. Those in England likewise converted, as with the political ascendancy of the English king they became more and more socially integrated. The fact that Eymund was found in a graveyard thought to have belonged to a small church or chapel strongly suggests that he and/or his parents were among those who successfully converted.

Full-body reconstruction of Eymund, with facial features recreated by sculptor Lynn O'Dowd based on scans from the original skull as excavated from a cemetery of *c.* 1000 AD at Fishergate, York. The clothes are based on known Viking fashions of the period.

16

THE KING WHO TRIED AGAIN 1329

T he day was 23 June 1314, the location a few miles from Stirling Castle, one of the fortresses through which England's late king, Edward I, had subjugated the Scots. Recently, however, the Scots had proved very unruly, and the castle's governor had sent word to London that he would have to surrender it unless he received reinforcements.

It was precisely in answer to that plea that the Earl of Hereford's nephew, Sir Henry de Bohun, was proudly riding at the head of the huge army that King Edward II had brought for Stirling's relief when, just before the castle, he espied a lone man on a pony. This individual was inspecting a group of foot-soldiers half-hidden in woodland, and from the gleam of a gold circlet, de Bohun immediately recognised Robert the Bruce, the King of Scots, whose troublemaking had prompted this whole expedition. Because there survives no reliable contemporary portrait of the Bruce, seven hundred years later we might never have known the face that de Bohun looked on that day but for a fine reconstruction produced by Richard Neave and his colleagues.

For de Bohun, recognition of that royal face was to have the direst consequences. Feeling invincible in full armour astride a magnificent war-horse, against which the Scottish king's battle-axe and pony must have seemed all too tempting a target, he impulsively lowered his visor, couched his lance, and spurred his mount full tilt in a fearsome charge that he had practised a thousand times before in the lists.

To the amazement of observers, King Robert made no attempt to flee to the cover of the nearby woodland. Instead, stolidly waiting until de Bohun's lance-point was almost on him, he neatly dodged it, stood up to his full height in his pony's stirrups and smashed his battle-axe down on to the knight's head with such force that helmet, skull and axe handle all split asunder in unison. As the English war-horse sped on, de Bohun's corpse dangling bloodily from its stirrups, the partly concealed Scottish ranks let out a huge roar, while the English cavalry, immediately behind, unsettled by some skilfully disguised pits with which the Scots had peppered their path, turned in confusion and fled. Such was the psychological effect, combined with the Bruce's

It was against an English knight, mounted, armed and armoured much as seen here that Scotland's king Robert the Bruce scored one of his most notable feats of combat. From the Luttrell Psalter, c.1340, British Library, London.

brilliance as a tactician, that the very next day the Scottish army, consisting predominantly of foot-soldiers, resoundingly defeated the flower of the English cavalry in the victory of Bannockburn.

In desperation King Edward II, whose aides physically hauled him from the battlefield when it was obvious that the day was lost, rode hard for the refuge of Stirling Castle. The castle's pragmatic governor, however, pointing out that Edward had failed to bring him the necessary protection, refused the royal party entry, and they were obliged to flee south in utter disgrace, abandoning the main army and leaving the entire baggage train and even England's Great Seal in Scottish hands. Intent on avenging such a humiliating defeat, in 1322 Edward attempted a second, even bigger expedition. But Robert the Bruce was again well prepared, and the result was a similarly resounding defeat, complete with the loss of a second baggage train and a second Great Seal.

Because Scotland was so under-developed a country in the early fourteenth century, art of any quality was hardly known. There survives no authoritative

Stirling Castle, a strategic English command post when Robert the Bruce began his reign in 1306. Its wily governor refused to give refuge to England's King Edward II following his crushing defeat by Robert the Bruce at Bannockburn.

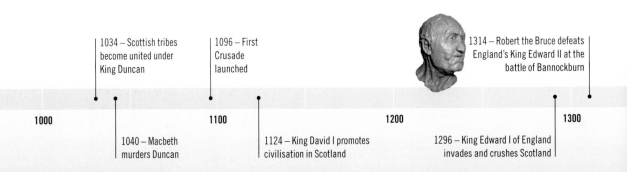

1034 – Scottish tribes become united under King Duncan

1096 – First Crusade launched

1314 – Robert the Bruce defeats England's King Edward II at the battle of Bannockburn

1000   1100   1200   1300

1040 – Macbeth murders Duncan

1124 – King David I promotes civilisation in Scotland

1296 – King Edward I of England invades and crushes Scotland

contemporary portrait of Robert the Bruce, and there may well never have been one. The commemorative equestrian statue that today looks out over the Bannockburn battlefield is based on no more than a modern-day sculptor's imagination. The vague profile to be seen on his coins offers no seriously meaningful likeness. Nor is there any clear description of him from the historical record.

However, in 1817 a major building programme was put in hand to refurbish the abbey church of Dunfermline, the traditional burial-place of Scottish kings, where King Robert is known to have been laid to rest in June 1329.[1] The entire abbey had been ruined during the Reformation, but on 17 February 1818 the workmen rebuilding the church came across a vault before the area where the high altar had been. The vault's size and position strongly suggested that it was an important royal tomb. When on 5 November 1819 it was formally opened in the presence of several Scottish notables and medical specialists, there was general agreement that the well preserved skeleton inside had to be that of Robert the Bruce. Not least of the reasons was that the chest could clearly be seen to have been sawn through. This was consistent with the historical record that on his death the Bruce's heart was cut from his body in order to fulfil his dying wish for it to be taken to the Holy Land and laid in the Holy Sepulchre. The honouring of that wish was duly undertaken by his most redoubtable aide, Sir James Douglas, who commissioned a silver and enamel casket in which to carry the heart around his neck; he was still wearing it when he was killed *en route* fighting the Moors in Spain. The heart was later recovered and buried in Melrose Abbey in the Scottish Borders.

Robert the Bruce is known to have died at the age of around fifty-five, and when the nineteenth-century medical specialists examined the skull, they noted the teeth of his lower jaw to be large and almost all intact. Four or five however, were missing in the upper jaw, seemingly having been lost in some trauma which had also fractured his upper jaw-bone. From their measurement of the long-bones the specialists estimated the king's height to have been

Coin of Robert the Bruce, its artistry clearly inadequate to provide a reliable guide to the king's likeness.

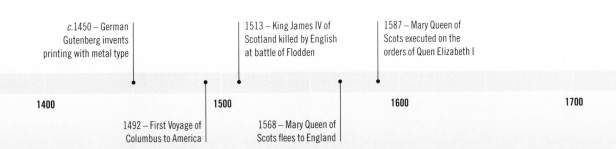

c.1450 – German Gutenberg invents printing with metal type

1513 – King James IV of Scotland killed by English at battle of Flodden

1587 – Mary Queen of Scots executed on the orders of Quen Elizabeth I

1400

1500

1600

1700

1492 – First Voyage of Columbus to America

1568 – Mary Queen of Scots flees to England

around five feet eleven inches (1.8m), though more recent evaluation of the same measurements has scaled this down to five feet six inches (1.68m).

Much more importantly, before Robert's skull was returned to the vault it was passed to an artist, a Mr Scoular, for the making of a plaster cast. This cast was recorded at the time as having been 'executed with great skill',[2] and it ultimately passed into the care of Edinburgh University's Anatomical Department. Thanks to Scoular's skill, the survival of the cast, and the expertise of Richard Neave and his colleagues, today we have a much better idea of Robert the Bruce's personal appearance than anyone has had for the last six centuries.[3]

From Neave's facial reconstruction work, the immediate impression is of a very Churchillian face – an extremely strong jaw and a bull neck, befitting a man who had spent most of his early years as a guerrilla living by his wits and his physical strength. The loss of his upper teeth and the jaw fracture may well have been sustained during a particularly close shave that he suffered shortly after his coronation at Scone in 1306. Camped for the night near Methven, he and his party were taken by surprise by the enemy Earl of Pembroke. He was three times unhorsed in the fighting, lost a number of his closest aides, and only narrowly escaped with his life. Shortly after this setback he suffered the capture and execution of his brother Nigel and other Scottish aristocrats, along with the imprisonment of his wife and other Scottish noblewomen, some of whom the English treated with unspeakable cruelty.

The face of King Robert the Bruce (1274-1329), as reconstructed by Richard Neave and colleagues. This reconstruction was only made possible thanks to a well-produced plaster cast of the king's skull that was created back in 1819.

But, as is well known to schoolchildren, when Robert was at his lowest ebb, hiding in a cave in the wake of this disaster, he watched a spider repeatedly trying to bridge the cave with its web, failing six times before succeeding on its seventh attempt. This inspired his famous dictum that if at first you don't succeed, you should 'try, try and try again', and he resolved to fight another day. Whereupon, as history relates, it was ultimately his English counterpart, the profligate King Edward II, who came off worst, not only suffering the humiliating defeats at Bannockburn and later, but alienating most of his court, including his own queen, Isabella of France, by his relationships with unworthy favourites such as Piers Gaveston and the utterly unscrupulous Despensers. Ultimately forced to resign the throne in favour of his son, the altogether abler Edward III, Edward II was kept a prisoner in Berkeley Castle in Gloucestershire, where he was horribly murdered at the instigation of his wife and her lover. And even when the fifteen-year-old Edward III, on succeeding his father, led a fresh campaign against Scotland, the result was again such a humiliating defeat that in 1328 he was obliged to sign a peace treaty formally recognising that 'the kingdom of Scotland… shall belong to our dearest ally and friend… Lord Robert… King of Scotland' and should be 'separate in all things from the Kingdom of England, whole, free and undisturbed in perpetuity'.[4]

In 1328, when the Bruce was already in his fifties, in the penultimate year of his reign, such a total capitulation by England can only have been of enormous satisfaction. The Scotland in which he had grown up had a total population of less than 500,000, and was a very much weaker, poorer place than its prosperous southern neighbour. In his younger days his father the Earl of Carrick's great rival John Balliol held the Scottish throne, and Robert could only look on helplessly as King Edward I crossed the River Tweed, butchered most of the population of Berwick, and proceeded ruthlessly to impose his will on Scotland. Robert might well have felt equally helpless when, eight years after Sir William Wallace's stirring victory over the English at the battle of Stirling Bridge (September 1297), Wallace was betrayed, captured, and transported four hundred miles (640km) to London. There he was hauled four miles (6km) through the streets chained to a hurdle, publicly hanged, cut down, castrated and disembowelled while still alive, finally beheaded and his body cut into quarters. In the light of the fate meted out to those who dared resist English might, Robert the Bruce surely had every reason never to try at all.

But try he did, in 1306 seizing his chance at the throne, formally receiving the crown at Scone, and thereupon, despite the serious initial setbacks he suffered, skilfully deploying the greater resilience and mobility of his fighting men *vis-à-vis* the English. This was most vividly described by the contemporary French chronicler Jean le Bel:

These Scots are exceedingly hardy through their constant wearing of arms and experience in combat. When they enter England they will in a single day and night cover twenty-four miles, for they ride on sturdy horses and bring no wagons with them. They carry no provisions of bread and wine for their abstemiousness is such that they will live for a long time on stewed meat and drink river water. They need neither pots nor pans for wherever they invade they find plenty of cattle and use the hides of these in which to boil the flesh. Each man carries under his saddle an iron plate and behind the saddle a little

bag of oatmeal. When they have eaten the stewed meat they place the plate on the fire and when the plate is hot they spread on it a little paste made of oatmeal and water, and make a thin cake in the manner of a biscuit to comfort their stomachs. So it is no wonder that they can travel farther in a day than other soldiers.[5]

Five centuries later Australian bushmen would make 'damper' bread on their camp-fires in much the same way as the Bruce's Scotsmen. It was thanks to such frugal self-reliance, and despite many a close personal brush with capture and death, that Robert succeeded in overthrowing the English yoke and avoiding Wallace's martyrdom. We know that he died of natural causes at the simple manor house that he had built for himself and his wife Elizabeth (whom he outlived by eighteen months) at the village of Cardross, near Dumbarton. Death came after a long illness that had repeatedly incapacitated him in his final months, though exactly what it was remains a matter of some debate.

According to later medieval writers it was leprosy. Most modern commentators, however, think this unlikely, since throughout the Middle Ages the quarantine of lepers was strictly enforced, and not even kings were exempt. Besides, as part of the peace treaty with England, Robert's four-year-old son David was married to Edward III's six-year-old sister Joan. The ailing Robert shortly afterwards entertained the newly-wed youngsters at Cardross (having been too ill to attend their wedding), and he would surely not have risked infecting two children had he known his disease to be anything as feared and supposedly contagious as leprosy.

If we still had access to the king's skeleton it might be feasible at least to eliminate leprosy as a possibility, for in advanced cases of this disease the bones are always affected. Without such access, however, the only possible clue is a pitting on the surface of the cast of his skull, the explanation of which might be as simple as slight imperfections to Scoular's method of casting in 1819. It has been suggested that Robert's true illness might have been syphilis, which before modern medicine was often wrongly diagnosed as leprosy. Certainly this disease was rife in the Middle Ages, and reached epidemic proportions in the fifteenth century. Although Robert was devoted to his wife Elizabeth, he did spend eight years of his marriage separated from her while she was imprisoned in England; during this time, in common with many royal figures before and since, he sired several illegitimate children by unknown mothers.[6]

Whatever the nature of the illness from which Robert the Bruce died, he has by any score to rank as one of Scotland's greatest, bravest and most successful of kings. And if, within a generation, much of what he had so brilliantly achieved would sadly be lost again by his son, David II, England in its turn was far from exempt from reverses of fortune.

...us dei gracia Lex Ungliae
...et dominus hibernie

hamenus   sanctus

ley   trahor   propt

Regina Elizabetha
Edwardi dei gracie

AN UNKNOWN SOLDIER IN THE WARS OF THE ROSES 1461

In any age he would have stood out as a big, muscular man, attributes which no doubt led to his early recruitment as a professional soldier. And despite suffering an earlier face-wound, even in his late forties he must still have been highly vigorous. Hence his involvement in the Battle of Towton on Palm Sunday, 29 March 1461, an episode in the Wars of the Roses fought in what are today pleasantly undulating fields beside the A162, ten miles east of the Yorkshire city of Leeds.

But to our soldier's misfortune, blowing that Palm Sunday was an unseasonably fierce blizzard, which drove blinding gusts of snow directly into his and his fellow-Lancastrians' faces, seriously impeding their aim and firepower and greatly aiding their Yorkist opponents. Beset with such difficulties, at some point he and his companions appear to have turned and fled the field, only to be cut down and savagely killed. Their bodies were stripped and tightly packed together into a mass grave, there to lie undisturbed until August 1996 when they were unexpectedly found by construction workers laying the foundations for an extension to Towton Hall.

University of Bradford osteologists and archaeologists were summoned, and methodically set about uncovering and recording what proved to be forty-three well-preserved skeletons readily identifiable, not least from the radiocarbon dates, as victims of the Towton battle. Many had suffered appalling injuries, and as none bore any form of identification, all might be classed as 'unknown soldiers' in the Wars of the Roses. Because Number 16 of the archaeologists' notation stood out from the rest, he was chosen for facial reconstruction by Richard Neave's Unit of Art in Medicine at Manchester University. It was a task that fell principally to Caroline Wilkinson, and the result has exceeded all expectations. As well as confronting us with a most convincing facial likeness of a man born around the time of Agincourt, it also presents some harrowing glimpses of what life – and death – were truly like for the professional soldier serving during that turbulent fifteenth-century period.[1]

The Battle of Towton was one of the bloodiest encounters in the Wars of the Roses.[2] Contemporary estimates put the total number slain at 28,000,[3] which if true would

King Edward IV (1442-1483) and his queen Elizabeth Woodville, as portrayed on the Royal Windows in Canterbury Cathedral. It was against the eighteen year old Edward's Yorkist army that the 'Unknown Soldier' fought at the battle of Towton, with fatal consequences. Despite Edward marrying into the Woodville family, who were Lancastrians, this failed to end the Yorkist-Lancastrian bitter feuding.

be more than on the first day of the Battle of the Somme, though the figure is widely disbelieved by modern-day historians. The rightful English monarch of the time, albeit more in name than disposition, was Henry V's son, the unworldly Henry VI, who had inherited a tendency to periods of mental confusion from his insane grandfather, Charles VI of France. It was during one of these bouts in 1453 that Henry's cousin Richard Duke of York, aided by the Earl of Warwick, took the king under his 'protection', imprisoning him and forcing him to declare him as his heir. When this 'protectorship' was fiercely contested by Henry VI's strong-willed queen Margaret of Anjou, the stage was set for the start of the 'Wars of the Roses' – so called because the Yorkists' badge was a white rose while that of Henry VI's royalists (Lancastrians, after his great-grandfather John of Gaunt, Duke of Lancaster) was supposedly a red one.

The advance of the Yorkist archers at Towton. Their firepower was able to be devastatingly effective because a blizzard blowing in their opponents' faces robbed the latter of their aim and effectiveness.

1215 – Signing of
Magna Carta

1461 – 'Unknown
Soldier' killed at
battle of Towton

1492 – First Voyage
of Columbus to
America

1200   1300   1400

1348 – Black Death
ravages Europe

1474 – First book
printed in England

On 30 December 1460 Queen Margaret's Lancastrian forces, comprising many northerners and wild Welshmen, soundly defeated those of Richard of York at the Battle of Wakefield. Richard himself was killed and his head stuck on the walls of York, crowned with a paper cap. This royalist victory was followed by a second on 16 February 1461, in the environs of St Albans – the first English battle in which firearms were used – and again the Yorkist army found themselves outnumbered and had to beat a hasty retreat.

But then Queen Margaret's Lancastrians disgraced themselves, and not for the first time. While she and her hapless husband enjoyed the hospitality of the monks at St Albans, her unruly troops ransacked the town and convent. When news of this reached London, the citizens refused to open the gates to them, welcoming instead

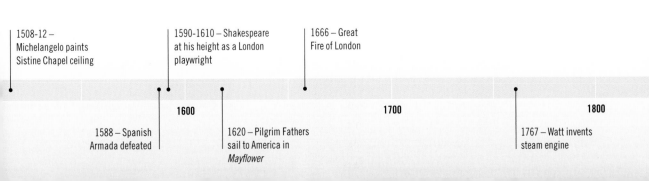

1508-12 –
Michelangelo paints
Sistine Chapel ceiling

1590-1610 – Shakespeare
at his height as a London
playwright

1666 – Great
Fire of London

1600

1700

1800

1588 – Spanish
Armada defeated

1620 – Pilgrim Fathers
sail to America in
Mayflower

1767 – Watt invents
steam engine

Richard of York's eighteen-year-old son Edward, Earl of March, whom on 4 March 1461 they proclaimed King Edward IV.

While Queen Margaret had little option but to lead her army back to its northern roots, the tall Edward (six feet three inches, 1.9m) and his mentor Warwick quickly re-mustered their dispersed followers. They then pursued the Lancastrian troops northwards in an all-out bid to avenge the death of Edward's father and establish Yorkist sovereignty. And it was in the environs of the tiny village of Towton that they caught up with them, finding them encamped on a plain bounded by the Cock brook on one side and the road to Tadcaster on the other. The battle reportedly raged for ten hours, and despite the favourable wind direction for the Yorkists, the royal army's sheer size initially seemed to give it the advantage – until the late arrival on to the scene of the Duke of Norfolk. As Norfolk's men fell upon the left flank of Margaret and Henry's troops they faltered and collapsed, whereupon the Yorkists suddenly found themselves gaining the upper hand. It was one of the holiest days of the year, yet the leaders of both sides had ordered no mercy. And whether or not the figure of 28,000 dead is to be believed, undoubtedly the Yorkists drove many of the fleeing Lancastrians into the Cock brook and there slaughtered them. Reports of the time describe the waters running red with blood long afterwards.

Clearly the cache of forty-three skeletons discovered in 1996 was just one of a number of pits that were hastily dug to bury those killed that day. But the painstaking forensic work carried out by the University of Bradford archaeologists and osteologists has enabled a great deal to be learned even from this single discovery. From the outset the archaeologist in charge, Tim Sutherland, although under pressure to clear the site quickly, presciently arranged for each bone's position to be carefully mapped on to a computer. This work revealed far more clearly than any photograph how the bodies of the dead had been randomly heaped one on top of the other, squeezed into a comparatively shallow trench twenty feet long by six and a half feet wide (6 x 2m). All were male, aged between sixteen and about fifty. Their heights ranged from five feet two inches to just over six feet (1.6 to 1.8m), and most were of significantly more robust build than the average individuals found in medieval cemeteries. The absence of any accompanying accoutrements strongly indicated that all had been stripped naked.

The skeletons were mostly well preserved. Almost all of them showed damage from bladed and spiked weapons, so lethal that the injury could only have been sustained on the

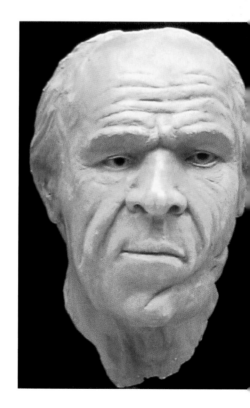

Frontal and side view of the Unkown Soldier's facial features, as reconstructed by Caroline Wilkinson. This reconstruction was created from a cast made of the soldier's skull as found in one of the pits dug for those killed during or after the Towton battle. Medical experts are agreed that the great facial wound has to have been sustained during some earlier combat. Medieval physicians used some surprisingly impressive procedures to treat this injury, which given its severity has healed remarkably well.

day of Towton. In many instances the shapes of the injuries match surviving fifteenth-century weapons preserved in Britain's Royal Armouries. But a quite unexpected finding was that around a third of the skeletons bore scars of weapon-inflicted injuries, often serious, that could only have been sustained some time earlier and had healed. This strongly suggested that they were professional soldiers for whom Towton was not their first battle.

Another important observation, reinforcing the identification as professional soldiers, was that the bones of many exhibited a muscular development that was particularly marked to the left side of the body and to the left forearm. Intrigued by this, the osteologists arranged for CT scans to be made of the body of a local archery enthusiast, Simon Stanley, known to have practised drawing the longbow from a very early age. As the scans revealed, Stanley's bones exhibited marked localised muscular developments strikingly similar to those on the Towton skeletons. The strong inference was that many of the Towton victims had spent much of their lives practising archery. In the late Middle Ages it was English strength and skill in the use of the longbow that often played a key role in winning battles, as in the fourteenth- and early fifteenth-century victories against the French. The difference here was that it was English archer against English archer, with the Lancastrians at a disadvantage half-blinded by the blizzard blowing in

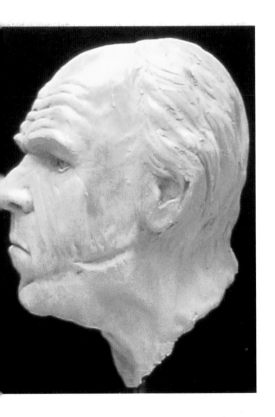

their faces. Hence the likelihood that our 'unknown soldier' and his companions were Lancastrians.

Among the Bradford osteologists was Shannon Novak, an American seconded from the University of Utah following her studies of the war graves in Croatia. She and her colleagues found particularly fascinating among the bone injuries the great facial wound that the exceptionally big-built soldier 'Sixteen' had sustained at some earlier stage in his life. As the Wilkinson facial reconstruction vividly shows, this took the form of a pronounced gash on the left side of his face, running almost from ear to chin. Clearly, in some battle several years before Towton 'Sixteen' had been struck full across the side of the face with a large-bladed weapon that had severed part of the jaw and chin, including almost certainly the tongue.

In the face of this injury, one especially impressive feature is the surprisingly expert medical attention that he must have received in order to be fit enough to fight another day. Surviving medieval texts describe surgical and medical treatment procedures, mostly learned from the Arabs, for tending battle injuries to the face. These prescribe the application of wax where the bone has been cut through, then a dressing, accompanied by a splint the length of the jaw; the wound is bandaged, and the whole ensemble is then sewn to a skull cap to keep it in place. Although historians had mostly been highly sceptical that such procedures were ever actually carried out, the evidence from 'Sixteen' and some of his companions not only confirms that they were, but also shows that they were used even on comparatively humble serving men.

The presumption has to be that 'Sixteen' and others with earlier war-wounds were retainers in some noble household whose great lord had the means to finance such skilled medical treatments and considered it worthwhile from the track record of results. For another surprise, as indicated by the studies of 'Sixteen' and others, is just how well the injuries had healed in the wake of the treatment. Any slicing to the bone with an unsterilised weapon might normally be expected to lead to serious bacterial infection, but in case after case the Towton soldiers' bones had healed cleanly, with no sign of any such complications. This argues for medieval medical know-how, particularly in relation to hygiene, being rather better than has previously been credited.

But what really surprised the osteologists was what they discovered from the injuries that the soldiers had sustained on the day of Towton itself, from which they had died. In only one instance was there evidence of an archer's arrow. In almost all other cases, including Sixteen, the main injuries were terrible blows from swords, daggers and pick-like battle-axes that had been rained on the men's faces and heads with excessive savagery. Ancillary wounds to the limbs indicated that the victims had often raised their arms instinctively, but uselessly, in self-defence.

Since helmets were standard issue for medieval soldiers, when these individuals met their deaths they can only have lost any such head protection, or had it

Weapons that well-armoured 15th-century nobles used during hand-to-hand combat. The 'Unknown Soldier' and his companions appear to have been brutally hacked to death by individuals wielding weapons that were essentially near identical.

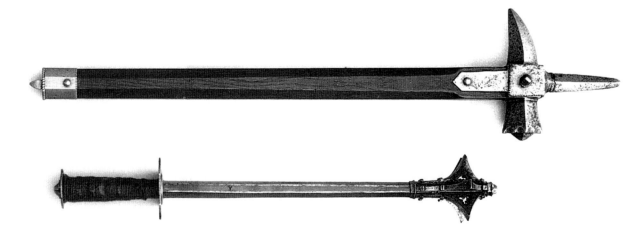

Edward V, the elder of Edward IV's two sons, who succeeded to the English throne in 1483, at the age of thirteen. Richard, Duke of Gloucester was uncle to the new king and his brother, and under the guise of protecting the pair he imprisoned them in the Tower of London, from which they would never emerge alive – the famous 'Princes in the Tower'. Richard thereupon became king, as the notorious Richard III.

removed, before receiving this final, fatal battering. In some instances there were indications of noses and ears being sliced off. And some of the major wounds were so savage and repeated that they went far beyond what it would have been either necessary or prudent to inflict in any ongoing battle. In Sixteen's case virtually the entire upper left-hand side of his face had been hacked away, obliging Caroline Wilkinson to reconstruct it from the surviving right side.

The strong implication, therefore, is that these men, Sixteen among them, were Lancastrians who had been overtaken in flight. Having captured them, the already victorious Yorkists clearly had no compunction in torturing and massacring them, consistent with the teenage Edward of York's stated determination that the maximum vengeance should be wrought for his father's death at Lancastrian hands.

The medieval England that Sixteen knew was in many ways a highly attractive place, with churches richly decorated in the brightest colours, an annual calendar of colourful festivals and entertainments, and a rapidly improving lifestyle being enjoyed by an increasingly affluent middle class. During his lifetime Sixteen probably never had to put his hand to a plough. Instead he had his food, lodging, clothing, armour and weapons supplied by a noble household, quite possibly the royal one itself, in return for which he trained long and hard in the arts and discipline of warfare.

But while the medieval era, at least in its earlier centuries, is known as 'the age of chivalry', Sixteen's grim fate after Towton makes it clear that the actuality of its warfare, certainly for the ordinary serving soldier, was significantly harsher and less romantic than most historical novels and films would have it. Whatever our unknown soldier's name may have been, he was undoubtedly a seasoned and terrifying-looking veteran who had taken part in a battle well before Towton. On this earlier occasion he had received injuries that might have killed him there and then, only to recover from these to fight again. And had it been his side which had won at Towton, we can guess that, given the chance, he would have been just as ruthless to the Yorkists as they were to him.

However horrifying such brutality on English soil might seem to us, at least the two opposing sides, Yorkists and Lancastrians, were relatively evenly equipped and matched. This cannot be said for the victims of our next 'face', that of another highly professional fighting man. In this instance we not only know the man's name – it is one well known to world history. And he would be born in Spain a mere fifteen years after our 'Sixteen' had breathed his last.

18

Butcher of the Incas 1541

This face in 1533 greedily gazed on more tonnage of gold than most of us might expect to see in a hundred lifetimes. When, eight years later, he died fighting off assassins, he was in his mid-sixties, a robustly built individual around five feet nine inches (1.75m) tall. We can put a name to him: he was Francisco Pizarro, the Spanish soldier primarily responsible for conquering the Inca empire of Peru. And although no reliable contemporary portrait of him has survived, we can also put an authentic face to him, thanks to the skill of the veteran American specialist Betty Pat Gatliff, whose facial reconstructions of Pizarro are to be found in museums on both sides of the Atlantic.[1]

Born some time around the mid-1470s in Trujillo, Spain – an ancient Castilian town which today boasts his equestrian statue in its main square – Francisco Pizarro was the illegitimate son of a veteran soldier, Gonzalo Pizarro, and a labourer's daughter, Francisca Gonzales. Brought up in the house of his mother's parents, he was never taught to read, and was still in his teens when Columbus set out on the fateful voyage on which he would 'discover' and open up the New World. In 1502, while Columbus was still alive, Francisco set off on his own fortune-seeking venture across the Atlantic, personally doing much to exterminate the naked and defenceless Taino Indians who had so enchanted Columbus twenty years earlier, before setting up as a cattle rancher in Panama. And it was while he was in Panama that he first heard tales of the glittering and as yet undiscovered Inca empire to the south.[2]

In partnership with the adventurer Diego de Amalgro, Pizarro made two reconnaissance expeditions in search of this fabled domain. Neither expedition was successful, but the interception of a raft carrying goods destined for Inca territory proved that the empire existed, encouraging Pizarro to journey to Spain to request from the Holy Roman Emperor Charles V the necessary royal licence to carry out a conquest. By good fortune the conquistador Hernándo Cortés was at the Spanish court at the time, creating a deep impression with the wealth amassed from his conquest of the Aztec empire. So Pizarro easily gained his licence, together with the

Francisco Pizarro (c.1476–1541) as depicted in a near-contemporary portrait of doubtful reliability, portraiture as thin-faced and aristocratic being fashionable among the Spanish nobility of the time. Betty Gatliff's facial reconstruction from Pizarro's actual skull has revealed an altogether more strong-jawed cast cast of countenance.

Left: Pizarro's half-brother, Hernando and his posse of mounted envoys making the first rendezvous with Inca Emperor Atahualpa at hot springs just outside Cajamarca. At that time the peoples of South America had no form of animal transport, and the Spaniards' horses and skilled horsemanship played a potent part in bringing about the Inca's downfall.

Right: Artist's rather fanciful impression of Francisco Pizarro's momentous encounter with Atahualpa in Cajamarca Square, with, between them, Pizarro's Dominican chaplain, Fr. Vicente de Valverde. When Atahualpa threw Fr. Vicente's breviary to the ground, Pizarro signalled for his forces to attack. In actuality Atahualpa was loftily enthroned on a litter at the time.

title of viceroy of the territory yet to be conquered. In 1531 he was back in Panama, at the head of a force of some 180 heavily armed men that included his half-brothers Hernando and Gonzalo.

As these gold-hungry Spaniards sailed south from the Pacific side of the Panama isthmus, the relatively new Inca empire that they approached held good claim to being the largest and most advanced in South America. It stretched from present-day Colombia/Ecuador to central Chile, and from the Andes' eastern slopes to the Pacific Ocean. But, again to Pizarro's good fortune, it was currently being ravaged by an epidemic of smallpox, one of the gifts that the Spanish had brought with them from the Old World to the New. This was probably the cause of the death of the Inca ruler Huayna Capac, following which civil war had broken out between the

1250–82 – Spanish science and literature flourish under Alfonso the Learned of Castile

1347–9 – Black Death ravages Europe

1469 – Marriage of Ferdinand of Aragon with Isabella of Castile unites Spain

1200

1300

1400

1271 – Marco Polo travels to China

1492 – First Voyage of Columbus to America

legitimate heir, Huáscar, and his half-brother Atahualpa, a weakness that would turn out to be to the Spaniards' advantage.

Merely to reach the Inca empire from Panama involved a most gruelling journey in tropical temperatures. And on learning that Atahualpa, having defeated Huáscar, was staying only a relatively short distance inland from them, at the mountain town of Cajamarca, Pizarro and his men took a huge risk by tackling the steep mountain tracks to reach it. Encumbered as they were by heavy armour, and hauling heavy cannon, they could easily have been fatally ambushed while they were negotiating such difficult terrain. But they were not, and as the route at last opened out into a lush valley, they suddenly found Cajamarca, with its huge plaza and ceremonial platform, stretched out below them, and beyond, the camp of Atahualpa's vast army, estimated at 80,000 men.

Completely undismayed that the Incas so vastly outnumbered his own force of 180, Pizarro coolly despatched a posse of envoys on horseback to the new emperor, then relaxed at hot springs some way from the main town. Atahualpa received the envoys graciously, granted the Spaniards permission to lodge in some empty buildings around Cajamarca's square, and promised that he would meet Pizarro there the next day. He duly honoured this promise, arriving at the head of a magnificent procession, on a litter borne by eighty of his nobles, with battalion after battalion of his superbly drilled army taking up positions around him.

It was a sight that according to one chronicler caused many of the Spaniards to wet themselves on the spot 'without noticing it, out of pure terror'. But Pizarro had strategically stationed his cannon, his horsemen and his foot-soldiers all around the square. And when, during the preliminary speechmaking, Atahualpa contemptuously tossed to the ground a Christian breviary that a priest in the Spanish entourage had proffered to him, Pizarro calmly gave the signal to attack. Taking full advantage of the shock and confusion that followed the first cannon fusillade, the Spaniards ruthlessly slashed their Toledo steel sword-blades left and right into the thickest ranks

1519 – Spanish Hernando Cortés begins conquest of Aztec Mexico

1588 – England of Queen Elizabeth I defeats Spanish Armada

1768–79 – Captain Cook creates first modern map of Pacific Ocean

1600

1531–41 Spanish conquistador Francisco Pizarro conquers Inca Peru

1620 – Pilgrim Fathers sail to America in *Mayflower*

1700

1776 – American War of Independence

1800

of the Inca soldiers, whose lack of body armour or metal weapons left them virtually defenceless. Not only was every single one of Pizarro's men able to inflict huge carnage, Atahualpa himself almost literally fell into their hands. As Pizarro personally hacked at the bare arms of the nobles carrying the emperor's litter, his horsemen toppled it, and Atahualpa was ignominiously tumbled to the ground as their prisoner. Six or seven thousand of his men were dead or dying around him, and the rest had either fled or were nearly paralysed with fear at their impotence.

Confronted with this predicament, Atahualpa offered Pizarro a bargain that few men in history can have ever been in a position to make, let alone fulfil. In return for his freedom he promised that he would fill a room twenty-two feet long and seventeen feet wide (7 x 5m) with gold and silver. And to Pizarro's and his fellow-Spaniards' incredulity, throughout the early months of 1533 a vast stream of the promised treasure poured into the appointed room, gathered from all corners of Atahualpa's empire.

Yet the physical sight of so much gold – four-fifths of it was melted down and divided

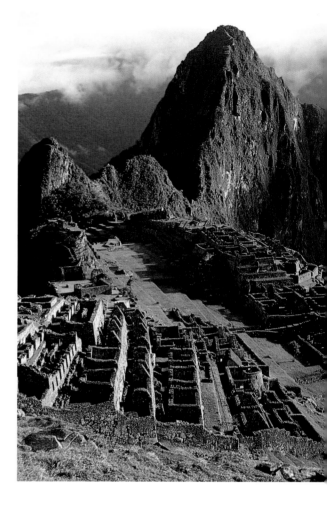

Macchu Picchu, a precipitously-located city in the Peruvian Andes that is thought to have been used by Inca emperors as a pleasure resort. Although Pizarro and his companions never found it, it was abandoned by the Incas and only rediscovered, remarkably well preserved, as recently as 1911.

among the army, and one fifth was sent back to the Emperor Charles in Spain – simply motivated Pizarro to dishonour his part of the bargain. Instead of releasing Atahualpa, he coldly put him to death. He used the ensuing turmoil to march upon the Inca capital, Cuzco, seize it, and install his own choice of puppet-king, a relative of Huáscar's. Pizarro then set about consolidating his conquest, granting each of his senior conquistadors the best of the former empire's lands and thousands of Inca slaves. He built seven towns, all of which have survived, among them the present-day capital, Lima, which he made his personal centre of operations, complete with a cathedral and a palace for himself as viceroy.

There he might have lived on and died in his bed but for the huge animosity generated among the followers of his former partner, Diego de Amalgro. These had arrived too late to play a key part in the seizure of Peru, and were thereby denied a share of its enormous wealth. Had they found as rich a territory in Chile, to the south – to which they had been granted title – their passions might not have been so intense. But on finding this land ostensibly worthless they returned to try to seize Cuzco, only to be soundly defeated by Pizarro's half-brother Hernando, who then duly executed Amalgro.

Tactically this was a mistake, since it not only angered the Spanish emperor, whose authority it usurped, but it left Amalgro's surviving followers intent on wreaking revenge. Pizarro was warned that there could be trouble, but even so his security was lax when on 26 June 1541 he took a leisurely lunch with guests at his palace. Suddenly a heavily armed band of the conspirators noisily made their presence known outside the palace. Moments later they had burst through the doors before these could be properly secured. The lunch guests, without means of protecting themselves, made undignified exits through the gardens, while Pizarro's aides did their best to hold the conspirators back so that he could get to his bedroom and buckle on his armour. But they were quickly overcome, and Pizarro had no option but to abandon his armour, grab a shield, and set about defending himself as best he could in his bedroom doorway. By now in his sixties, he succeeded in killing at least two of his assailants. But a moment's delay in withdrawing his sword from the body of a third let through a vicious and instantly disabling thrust to his throat. Moments later the whole fury of his attackers was unleashed on him and amidst a flurry of flashing sword-blades he collapsed dead to the floor.

That evening Pizarro's corpse was hastily buried behind the brand-new cathedral that he was having built in Lima. Four years later the remains were exhumed and placed in a wooden box stored in the cathedral's main altar. During successive enlargements and alterations the box was repeatedly moved, inevitably creating confusion. However, a notice of 1661 clearly recorded that the cathedral housed two boxes, one of wood, the other of lead inscribed *'AQUI ESTA LA CABECA DEL SEÑOR MARQUES DON FRANCISCO PIZARO QUE DES-CUBRIO Y GANO LES REYNOS DEL PIRU Y PUSO EN LA REAL CORONA DE CASTILA'*: 'Here is the head of the Marquis don Francisco Pizarro who discovered and won the kingdoms of Peru and brought them under the royal crown of Castile.'[3]

During the ensuing centuries Lima was hit by earthquakes, and the cathedral had to be completely rebuilt. In 1891, the 350th anniversary of Pizarro's death, a specially appointed commission formally identified as his a mummified body found in the crypt under the altar.[4] Solemnly deposited in a special glass sarcophagus in the cathedral, this mummy was universally assumed to be Pizarro – until 1977.

In that year four workmen deputed to clear the cathedral crypt found, bricked up beneath the altar, a wooden box containing an assortment of bones, together with a lead box which contained a skull and bore the inscription quoted above. Suspecting that the wrong identification had been made in 1891, in 1984 the

Lima authorities invited the Florida-based American anthropologist William Maples to give his opinion on the new-found remains. Maples determined that the skull in the lead box matched a headless skeleton in the wooden box and belonged to an elderly man who had suffered numerous blade-wounds readily corresponding with what was known of Pizarro's assassination. The official 'Pizarro' mummy, on the other hand, bore no such wounds. From this Maples firmly concluded that the 'official' mummy in the sarcophagus had to be of some unknown person, probably a churchman. On the other hand, the skull and matching body that had been found in 1977, despite their separate storage containers, were the true remains of Peru's conqueror Francisco Pizarro.[5]

And to the expert eye, tell-tale marks on these 'true Pizarro' bones spoke volumes about the violent manner of his death. One stab from a double-edged blade had sliced into his first cervical vertebra, indicating that it would have severed his right verte-

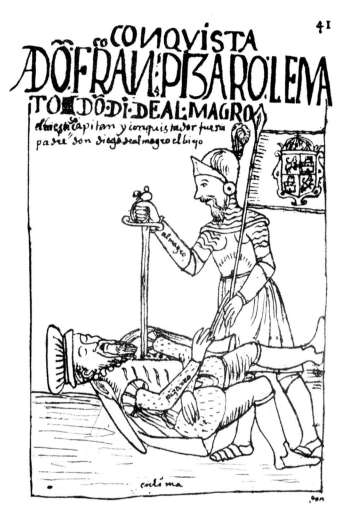

Pizarro's fatal stabbing in the neck as depicted in an early 17th-century Spanish chronicle.

bral artery, inevitably causing an incapacitating spurt of blood. This was probably that first thrust to the throat historically recorded as having been delivered by his assassins. The right sides of the second, third and fourth cervical vertebrae likewise exhibited sword damage, with some parts completely cut away. Another blow between the fourth and fifth vertebrae probably hit his spinal cord. His right arm had received a savagely disabling sword cut that sliced away part of the humerus bone. Another blade had hit his nose. Another, probably delivered after Pizarro had collapsed face down, had smashed in the back of his skull.

With this single exception, all the wounds had come from the right oblique front, the very side that a right-handed swordsman would have presented to an adversary.[6] From the forensic evidence, therefore, there can be absolutely no doubt that Pizarro fought to his last breath as gamely as the contemporary descriptions attest. A large sword found beside his skeleton in the wooden box is likely to be the very one with which he defended himself so vigorously during his final, fatal skirmish.

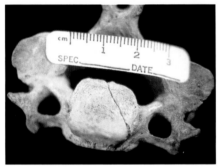

Top: Reconstruction of Pizarro's facial features, created by Betty Gatliff from a cast of the original skull discovered in a lead box in Lima Cathedral. The styling of the beard is based on contemporary Spanish fasion, and what can be gleaned from portraits.

Bottom: Close-up of a bone from Pizarro's neck, showing clear evidence of damage from the sword of one of his assaassins that would almost certainly have injured his spinal cord.

But what did he actually look like, this man who, more than any other, destroyed the entire Inca empire? In July 1984 at Lima cathedral William Maples' colleague Robert Leavy of the Florida Museum of Natural History made a careful cast of the skull that is now identified as Pizarro's. Maples sent this cast to the forensic sculptor Betty Pat Gatliff in Norman, Oklahoma, who at her 'SKULLpture Lab' duly set to work to build up features on it, following the so-called 'American method' described earlier.[7]

The result undoubtedly provides us with a very much better idea of Pizarro's facial appearance than any of the 'official' portraits or sculptures. Most of the latter seem to have been created at second or third hand, the only one of some possible veracity being a bust carved on the corner of the house that his half-brother Hernando built in their Spanish home town of Trujillo.[8] Gatliff's reconstruction shows most distinctively that he had wide, peasant-like jaws, quite unlike the long thin aristocratic face of the official portraits, which simply followed the Spanish courtly fashion of the time. And although Pizarro would undoubtedly have worn a full beard as on the Trujillo bust – a beard duly provided for the main reconstruction – Gatliff has also usefully produced a beardless version, thereby giving us a much clearer view of Pizarro's facial character. Subjective though any personality assessment from it must be, it is a countenance that it is easy to see belonging to a man of strong leadership and decisiveness.

Although Francisco Pizarro never formally married, he had a son and daughter by Atahualpa's daughter, therefore of the royal Inca line. The son did not live to adulthood, but the daughter did, subsequently marrying her uncle Hernando. The third generation of Pizarro's descendants became recipients of a royal pension awarded in their ancestor's honour, and according to the great nineteenth-century historian of the Peru conquest, William H. Prescott, some descendants were still living in the environs of Trujillo as late as the 1850s. No doubt it might be an interesting exercise one day to match DNA from the Pizarro skeleton in Lima with that of individuals bearing the Pizarro name still living in Trujillo – though Maples's and Gatliff's fine work has made identification of the Lima skeleton so conclusive that this hardly seems necessary.

ГРАЖДАНИНУ МИНИНУ И КНЯЗЮ ПОЖАРСКОМУ
БЛАГОДАРНАЯ РОССІЯ. ЛѢТА 1818

19

TSAR IVAN THE TERRIBLE 1584

Soon after Tsar Ivan IV's death in 1584, his fellow-Russians gave him the nickname 'Grozny', variously translated into English as 'Dread' or 'Terrible'. At the age of fifty-four, after having held power for all but three of those years, he suffered a severe stroke while playing a game of chess. Conscious that he was dying, and fearful of how he might be judged in the afterlife, he called for the habit and cowl of a monk, and died wearing them. His corpse was solemnly buried, according to the rites of the Eastern Orthodox Church, in the Archangel Cathedral of the Moscow Kremlin, Russian royalty's traditional burial place. There it lay undisturbed for more than three and a half centuries, until a month after the death of Josef Stalin.

On 23 April 1953 a group of Soviet Ministry of Culture officials and workmen entered the Archangel Cathedral, walked up to the brick-built tomb bearing Ivan's epitaph, and proceeded to chip away its coating of plaster. After removing several lower layers of bricks and shoring up the rest, they came to the white stone sarcophagus containing Ivan's body. In it was a skeleton covered with the vestiges of a monk's habit, its skull still partly hidden by the cowl and embroidered prayer texts. Despite much fleshly decay there were wisps of hair and beard, and to the left of the head a dark blue glass drinking-cup decorated with yellow enamel. A monkish embroidery on the chest bore a crucifixion scene in the Byzantine style. The body had been laid out on its back, the right forearm bent sharply upwards so that the fingers touched the chin, the left diagonally across the body. The remains were solemnly handed over to Moscow's Research Institute of Forensic Medicine, which allowed the Russian facial reconstruction pioneer Mikhail Gerasimov to take a cast of the skull. From it Gerasimov methodically reconstructed the facial features of Ivan Vasilyevich 'the Terrible', first Tsar of all the Russias.

Ivan was born in 1530, the son of Grand Prince Vasily III of Muscovy's Rurik dynasty and his second wife Yelena Glinskaya, herself descended via her mother from the former Byzantine empire's Palaeologus imperial dynasty. In most other European

Testament to some of Tsar Ivan IV's more positive qualities? The breathtaking domes and spires of St.Basil's Cathedral, Moscow, commissioned by Ivan as an expression of thanksgiving for his victory over the Tartars. However, a darker legend has it that Ivan had his architect blinded, so that he might never again create anything so beautiful.

countries strong monarchies had emerged from earlier baronial strife – England, for instance, following the Wars of the Roses, was now ruled by Henry VIII. Muscovy, by contrast, was just one of a number of poorly developed Russian principalities, land-locked, surrounded by hostile neighbours such as Poland and Lithuania. Marauding Tartars had recently ravaged it, their menace still far from over, while its barons, the boyars, constantly feuded with each other. Moreover, although Ivan's father had gone some way to improve the machinery of government, he died in 1534, of necessity bequeathing his 'grand princedom' to the three-year-old Ivan. Although Ivan's forceful mother Yelena quickly and capably took over as regent, the boy was only seven when she died in her turn, probably poisoned by one of the boyar factions.

For six years anarchy reigned, with bloody power-jostling between boyar and boyar. They carried out murders even within the Kremlin palace, while the ordinary people's economic plight went badly neglected, and even the child 'grand prince' himself often went cold and hungry. Reportedly the young Ivan behaved little better than those around him. As soon as he could ride he would gallop through the streets of Moscow slashing at all in his path, deriving pleasure from witnessing both human and animal suffering. Many of the Eastern Orthodox clergy were as dissolute as the populace, indulging in gambling and heavy drinking. Only one man, Moscow's Metropolitan, Makary, exerted a deep influence on the young prince, instilling in him at least some principles of social justice, should he ever gain the opportunity to implement them.

In the event Ivan seized that opportunity with surprising speed. In 1543, when he was only thirteen, he suddenly and publicly upbraided the boyars for their misdeeds. Arresting the most troublesome, Andrei Shuisky, he had him thrown to a pack of wild dogs and simultaneously publicly hanged thirty of Shuisky's supporters. These savage measures earned him some much-needed respect from the boyars and – far more importantly – widespread popular approval. Four years later, on 16 January 1547, the seventeen-year-old Ivan had himself proclaimed 'tsar and grand prince of all the Russias'. Hitherto 'tsar' (derived from 'Caesar') was the title used for the former Byzantine emperors, so he was assuming imperial status. A month later he consolidated this by marrying Anastasia Romanovna, daughter of the court chamberlain and ancestor of Russia's ill-fated Romanov dynasty.

988 – Byzantine missionaries convert Russians to Christianity

1238 – Russian independence overthrown

1300 – Kremlin built

900   1000   1100   1200   1300

1224 – Mongolian 'Golden Horde' invasions of Russia

1271 – Marco Polo travels to China

Soon afterwards, the outbreak of disastrous fires reduced much of Moscow to ashes. There was a riot in which Ivan's uncle was murdered in church, following which the mob marched to the young Tsar to demand that his unpopular grandmother be handed over to them. Ivan coolly resolved this by executing the mob's spokesmen. But, to his credit, Ivan then began implementing an ambitious programme of reforms. He summoned the first-ever Zemski Sobor, or Russian parliament, formed from boyars, clergy and specially elected lay representatives.

This initiative aside, wherever he could, Ivan continued pointedly to undermine the boyars' powers and instead elevated the lower gentry, on whose loyalty he could better rely. From among these that he chose his chamberlain, or prime minister, Alexei Adashev, who, along with Ivan's chaplain the monk Sylvester, and his very sensible wife Anastasia, represented his closest advisers. Under their influence there was a marked improvement in the moral climate in which court business was conducted. Ivan also overhauled the justice system, reducing and ultimately abolishing its hierarchy of rapacious, self-serving governors in favour of centrally appointed sheriffs. The army that he inherited drafted in its soldiers on a casual basis, and was riddled with commanders appointed purely because of aristocratic birth; he introduced a proper, regular army with officers who were selected and promoted for their ability.

It was not long before such measures began to bear fruit. In 1552, when Ivan was just twenty-two, he led his troops against the Mongol Tartars' stronghold at Kazan. Despite fierce resistance, his highly effective tactical deployment of cannon led to the town's capture, following which he was able to take over Astrakhan, the Tartar-held territory to the south. He thereby gained control of the Volga river, and with it economically vital access to the Caspian Sea. The splendid St Basil's Cathedral, jewel of Moscow's Red Square, originally dedicated to the Virgin Mary, was built by Ivan in thanksgiving for these hard-won and outstanding victories.

Up to this point Ivan had earned a hero's reputation, and considerable confidence handling the ever-untrustworthy boyars. When an English expeditionary ship got into difficulties in Russian waters, he was able to exploit the incident to open diplomatic and trading contacts with western Europe. But now, against the strongest advice of Adashev and Sylvester – a rift exacerbated by the loss of his wife in August

1453 – Constantinople falls to the Turks

1534–84 – Reign of Ivan IV the Terrible in Russia

1689 – Peter the Great becomes tsar of Russia

1776 – American War of Independence

1400   1500   1600   1700   1800

1480 – Invasion of Tartars checked

1588 – England of Queen Elizabeth I defeats Spanish Armada

1762–96 – Catherine the Great empress of Russia

1560 – he directed his army's new-found military prowess towards Livonia, present-day Latvia and Estonia, hoping to gain free access to the Baltic, with all the trading opportunities this might open up.

But this resulted in Livonia's powerful neighbours Lithuania and Poland forming an alliance against Russia. It provided a ready fuse to conspiracy among the boyar faction. And it sparked off a protracted war that would drain too many of Russia's precious resources. To make matters worse, in 1564 Ivan received perhaps the rudest shock of his life. One of his leading and most trusted commanders, Prince Andrei Kurbsky, deliberately engineered a defeat in the Livonian campaign, and promptly defected to the Polish side. Kurbsky immediately followed this up with an extremely abusive letter to Ivan, which he sent by messenger to the Moscow court.

Ivan read the letter, had the messenger summoned, and drove his staff through the man's foot, leaning on it with his full weight while the letter was read out to the court. Then he sent a suitably robust response to Kurbsky. Such a display of cruelty was an attempt to disguise the deep psychological effect that the entire affair had had upon him, bereft as he was without Anastasia or his other former close advisers to confide in.

On 3 December 1564, in the depths of the Russian winter, he left Moscow with his family and bodyguards for his country seat at Alexandrov. A month later he sent

Shadow of a tyrant - Ivan IV's tactical withdrawal to his country seat at Alexandrov prior to his reign of terror. One of the many memorable scenes from Russian director Sergei Eisenstein's film epic *Ivan the Terrible*.

two letters to Moscow, the first to the Metropolitan, declaring that the boyars made life so impossible for him that he had decided to quit Muscovy. The second was to Moscow's citizens saying that he was not blaming them for his decision. Horrified that Ivan might leave them to the boyars' mercy, a great embassy of Muscovites trudged through the snow to Alexandrov to plead for their tsar to return, an episode immortalised in the Russian director Sergei Eisenstein's epic film *Ivan the Terrible*.

Ostensibly with reluctance, Ivan consented to the delegation's requests, but insisted that they agree to let him deal with any traitors as he thought fit, and allow him to form the Oprichnina, a special state within Muscovy that was to be free of all potentially disruptive boyars. This was to be staffed by 6000 troops and other functionaries, many of lowly birth, recruited specifically for their sworn personal loyalty to him. These Oprichniki adopted for their badge an axe, a dog's head and a broom, signifying that any traitors would be beheaded, eaten by dogs and swept away. With their aid Ivan, whose whole appearance was said to have become wild and dishevelled on his return from Alexandrov, launched into a seven-year pogrom or extermination programme that, whatever meaning may be attached to *grozny*, earned him his 'terrible' reputation.

Because much historical documentation from this reign of terror was lost through fire, many details are sketchy in the extreme, and some are quite possibly exaggerated. But Ivan himself left a book in his own hand recording the masses he had ordered for 3470 victims. With little doubt, many boyars and other aristocracy were wilfully murdered during this period, executions that the Oprichniki carried out under scant supervision and often with the grossest barbarism and cruelty. Totally abandoned were the social justice reforms and rights of appeal that Ivan himself had introduced only a few years earlier. Even the Metropolitan Philip, whom Ivan had personally appointed, was ruthlessly arrested at his own altar, thrown into prison and strangled for daring to plead for the Oprichniki's abolition.

An estimated 60,000 died in the mayhem, exacerbated by plague and famine. To make matters worse the Tartars seized their opportunity to wreak revenge, in 1572 streaming virtually unchecked into Muscovy to set Moscow ablaze yet again. Amidst it all Ivan maintained a remote, uncaring stance, indulging in excessive eating, heavy drinking and debauchery, and marrying five wives within nine years. Quite evidently he was conscious of such failings, since in 1572 he wrote in his will, with characteristic literary fluency:

My understanding was infamous and my spirit corrupt, so also my mind was defiled by a liking for unworthy things, my mouth by words of murder, lewdness and other bad acts, my tongue by self-praise, my throat and chest by pride and arrogance, my hands by indecent contacts, by theft and assassination, my inner urge by shamelessness, debauchery and drinking, my belly by grave offences of the flesh and a readiness to commit all sorts of evil…[1]

But if he was minded to set to rights such unstable and anti-social behaviour, the closing years of his reign saw no change of heart, but instead more excesses and instability. In 1575 he seems to have mysteriously abdicated for a year in favour of a Tartar. In 1581, in a fit of temper, he struck his own son Ivan so hard with an iron rod that he killed him. This was to have grave repercussions, for young Ivan was the only one of his offspring with the calibre to succeed him. Since his next rightful heir, Fyodor, was weak and more suited to the life of a monk, this action would lead directly to the extinction of the Rurik dynasty as possessors of the Russian throne.

Perhaps surprisingly to the twentieth-century mind Ivan was greatly mourned, in spite of his murderous excesses. It is important to see these within the context of a culture that had inherited malevolent intrigue from its Byzantine roots, a culture in which coarseness and brutality were so ingrained as to be ordinary. It is also important to recognise that Ivan's strong stance against the boyars had been very necessary, just as other European monarchs had earlier been obliged to clip the wings of their aristocracies. And although Ivan left Russia economically bled dry by the Livonian War, in other respects, such as his encouragement of printing, architecture, foreign trade and the development of a centralised administration, his mark on the country was highly beneficial.

Even so, Ivan's psychological make-up was sufficiently unstable, particularly in the wake of his nervous collapse in 1564, to warrant some underlying explanation. And at least part of this may be found in the forensic study of his physical remains that accompanied Mikhail Gerasimov's work on the facial reconstruction. Ivan had been a tall man, nearly six feet (1.8m), and his skull showed Mediterranean Caucasoid characteristics that were no doubt an inheritance from his Greek grandmother, Sophia Palaeologus. He had no congenital abnormalities, and his teeth were surprisingly intact, having apparently erupted very late in life.

But other features of his medical condition were altogether more serious. Irregular growths on many of his bones and joints indicated severe metabolic disturbances that had almost certainly arisen from his immoderate lifestyle and his failure to take proper exercise. Although Eisenstein's film portrayed him as thin and ascetic, supported by non-contemporary illustrations in pictorial history books, the reality, as Gerasimov gauged from the powerful neck and other clues on his skeleton, is that at his death he was very fat. His estimated weight was around 210lb (95kg). This would appear to have caused severe arthritis, which would have given him intense pain and a pronounced stoop.

Pioneering Russian Mikhail Gerasimov's forceful reconstruction of Ivan the Terrible, as based on casts made from the tsar's skeleton when his Kremlin tomb was opened up in 1953. The clothed bust shows Ivan with the beard that is known from contemporary portraits. Behind is a reconstruction of how he would have appeared without the beard, and the cast from which the reconstructions were made.

This makes sense of another finding from a test on his bones for traces of arsenic and mercury. Although the arsenic level was nothing out of the ordinary, the mercury level was excessively high. The likelihood is that it derived from the mercury ointment that Ivan used to ease the arthritic pains in his limbs, pains that could hardly have improved his ever friable temper.

Gerasimov made two reconstructions of Ivan, both of them head and shoulders. The first of these, the naked and hairless version, shows him, on the evidence of his skeleton, as powerfully built, with a very strong, determined jaw, and (based on his teeth) a set of the mouth that would have given him an almost permanent sneer. The second version, utilising information from the few poor contemporary portraits (Russian art, deriving from Byzantine, set very little store by photo-realism), adds to the first the probable styling of Ivan's hair and beard. It also conveys something of the clothing that he is likely to have worn.

Through the magic of Gerasimov, Ivan Grozny appears before us, not as the thin, hawk-nosed, Machiavellian tyrant purveyed by Eisenstein, but as a seriously overweight old man riddled with arthritis. The image may not have quite the same appeal for melodrama, but historically it may be rather more credible and allow for more understanding.

20

A Frenchman in the Americas 1686

He was a French *matelot* or seaman, who stood some five feet five inches (1.65m) tall, and was aged around forty when he died. From the inscription on a small bowl found next to the body, he was possibly surnamed 'Barange'.[1] At the time of his death, January 1686, he was thousands of miles from his home in France, and just a few miles off the coast of Texas. He was serving as a crew-member on *La Belle*, one of four vessels of a fleet commanded by the French nobleman René Robert Cavelier, Lord of La Salle. As befits a sailor, his grave was a watery one, thanks to a violent storm that blew up in the Gulf of Mexico, causing *La Belle* to founder. Although the other crew managed to escape, he went down with the ship. This was among the first of a series of ever-worsening disasters that befell La Salle's expedition.

Four years earlier, Commander La Salle had been at the height of his success. As the first European to travel the length of the river Mississippi, from the Great Lakes to the Gulf of Mexico, he had claimed the vast river basin for the French crown as 'Louisiana'. In November 1682 he sailed back to France to urge that it be made a French colony. At the court of King Louis XIV – the 'Sun King' who created Versailles – he was fêted and his report on 'the savages of the French provinces in America' formed the subject of a ballet.[2] Duly receiving the appropriate backing for his colonisation scheme, on 24 July 1684 he proudly sailed out of the port of La Rochelle at the head of a fleet of four ships carrying some 300 would-be colonists and accompanying crewmen. Our *matelot* would have been among them.

By September the fleet had reached the French-controlled western end of the island of Santo Domingo, where the three main vessels were re-supplied, the fourth, a small ketch called *St François*, having been captured by Spanish pirates before reaching port.

Then, as the already diminished fleet proceeded onwards into the Gulf of Mexico, La Salle's over-authoritarian manner began seriously lowering morale. Through a

The skeleton of the French matelot as found in the *La Belle*'s bow. To the left of his body can be seen the ship's coiled anchor rope, while in the lower part of the picture is a willow-hooped drinking vessel. Also found close to the body was a pewter porringer inscribed 'C. Barange'.

navigational error, or perhaps by design, the three remaining vessels missed the Mississippi by 400 miles (640km), in January 1685 arriving at Matagorda Bay in what is today the central Gulf Coast of Texas between Galveston and Corpus Christi. There is an extensive complex of waterways in this region, with numerous small rivers flowing into the broad San Antonio and Matagorda Bays. Lacking the means of checking his position – the technology for calculating longitude was not yet invented – La Salle mistook these for a western arm of the Mississippi. As his supply ship *Aimable* entered Matagorda Bay it ran aground and sank with much of the expedition's food, medicines and tools. Faced with this loss many of the would-be colonists, already disillusioned and homesick, decided to return home on their third vessel, the *Joly*. This left La Salle with only his fourth and last vessel, *La Belle*.

La Salle now urged the 180 colonists who remained to start building a proper settlement. They began erecting a stockade and permanent buildings as Fort St Louis, located on what is today Garcitas Creek, Texas. Meanwhile La Salle began a series of expeditions to try to locate the Mississippi river. During his absence many of those left behind became dispirited by the inhospitable Gulf Coast region. Abundant though it was in bison, fish and bird-life, it was flat and mosquito-ridden. Some of the would-be colonists died from dysentery, smallpox and snake-bite, others at the hands of local Indians who, though friendly at first, soon turned hostile.

La Belle, which had been anchored offshore with a crew of about twenty, now ran out of drinking water. Reportedly some on board even died of thirst before the pilot, who had been consuming the stock of wines and spirits, hoisted sail for Fort St Louis. At this point there blew up the severe gale that sank the vessel, our *matelot*, as we have already learned, going down with it. Of the fate of the remaining crew all that is known is that only six made it back to Fort St Louis.

La Salle, now seriously concerned for his fledgling colony's survival, in January 1687 set out with seventeen men to try to get help. Two months later five of his companions ambushed him, shooting him through the head and leaving his body in the brush by the Navasota river just up from its junction with the Trinity river. Five loyal survivors, including Henri Joutel, famous for his journal of the La Salle expedition, La Salle's older brother, Abbé Cavelier, his nephew, Colin Cavelier, and Friar Anastase Douay, managed to make their way a thousand miles northwards to

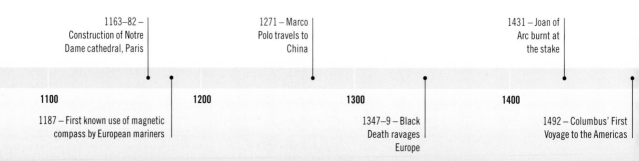

1163–82 – Construction of Notre Dame cathedral, Paris

1271 – Marco Polo travels to China

1431 – Joan of Arc burnt at the stake

1100

1200

1300

1400

1187 – First known use of magnetic compass by European mariners

1347–9 – Black Death ravages Europe

1492 – Columbus' First Voyage to the Americas

Artist's impression of French explorer La Salle claiming the Mississippi for the 'Sun King', Louis XIV of France. The crewman found on *La Belle* took part in La Salle's ill-fated attempt to fulfil this claim – an expedition dogged from the outset due to a navigational error by which it reached, not the Mississippi, but an inhospitable region further to the west.

1620 – Pilgrim Fathers sail to America in *Mayflower*

1684 – French matelot takes part in La Salle expedition to Gulf of Mexico

1734 – English clockmaker John Harrison develops first chronometer for measuring ship's longitude

1600

1609 – Telescope invented by Galileo

1700

1661 – King Louis XIV initiates construction of Palace of Versailles

1776 – American War of Independence

1800

1792 – French Revolution

1825 – First passenger train

1900

Canada, whence they sailed for France, arriving in late November 1688. But Louis XIV proved deaf to their pleas to send help to those left behind at Fort St Louis, and consequently those stalwarts who had stayed on at the outpost quickly died out from disease and from raids by neighbouring Indians. With their demise there faded any lingering hopes of a French colonisation of this region, though in 1699 Pierre Le Moyne d'Iberville, with the help of two La Salle expedition survivors who had integrated with the Texas Indians, managed to establish a temporary French foothold in what is now Louisiana.

Many of the details recounted above we owe to the journal kept by Henri Joutel,[3] who had acted as La Salle's lieutenant at Fort St Louis during his leader's absences.[4] In addition, as early as 1687 a Spaniard reported a wreck with 'three *fleur-de-lys* on her poop' that he had seen in Matagorda Bay. This description is generally thought to be of *La Belle*. However, it was not until 1995 that the vessel's story assumed fresh impetus when its remains were discovered about twelve miles (19km) north-east of Port O'Connor, Texas, and positively identified.

The ravages of more than three centuries had left intact only about one third of the original hull. Nevertheless, preliminary underwater exploration quickly brought to light some ornate cannon bearing the crest of the Comte de Vermandois. As Vermandois was the French admiral (in fact one of several illegitimate sons of the licentious Louis XIV) under whom La Salle had served, this confirmed the wreck as *La Belle*. And because the vessel lay in shallow water, at a depth of just twelve feet (3.65m), it proved practical, albeit expensive, to build a double-walled steel coffer dam around it. When the seawater was pumped out, *La Belle* could be excavated just as if it were on dry land. This allowed considerably more sophisticated techniques to be used than are possible in underwater archaeology.

As recorded in independently discovered historical sources, *La Belle* was not a big vessel, only fifty-one by fourteen feet (15.5 x 4.25m). But from the archaeological work within the coffer dam she has proved to be a veritable time-capsule of nearly one million recovered artefacts. Among these are three ornate 'Vermandois' bronze cannon,[5] a ceramic jar filled with mercury, decorative candlesticks, a lady's ring, navigational dividers with inscribed initials, ceramic firepots with incendiary devices, wooden casks containing muskets, a wooden crucifix, bones of deer and dog, tools, leather shoes, and more than 700,000 glass beads. Though the beads were no doubt intended for trading with the Indians, they clearly had to be abandoned with the rest of the ship's cargo when the vessel foundered and all those on board had to swim for their lives – all, that is, except the *matelot* tentatively identified as Barange.

On 31 October 1996, while the archaeologists were still painstakingly removing the thick but highly preservative mud that had accumulated over the wreck, they came upon this *matelot*'s skeleton in the ship's bow, flexed on the anchor rope. As events

Excavation in progress within the coffer dam built around the *La Belle* wreck. Even though the vessel lay twelve feet below the waters of Matagorda Bay, after constructing the dam and pumping out the water, it proved possible to excavate much as if it was on dry land.

proved, his were the only human remains that they would find on board, which indicated that the other crew members escaped. His bones were so well preserved that they had retained some of his tissues. A liquor cask, its split-willow hoops still virtually intact, lay just next to him, together with a pewter porringer inscribed 'C. Barange', the lone and far from conclusive clue to his identity.

So if *La Belle*'s pilot had been as drunk as Joutel claimed, could our *matelot* perhaps have been his drinking companion, lying in a stupor when the ship went down, too drunk to make his escape with the rest? Or might he have been one of those who had died of dehydration through lack of drinking water, his body perhaps left unburied as the pilot at last set sail for land? However, since a dead body is unlikely to have been laid atop an anchor rope that needs repeatedly to be deployed, yet another explanation is that when the storm struck the *matelot* had been about to drop the anchor, only to fall through a deck hatch and down into the forward hold when the *Belle* suddenly grounded.

Whatever the explanation, we know with a fair degree of certainty what Barange – if that was his name – looked like. The Texas A&M University conservators in charge of conserving the *La Belle* hull and its related artefacts decided to have a special replica made of his skull using stereolithography. This is a process akin to the milling machine that we saw in the story of Esamun and 'Eymund', and it enables the interior and exterior features of an object to be reproduced three-dimensionally, yet without making a cast. The first step was to have the skull CT-scanned, and in March 1997 this was successfully performed at the Texas Scottish Rite Hospital for Children, Dallas, the scans clearly revealing that parts of the tissues of Barange's brain were still intact inside his cranium.

Using the computerised, digital data provided by the scans, the Arlington-based commercial company CyberForm International then made two exact resin replicas of the skull stereolithographically. One of these was passed to Professor Denis Lee, at that time head of the University of Michigan's Medical and Biological Illustration Department. Once a pupil of Betty Pat Gatliff, and long based in Ann

Arbor, Lee made his own cast from the replica and proceeded to build up in clay a facial reconstruction of Barange according to his version of the Gatliff method. He did this using Klean Clay, his preferred modelling clay because it contains no sulphur that can adversely affect silicon rubber. He then made a silicon rubber mould from the clay model so that he could create more permanent casts in the most suitable materials.

The most definitive of these casts, made in white dental stone to which Lee has added prosthetic eyes, an appropriate period hairstyle and a final application of paint in lifelike colours, has a positively Gallic air about it, with convincingly weather-beaten features. An accompanying skeletal analysis conducted by Dr Gentry Steele of Texas A&M University's Anthropology Department has revealed further details. From this we can be sure that our *matelot* was a stockily built European, definitely male. It is also certain that he had suffered some hard knocks earlier in life, most notably a break to the left side of his nose. Possibly as one consequence of the recent introduction of sugar into European diets, he had lost a number of teeth. Even those that remained had become badly affected by decay and by abscesses that had eaten through the bone just above the upper left teeth. He also suffered from lower back pain. Given such chronic afflictions, if he really was drunk at the time of his death, it is understandable that he might have been drinking to excess in order to relieve his pains.

Is there any more that we can know about him? Intriguingly, the most perfunctory of investigations in France have revealed that there are families bearing the name 'Barange' who still live in the vicinity of La Rochelle. This was the very port from which *La Belle* sailed under La Salle's command in 1684, with Barange probably recruited locally as a crewman. And since his skeleton should be able to provide DNA details of its original owner, if he was indeed C. Barange it may well be possible genetically to link him with living relatives and descendants.

As this book goes to press the Texas A&M University Conservation Research Laboratory and Texas Historical Commission team are finalising their plans for DNA testing of tissue samples from Barange's skeleton. When their findings become available, they will be published, in hard copy and on the Conservation Laboratory website. But it certainly looks as if, in due course, the *matelot*'s remains may have yet more to tell us before the archaeologists', conservators' and anthropologists' researches are finally completed.

The face of the French *matelot* found dead on *La Belle*, as reconstructed by Professor Denis Lee of Ann Arbor, Michigan. Like his earlier Roman counterpart, the 17th-century French matelot suffered badly with his teeth, though probably for very different reasons.

POSTSCRIPT: THE FUTURE

Postscript: What of the Future?

All that we have seen in this book represents a remarkable new artistic science, or scientific art, of putting faces to people from the past that few would have dreamt possible a couple of decades ago.

And it is a discipline that is still very much under development. Things are happening fast. While those who use the American method are producing some interesting and no doubt broadly accurate faces, arguably there is much that they can still learn from the rather more muscle-sensitive techniques that Richard Neave and his Art in Medicine Unit have been developing in England. Yet, as Neave himself anticipates, the ever more sophisticated computer software programmes that are being brought into this field are in their turn improving fast. Ultimately, therefore, they are almost bound to take over, wholly or partly, from his 'hands-on' experience, hard-won from long years of working in medical school dissection rooms. In the meantime, however, the sheer quality of facial reconstruction that Neave and his team can achieve, even without necessarily proceeding to a waxwork state of finish, should be apparent from the high proportion of examples featured in this book.

Similarly, the science of DNA analysis has been undergoing rapid and remarkable developments, which are likely only to accelerate following the recent successful mapping of the entire human genetic code.[1] The Oxford University geneticist Professor Brian Sykes – who worked on Cheddar Man – has recently announced that, from the mitochondrial DNA swabs that he has taken from some 6000 living Europeans, he can now trace the descent of almost every European to just seven clan-founding matriarchs who lived up to 45,000 years ago. According to Sykes:

> Every time a European takes a breath, he or she is using the same genes to metabolise the oxygen as one of those seven women. It brings it all alive to think that these were real people who had to survive, and that we have a direct, unbroken line to them.[2]

Equally intriguingly, we may be only a short distance from being able to recreate a picture – not dissimilar to those made from skulls – of a person from the past from the most minuscule of DNA samples. Kevin Sullivan, DNA research and development manager for the UK's Forensic Science Service, has predicted that within less than a decade it should be possible to make a Photofit picture, including details of height, shape of chin, ears, significant physical defects and so on, from a few flakes of skin left behind on a car steering wheel or a drinks can.[3] Once this science is applied to archaeology – as it will undoubtedly be – it should be possible to recreate at least the basics of an ancient face (scars and other physical injuries excepted) from as little as a lock of hair or a blood fragment.

In the future, therefore, there will be immense opportunities for putting faces to people from the past for whom we have either portraits of very doubtful reliability, or no surviving portraits at all. To take one example, there are preserved in the Cairo Museum the mummies of a number of ancient Egyptian pharaohs that were found just over a hundred years ago hidden in caches;[4] the mummification process, however, has often seriously altered the facial appearance that they would have had in life. And although statues and other images survive of these pharaohs, Egyptian artists idealised them rather than portraying them warts and all. A further difficulty is that, following the looting of the pharaohs' tombs in antiquity, and the mummies' subsequent rescue and reburial by priests, some of the ancient identification labels, hastily attached, are not necessarily reliable. In time, DNA studies will almost certainly be able to resolve the identification difficulties. Then it should be the turn of facial reconstruction specialists to recreate the true faces via CT scans and stereolithography of the mummy heads.

A particularly interesting mummy to reconstruct would be that of the 'heretic' pharaoh Akhenaten, whose reign was notable for a brief realistic phase of ancient Egyptian art; this reveals him to have almost caricature-like facial features and disproportionately wide hips, which some have suggested indicate Marfan's syndrome. Intriguingly, a recent study of the clothes found in Tutankhamun's tomb shows that Tutankhamun, thought to have been Akhenaten's son, had similarly wide hips, even though he was only around eighteen when he died.[5] There are grounds for believing that the mummy currently attributed to Amenhotep III is in actuality Akhenaten,[6] so a state-of-the-art facial reconstruction from 'Amenhotep' could provide valuable evidence for a re-attribution. Akhenaten is merely one of innumerable individuals from the past, not all from Egyptian cultures, for whom future reconstructions ought to be viable.

But, even assuming that in due time the relevant museum authorities grant the necessary approval for such projects, what right do we have to do any of this? While the town-dwellers of ancient Jericho and the Chinchorro peoples of Chile put faces

Egypt's pharaoh Tutankhamun (reigned *c.*1350 BC). A pharaoh who encouraged naturalistic portraiture, contemporary artistic representations indicate that he had highly exaggerated facial features. This would make him an interesting subject for facial reconstruction if his mummy can be correctly identified.

back on their dead for religious reasons, our motives are little more than scientific and historical curiosity. And since hardly anyone would wish to see their dead grandmother dug up for scientific purposes, what justification can we offer those who seriously disapprove of any disturbance of the dead in order to find out information from them, let alone recreate their facial likenesses in the manner featured in this book?

In 1990, for instance, inside a cave on the outskirts of Jerusalem, a first-century AD ossuary was found bearing an inscription suggesting that the elderly male skeleton among the bones inside was that of Caiaphas, the Temple high priest who features in the Christian gospels as interrogating Jesus and pronouncing the death sentence on him.[7] Although it would have been fascinating in the extreme to make a cast of this individual's skull and recreate what he once looked like, Israel's ultra-orthodox faction insisted on the skeleton's immediate reburial. Because of this attitude we have been deprived even of a documentary photograph of Caiaphas' skull, let alone a facial reconstruction of him.

Similarly, in the United States the Native American Graves Protection and Repatriation Act of 1990 now protects the bones of Native Americans from being indiscriminately dug up and subjected to scientific examination. It also provides for those remains that have long been gathering dust in museum vaults to be returned to Native American tribes for whom they represent an ancestral heritage. In 1996 this act was directly responsible for the seizure of one of the oldest-known skeletons ever discovered in North America, that of Kennewick Man. The bones in question were firmly withheld from any further scientific investigation, even though the indications are that this particular individual was unrelated to any of the present-day North American native tribes. Australian aboriginals have likewise been insisting on the return to them of remains of ancestors that were taken from them for 'scientific purposes' in the nineteenth century. In two different instances during the early 1990s, ancient aboriginal bones found in the Kow Swamp and the Lake Mungo region were formally handed back.

For anyone perhaps minded to deride indigenous peoples' sensitivities on these matters as mere superstitious nonsense, only a quick perusal of archaeological literature will reveal that even seasoned archaeologists can and do express qualms about the ethics of disturbing at least some of the human remains that they encounter. For instance, when a few years back the British archaeologist Julian Richards excavated a large grave near Stonehenge he found it contained the skeleton of a pitifully tiny child. As he has remarked with commendable candour of this discovery: 'I regretted excavating that child's burial ever since, and would feel much happier if I could replace the young bones where they were first buried over 3000 years ago.'[8] The Russian Natalya Polosmak, excavator of our 'Horse-Queen of the Icy Steppes', has described her thoughts as the girl's body and its wrappings began palpably to soften from their hard-frozen state: 'Somehow in that moment the remains became a person. She lay sideways, like a sleeping child… Forgive me, I said to her.'[9]

Even Howard Carter, discoverer of the tomb of Tutankhamun, remarked how much like an intruder he felt as he gazed upon the great star-spangled linen pall draped over the shrine containing the young pharaoh. In his words: 'The pall made us realise that we were in the presence of a dead king of past ages.'[10] When he lifted the lid covering the gold innermost coffin, he was similarly unnerved to see on it a tiny wreath of flowers that had almost certainly been laid by Tutankhamun's grieving young widow Ankesenamun as her last farewell to her dead husband:

> Amongst all that regal splendour… there was nothing so beautiful as those few withered flowers, still retaining their tinge of colour. They told us what a short period three thousand three hundred years was – but Yesterday and Morrow.

For this problem, according due respect to ancient human remains, yet at the same time trying to learn from them and to breathe life back into them, there are no easy solutions. For me, having visited Tutankhamun's now nearly empty tomb in the Valley of the Kings at Luxor, and having viewed the innumerable objects taken from it for Cairo's overcrowded Egyptian Museum, where they can never be ideally displayed, it is a matter of the greatest sadness that the tomb could not have been left as it was, with all its 'nesting' sarcophagi still one inside another rather like Russian dolls. It would have been the one pharaonic tomb to preserve intact the immense dignity and estate with which the ancient Egyptians buried their royal dead. Yet the reality is that, in that case, we could never have known the immense beauty of its innermost items, such as the gold face-mask and the solid gold sarcophagus. And, material values aside, the world would have been the poorer for this. In the same way, without violating human bones to the extent of at least making a cast from the skull, we could never have looked upon the face of a Minoan priestess or Robert the Bruce, 'Ötzi' or Philip of Macedon, as we have in this book.

It should also not be forgotten that there are some valid reasons why facial reconstructions of people from the past have been done, and continue to be done. If we already had some fully authoritative portrait gallery, stretching right back through time, that could bring us face to face with representatives of every one of humankind's past cultures, the work of Richard Neave and others in this historico-archaeological field would not be necessary, and they could concentrate purely on criminological reconstructions. But we do not have such a gallery, and it is useful to try to create one.

Very often the decision to disturb human remains, as in the case of several examples in these pages, may well have been taken by a local council or property developer

Russian archaeologists gazing down on the Ukok horse-queen's freshly excavated body. Natalya Polosmak, the archaeologist in charge of the excavation, has expressed an acute sense of unease at having disturbed the horse-queen's remains.

whose workmen have come across the bones while clearing land for redevelopment. Precisely this happened in the cases of the Severnside farmer, the Viking 'Eymund' and the Towton soldier featured in this book. By law such finds must always be reported, since a check needs to be made that the individual was not the victim of a recent homicide. After this the archaeologists are called in, and, when they have completed their work, it usually falls to them, whether they like it or not, to store all the bones found on the site, since these are the last thing that the developer wants returned to him. In this way, almost by default, museums become repositories for large numbers of skeletons, the Museum of London, for example, housing no less than 6500, a tally by no means exceptional among museums world-wide.

It should be appreciated that the techniques developed to reconstruct people from the past can also have great validity in preserving the appearance of people of the present. However much we may make disapproving comments about the genocidal behaviour of the sixteenth-century Pizarro, our own age has been little less culpable. All too many cultures that had survived tens of thousands of years have been snuffed out in the name of 'progress' within the last hundred.

Thus when, in 1905, it was recognised that the Khoisan bushmen of the Kalahari were in danger of becoming extinct, a meeting of the British Association in South Africa suggested the making of full-body plaster casts from living individuals so that their three-dimensional appearance might be preserved for posterity. The following year the South African Museum's director, Dr Louis Peringuey, specially commissioned for this project the Scotsman James Drury, who four years before had joined his museum as its taxidermist.

Drury proved a particularly inspired choice for this task. Conscientious and talented, he first experimented with taking casts from a volunteer museum employee, making several attempts before being satisfied that he had mastered the technique. Then he embarked on moulding his first 'field' subject, a bushman who was imprisoned in the De Beers convict station at Kimberley. Aware that groups of figures in related poses would be better than one, in 1907 he set off on the first of what became nine expeditions to bushmen communities scattered across South and South-West Africa.

Drury's technique, closely based on that of the eighteenth-century wax-workers, involved making sectional plaster moulds from the bodies of the subjects, then joining them up to create a full figure. Coating each chosen body section with petroleum jelly (the equivalent of Pepys' 'pomatum'), he marked its limits with a line of soluble dye so that when he applied the plaster this became transferred to the mould, guiding him where to cut each section so that it readily butted up to the next. To make the face and head casts, he provided the subject with mouth or nostril straws to enable him or her to breathe. Finally, he made detailed notes so that each figure could be accurately cast and reassembled at the museum, and could be supplied with accurate colouring, hair and accoutrements. He fitted in this work alongside his normal taxidermy duties, as well as skinning game animals killed by visiting aristocratic English 'white hunters', but still managed successfully to cast sixty-one full figures in this manner. In 1959 several of these were amalgamated into a diorama that is still on display in Cape Town's South African Museum (reproduced on p.27).[11]

The excellence of Drury's work is recognised to this day, but what gave it real purpose was that, even as he was making his models, much of the ancient hunter-gatherer lifestyle depicted in the diorama was indeed rapidly dying out, as the 1905 British Association meeting had predicted. Alongside decimation of the Khoisan bushman population through disease and trigger-happy Dutch colonists, surviving members of the tribe were being forced to work as labourers on farms, as a result of which they rapidly lost the hunter-gatherer lore and ways of their ancestors. Laurens van der Post more recently drew attention to this problem.[12]

In Australia during the last century much the same was happening with the aborigines. As the Melbourne anthropologist Donald Thomson, who was ahead of his time, told Australian governments in the 1930s: 'At every point where the Australian aboriginal has come into prolonged contact with a European or Asiatic population, his culture has commenced to decay, and degradation and racial extinction have followed.'[13] Though Thomson and others pleaded that surviving aboriginal tribes should be allowed viable territories where they could continue to live in the traditional lifestyle, governments too often ignored such pleas. A whole generation of aborigines was forcibly and most unhappily westernised – the so-called 'Lost Generation' – with consequences reverberating to this day. And not only did Australia have no model-making James Drury, a vital part of Donald Thomson's most dedicated work was irretrievably lost when unique film that he had taken of aboriginal communities still living the traditional hunter-gatherer lifestyle was destroyed in a fire.

The work of preserving three-dimensionally the appearances of people of the present is not just applicable to indigenous peoples whose ways of life are threatened by extinction. Even our own Western culture is undergoing such rapid changes that it is in need of some preservation by means other than still and motion photography. In the 1970s American artists of the Superrealist school, most notably John de Andrea and the late Duane Hanson, with no formal anthropological intent, hit upon very much this idea. Their methods, similar to those of Drury and his predecessors, involve covering the model in petroleum jelly while layers of bandages dipped into wet dental plaster are applied to sections of the head, trunk, arms and legs. After thirty to forty-five minutes the moulds are cut away, filled with flesh-coloured, fibreglass-reinforced polyester resin, and reassembled as a complete human body. This is painted to convey all the nuances of real flesh, and is given the necessary finishing touches, such as a wig, clothes, jewellery and so on. The near-ultimate realism than can be achieved is highly unnerving, as experienced by the American artist Carolyn Bloomer when she first encountered Duane Hanson's *Young Shopper* in the lobby of a museum:

> As I passed hurriedly through the entrance, I vaguely noticed a large woman loaded with shopping bundles. I thought her different from the usual museum-goer, but quickly dismissed this prejudice and hurried on into the museum. Later, upon returning to the lobby, I saw the same woman standing just as I had left her earlier. Incredulously, I realised that this was not a woman, but a shockingly lifelike sculpture. Approaching it I felt uncomfortable, as if invading the space of a real person. I forced myself to study the details of her physiognomy at very close range; I became even more ill at ease. I felt guilty, as if I were about to be lectured for staring impolitely at the flaws and curiosities of a real stranger's body. It would have been easy to dismiss these feelings, but by lingering and exploring my discomfort, I experienced a profound complex of personal and cultural inhibitions about personal space. The *Young Shopper* was a mini-session in sensitivity training.[14]

John de Andrea's work, because he specialises in nudes, evokes even more of a sense of impolite staring and invaded space than Hanson's, creating exactly the same feelings of human vulnerability as does the sight of a life-class model posing naked for an art class. The essence in both instances is the consciousness of human presence with a very real *sacredness* to it, a million miles removed from the nudity and killings that sex shows and the cinema so often exploit. The Khoisan hunter-gatherers whom James Drury approached with the intention of making moulds of their bodies very understandably exhibited similar reticence towards his intrusion on their space, and it required the greatest sensitivity on his part to overcome this and gain their trust and co-operation.

And this is pertinent to the issue of recreating faces from dead human remains. Not so long ago archaeologists tended to treat human bones irreverently, tossing them on to spoil heaps as among the least interesting of their finds. It is a different matter now that they know the wealth of information bones can yield, and just how much of the living person can be recreated. It is highly important, therefore, to keep in mind that work carried out on ancient human remains should be done with due regard for and consciousness of the fact that this was a real human being whose 'space' is being invaded, even in death.

In this regard, an admirable model of how archaeologists and anthropologists can handle such matters sensitively has recently come from Prince of Wales Island, Alaska, where in 1996 human bones were found in a cave that was known, from artefacts discovered earlier, to be very ancient.[15] Because of the Native American Graves Protection and Repatriation Act the archaeologist in charge, Terry Fifield, immediately contacted representatives of the local Tlingit and Haida Indians and invited their interest and involvement.

Although the Indians at first felt minded to tell Fifield to return the bones whence they had been found, the fact that he had approached them so sensitively and considerately aroused both their curiosity and their sympathy. They themselves became intrigued to know how old the bones might be, and whether they genuinely might have belonged to one of their ancestors. It then began to seem wrong to them that research on such matters should be stopped before anyone knew the answers. They therefore recommended to their people that consent should be given for the bones to be fully analysed, and the cave to be

Too 'real' for comfort? Duane Hanson's *Young Shopper*. Created in polyester resin in 1973 using plaster casts taken from a living model. Naturalistically coloured, fitted with real hair, dressed in real clothes, and supplied with a real handbag and shopping bags, the effect is so unnervingly lifelike that when the statue is exhibited some spectators feel it impolite to stare.

further explored, so long as the tribal assemblies were kept properly informed. In the event the bones were radiocarbon dated to around 10,000 years old, making them the oldest reliably dated human remains ever found in Alaska or Canada. The key lay in treating them, and those to whom they might be ancestrally meaningful, with sympathy and reverence.

In 1962 the American ethnologist Professor Carleton S. Coone, in his masterwork *The Origin of Races*, divided humankind into five basic human types, among whom he supposed that the Caucasoids or 'whites' had become 'sapiens' much earlier than the Congoids or 'blacks'. From this deduction he adjudged the latter culturally much less advanced and more 'primitive'. In a manner that Coone almost certainly never intended, US racist groups interpreted this as scientific proof of white supremacy, as a result of which his remarks caused great offence and hurt to those thus degraded. Today, thankfully, we know that Coone got it wrong and that it is in fact in the face of the nearly extinct bushman of southern Africa that we should see our own ancestry. And we know this at least in part because of DNA studies on some of the very bones around which the 'disturbance of the dead' issue most revolves.

Throughout this book, entirely due to the disturbing of ancestral bones, we have been able to study the past lives of people from every continent and every human era. We have been able to learn how different some of their cultures were from our own, and to appreciate something of the very different lives they led. We have seen how sometimes they did things that we would consider unthinkable, such as sacrificing another human being, or using technological advantage to commit what we would call genocide. But above all, thanks to the art and science of facial reconstruction, we have been able to view them as they would have looked in life, as if face to face.

And ultimately it is via this encounter, as we look into these actual countenances, that we are enabled to realise that there is hardly anything 'primitive' or alien about any of them. Instead, in spite of minor variations in skin colour and physiognomy, there is an underlying sense of familiarity. Quite unmistakably, these were people like ourselves. They all had thoughts, emotions and fears much like our own. As the geneticist Dr Peter Underhill of Stanford University has recently and most cogently summed it all up: 'We are all Africans at the Y chromosome level, *and we are really all brothers.*'[16]

Notes

Introduction

[1] Kathleen Kenyon, *Archaeology in the Holy Land*, London, Ernest Benn, 4th edn, 1979, p.34.

[2] See Bernardo Arriaza, 'Chile's Chinchorro Mummies', *National Geographic*, March 1995, pp.68ff.

[3] Quoted in Nick Fielding, 'Found: the world's oldest mummies', *Sunday Times*, 9 July 2000.

[4] Aidan and Eve Cockburn, *Mummies, Disease and Ancient Cultures*, Cambridge, Cambridge University Press, 1983 (abridged edn), pp.201-6.

[5] Brian Moynahan, 'The Oldest Face on Earth', *Sunday Times Magazine*, 13 June 1976.

[6] Salima Ikram and Aidan Dodson, *The Mummy in Ancient Egypt*, London, Thames & Hudson, 1998.

[7] Ben MacIntyre, 'Revealed: the faces no one has seen for at least 1,800 years', *The Times*, 27 August 1999.

[8] Boris Piotrovsky (ed.), *Treasures of the Hermitage*, New York (Portland) and Leningrad (Aurora Art), 1990.

[9] Anthony Harvey and Richard Mortimer (eds.), *Funeral Effigies of Westminster Abbey*, London, Boydell & Brewer, 1994.

[10] Giorgio Vasari, *Lives of the Artists*, Penguin, Harmondsworth, 1965, p.239.

[11] Robert Latham and William Hewer (eds.), *The Diary of Samuel Pepys*, London, G. Bell, 1976, vol. IX, p.442.

[12] ibid., p.449.

[13] Die Persistenz der Rassen und die Rekonstruktion der Physiognomie prähistorischer Schädel', *Archiv für Anthropologie*, xxv (1989), pp.329-59.

[14] M.M. Gerasimov, *The Face Finder*, London/Philadelphia, 1971.

[15] B.P. Gatliff, 'Facial Sculpture on the Skull for Identification', *American Journal of Forensic Medicine and Pathology*, 5, 1984, pp.327-32; 'Forensic Sculpture Adapts to Museum Use', *Scientific Illustration – 1986, Selected Papers from the 7th Annual Conference of the Guild of Natural Science Illustrators*, Washington, DC, 1986, pp.13-17.

[16] See *Scientific American Discovering Archaeology*, January/February 2000, pp.64-5.

[17] See article by Walter E. Rast in *Archaeology*, January/February 1987, p.49.

[18] Karen T. Taylor, *Forensic Art and Illustration*, Boca Raton, Florida, CRC Press, 2000.

[19] For the definitive account of Richard Neave's work see John Prag and Richard Neave, *Making Faces*, London, British Museum, 1997; reprinted in paperback, 1999, with corrections.

[20] Amit Roy, 'Making the Face Fit', *Sunday Times Magazine*, 27 May 1990.

[21] 'Negroid', 'Mongoloid' are loose descriptions, providing useful handles but not to be taken as rigid definitions.

[22] See for instance John Taylor, 'CT Scanning of a Mummy', *Egyptian Archaeology* no.4, 1994, pp.15-16.

[23] 35th edition (ed. Roger Warwick and Peter L. Williams), London, Longman, 1973, p.215.

[24] As widely publicised in the world's media, 27 June 2000.

Part I
Introduction

[1] See reports in *Science* magazine, 10 July 1998.

[2] Michael Pitts and Mark Roberts, *Fairweather Eden: life in Britain half a million years ago as revealed by the excavations at Boxgrove*, London, Century, 1997.

[3] H.L. Shapiro, *Peking Man: The Discovery, Disappearance and Mystery of a Priceless Scientific Treasure*, London, Allen & Unwin, 1974.

[4] *The Times*, 5 April 1997.

[5] R.S. Solecki, *Shanidar: The First Flower People*, New York, Alfred A. Knopf, 1971.

[6] Stanford University web-site article, 2 May 2000, 'The Human Family Tree: 10 Adams and 18 Eves'. Dr Peter A. Underhill and Dr Peter J. Oefner of Stanford University are among the world's leading researchers in this field.

[7] Steve Connor, 'DNA tests trace Adam to Africa', *The Times*, 9 November 1997.

[8] Colin Renfrew, *Archaeology and Language, the Puzzle of Indo-European Origins*, Cambridge, Cambridge University Press, 1988.

[9] The Neanderthals probably had language before them. Although the flesh components of our voice apparatus do not fossilise, the hyoid bone, from which the *homo sapiens* voicebox hangs, has been found in a 60,000-year-old Neanderthal skeleton discovered in the cave of Kebara in Israel (*National Geographic*, January 1996, p.30). This does not prove that they had language, but it is a strong likelihood.

[10] Neanderthal skeletons commonly show upper body injuries consistent with tackling large animals at close quarters. See *National Geographic*, January 1996, p.27.

[11] See R.G. Roberts, R. Jones and M.A. Smith, 'Beyond the radiocarbon barrier in Australian prehistory', *Antiquity*, 1994, vol. 68 (206), pp.611-16.

[12] J. Flood, *Archaeology of the Dreamtime*, Sydney, Angus & Robertson, 1995.

[13] Henri Lhote, trans. Alan Brodrick, *The Search for the Tassili Frescoes*, London, Hutchinson, 1960.

[14] M. Heun *et al.*, 'Site of Einkorn Wheat Domestication Identified by DNA Fingerprinting', *Science* 278, November 1997, pp.1312-14.

[15] This was first pointed out by the archaeologist V. Gordon Childe.

Chapter 1

[1] This was formerly transliterated as Choukoutien.

[2] Reported in *Science*, 10 July 1998.

[3] F. Sémah (ed.), '100 Years of hominid discovery in Java', *Bulletin of the Indo-Pacific Prehistory Association* 11, 1991.

[4] H.L. Shapiro, *Peking Man: The Discovery, Disappearance and Mystery of a Priceless Scientific Treasure*, London, Allen & Unwin, 1974.

[5] Richard Rudgley, *Lost Civilizations of the Stone Age*, London, Century, 1998, p.213.

[6] Statement by the UNESCO director Azedine Beschaouch, reported in Agence France-Presse, 11 November 1998.

Chapter 2

[1] 'Luzia' was presented under this name in an excellent BBC TV documentary, 'The Hunt for the First Americans', shown on BBC2 on 1 September 1999, to which this chapter is much indebted.

[2] W.A. Neves and H.M. Pucciarelli, 'Morphological affinities of the first Americans: an exploratory analysis based on early South American human remains', *Journal of Human Evolution*, 21, 1991, pp.261-73.

[3] A. Laming-Emperaire, *Le problème des origines Americaines*, Lille, 1980.

[4] J.M. Adovasio, T.D. Dillehay and D.J. Meltzer, *Antiquity* 68, 1995, pp.695-714.

[5] See examples in the article by N.Guidon, 'Prehistoric rock art', in the Mitchell Beazley *World Atlas of Archaeology*, London, 1985, pp.358-9.

[6] J. Allen and P. Kershaw, 'The Pleistocene-Holocene transition in greater Australia' in L.S. Strauss, B.V. Eriksen, J.M. Erlandson and D.R. Yesner (eds.), *Humans at the End of the Ice Age. The Archaeology of the Pleistocene-Holocene Transition*, New York, Plenum, 1996, pp.175-99.

[7] Grahame L. Walsh, *Bradshaws: Ancient Rock Paintings of North-west Australia*, Geneva, Carouge (limited edn), 1994.

[8] Mike Lee, 'Tri-Citians sculpt theoretical look for Kennewick Man', *Tri-City Herald*, 10 February 1998.

[9] Walter Neves and Max Blum, 'Were the Fuegians remainders of a Paleoindian non-specialized morphology in the Americas?' (forthcoming).

[10] Charles Darwin, *Voyage of the Beagle*, 1839.

[11] See for instance Laurens van der Post, *The Lost World of the Kalahari*, London, Hogarth, 1980. Intriguingly, Darwin noted the Tierra del Fuegians to be excellent mimics, repeating 'with perfect correctness each word in any sentence we addressed them'. He also noted being told 'almost in the same words, of the same ludicrous habit among the Caffres [Bantus of Africa]'. Charles Darwin, *Naturalist's Voyage Round the World*, London, John Murray, 1890, pp.194-6.

Chapter 3

[1] Michael B. Collins *et al.*, 'The Paleoindian Sequence at the Wilson-Leonard Site, Texas', *Current Research in the Pleistocene* 10, 1993.

[2] Now preserved at Washington State University. See *National Geographic*, September 1979, p.333.

[3] J.M. Adovasio and D.C. Hyland, 'The Need to Weave: The First Americans used more Fibre than Flint', *Scientific American Discovering Archaeology*, January/February 2000, pp.36-7.

[4] In fact the Jomon culture of Japan is one exception, since they have recently been found to have been using pottery millennia earlier than the peoples of the Near East.

Chapter 4

[1] For further information on the story of this reconstruction, and much of the other background material in this chapter, see Larry Barham, Philip Priestley and Adrian Targett, *In Search of Cheddar Man*, Stroud, Tempus, 1999.

[2] In order to be preserved the impressions must have been made when the sea-level was at a temporary peak, and later overlaid with a peat layer.

[3] For further background, see Chris Stringer, 'The hominid remains from Gough's Cave', *Proceedings of the University of Bristol Spelaeological Society*, 17 (2), 1985, pp.145-52.

[4] Entitled 'In Search of Cheddar Man', this documentary was produced by Philip Priestley of HTV, Bristol, and shown in 1997 as part of the HTV series *The Time Traveller*.

Chapter 5

[1] David Roberts, 'The Ice Man: Lone Voyager from the Copper Age', *National Geographic*, June 1993, pp.36-67.

[2] The details concerning Ötzi's equipment have been assembled from sources which have constantly updated and corrected earlier findings that proved inaccurate. Among the best sources are Konrad Spindler, *The Man in the Ice*, London, Weidenfeld & Nicolson, 1994; also Lawrence Barfield, 'The Iceman reviewed', *Antiquity*, 68, 1994, pp.10-26.

[3] L. Dorfer, M. Moser, K. Spindler, F. Bahr, E. Egarter-Vigl and G. Dohr, '5,200-Year-old Acupuncture in Central Europe', *Science* 282: pp.242-43.

[4] D. Zur Nedden and K. Wicke, 'The Similaun Mummy as Observed from the Viewpoint of Radiological and CT Data', in F. Höpfel, W. Platzer and K. Spindler (eds.), *Der Mann im Eis* vol. 1, Innsbruck, University of Innsbruck, 1992, pp.131-48.

[5] The Canadian-born Tom Loy works at the University of Queensland's Centre for Molecular and Cellular Biology.

[6] Tom Loy, article in *New Scientist*, 12 September 1998, pp.40-43.

[7] Fax to the author, 19 September 1994.

Part II
Introduction

1 Findings of an international symposium, 'The Late Quaternary in the Eastern Mediterranean', held in Ankara, Turkey, spring 1997, as reported in William Ryan and Walter Pitman, *Noah's Flood*, New York, Simon & Schuster, 1998, p.177.

2 James Sauer, 'The River Runs Dry', *Biblical Archaeology Review*, July/August 1996, p.57.

3 James Mellaart, *Çatal Hüyük – a Neolithic Town*, New York, McGraw Hill, 1967.

4 This occurrence has only recently been determined from the Black Sea's freshwater mollusc deposits being radiocarbon dated to pre-5600 BC, and the seawater varieties as all more recent than that date. See Ryan and Pitman, *op. cit.*, chapter 14.

5 Larry Barham, *In Search of Cheddar Man*, Stroud, Tempus, 1999, p.95.

6 S.N. Kramer, *The Sumerians*, Chicago, University of Chicago Press, 1963.

7 Evan Hadingham, 'The Mummies of Xinjiang', *Discover*, April 1994, pp.68ff.

8 Patrick E. McGovern, Stuart Fleming and Solomon H. Katz (eds.), *The Origins and Ancient History of Wine*, Philadelphia, University of Pennsylvania Museum/Gordon & Breach, 1996.

9 See *The Oldest Gold in the World – Varna, Bulgaria*, Jerusalem, Israel Museum, 1994.

10 The Early Bronze Age is generally dated as 3200-2000 BC, the Middle Bronze Age 2000-1550 BC, and the late Bronze Age 1550-1200 BC, with further divisions within these, but the dates constantly shift between one archaeologist and another.

11 M.N. Cohen and G.J. Armelagos (eds.), *Palaeopathology at the Origins of Agriculture*, New York, Academic Press, 1984.

12 One of at least thirty diseases that can be transmitted via milk.

13 Believed passed to man from the Asian water-buffalo.

14 The Iron Age is generally divided into Iron Age I (1200-1000 BC), Iron Age II (1000-586 BC), and Iron Age III (586-330 BC).

Chapter 6

1 This was originally read as 'Shubad', the name given to her in the earliest archaeological reports, including Sir Leonard Woolley's.

2 Sir Leonard Woolley, *Ur 'of the Chaldees'*, the final account, *Excavations at Ur*, revised and updated by P.R.S. Moorey, London, Herbert Press, 1982, p.69.

3 ibid.

4 Quoted in P.R.S. Moorey, 'What do we know about the people buried in the Royal Graves?', *Expedition* 20 (1), Fall 1977, pp.24ff.

5 Woolley, ed. Moorey, *op. cit.*, p.102.

6 ibid., p.67.

7 ibid, p.69.

8 Dr. Naomi F. Miller, article in *Expedition* magazine, vol 40, no.1.

Chapter 7

1 See chapter 7 of John Prag and Richard Neave, *Making Faces*, London, British Museum Press, 1997, pp.146-56.

2 For a popular account of the Sakellarakis excavations as they pertain to this chapter, see Yannis Sakellarakis and Efi Sapouna-Sakellaraki, 'Drama of Death in a Minoan Temple', *National Geographic*, February 1981, pp.203-22. Their more definitive account is J. & E. Sakellarakis, *Archanes*, Athens, 1991.

3 Dr John Prag has pointed out that the original building may be incomplete as excavated, the earthquake having possibly caused a large section to fall away down the hill.

4 e.g. a sarcophagus from Hagia Triada, Crete, dating *c*.1400 BC, as preserved in the Herakleion Museum.

5 Although this has been suggested as the cause of the fire, ancient sacrifices, both animal and human, often involved burning the victim after blood-letting, as was about to happen in the biblical story of Abraham. Possibly, therefore, those at the temple had already lit a fire for the sacrifice, which went out of control during the circumstances of the earthquake.

6 The Sakellarakises found evidence of some peripheral intrusion from 'treasure-hunters' – see their *National Geographic* article p.212 – but these did not reach the area where the bodies lay.

7 For detailed anatomical information, see J.H. Musgrave, R.A.H. Neave, A.J.N.W. Prag, E. Sakellarakis and J. Sakellarakis, 'The Priest and Priestess from Archanes-Anemospilia', *Annual of the British School at Athens*, 89, 1994, pp.89-100.

8 See Christos Doumas, *The Wall Paintings of Thera*, Athens, The Thera Foundation, 1992.

9 For a popular though now dated introduction to the Minoans, see Arthur Cotterell, *The Minoan World*, London, Guild, 1979.

10 Dr John Prag points out that he and his colleagues are currently working on a DNA project associated with the Mycenaeans, who later took over Minoan Crete. He hopes to follow this with a similar study of Minoan DNA.

Chapter 8

1 Quoted in A.R. David and E. Tapp (eds.), *The Mummy's Tale: The Scientific and Medical Examination of Natsef-Amun Priest in the Temple at Karnak*, London, Michael O'Mara Books, 1992, p.65.

2 B. Porter and R.L.B. Moss, *Topographical Bibliography of Ancient Egyptian Hieroglyphic Texts, Reliefs and Paintings*, Vol.11, *The Theban Necropolis*, Part 2: Royal Tombs and Smaller Cemeteries, 2nd revised edition, Oxford 1989, p.637.

3 Although the dating of Egyptian pharaohs is often quoted in exact years, as here, Egyptologists differ in their chronologies, some preferring a so-called 'high' chronology, others a 'low'. The datings from this time must therefore be regarded as approximations only.

4 Herodotus, *The Histories*, Book II, trans. Aubrey de Selincourt, Harmondsworth, Penguin, 1954, p.116.

5 See W. Osburn, *An Account of an Egyptian mummy presented to the Museum of the Leeds Philosophical and Literary Society by the late John Blayds, Esq.*, Leeds, 1828.

6 A.R. David and E. Tapp, *op. cit.*, p.118.

Chapter 9

1 Much of the background to this chapter has been based on the Russian archaeologist Natalya Polosmak's article in *National Geographic* magazine, October 1994, pp.80-103, and Peter Bogucki's chapter 'Pazyryk and the Ukok Princess' in Paul G. Bahn (ed.), *Tombs, Graves and Mummies*, London, Weidenfeld & Nicolson, 1996, pp.146-51.

2 Herodotus, *The Histories*, Book IV. See the Penguin edition, with translation by Aubrey de Selincourt, p.257.

3 ibid., p.264.

4 S.I. Rudenko, *Frozen Tombs of Siberia: the Pazyryk Burials of Iron Age Horsemen*, trans. M.W. Thompson, Berkeley, University of California Press, 1970.

5 Herodotus, *op. cit.*, p.265.

6 Entry for 'Altaics' in *The Red Book of the Peoples of the Russian Empire*, http://www.eki.ee/books/redbook/altaics.html.

Chapter 10

1 For the prime account of this reconstruction, see A.J.N.W. Prag, J.H. Musgrave and R.A.H. Neave, 'The Skull from Tomb II at Vergina: King Philip II of Macedon', *Journal of Hellenic Studies* 104, 1984, pp.60-78; also, for the most up-to-date, John Prag and Richard Neave, *Making Faces*, London, British Museum, 1997, chapter 4.

2 Didymus Chalcenterus, *Philippic*, xi, 22, in *Kommentar zu Demosthenes*, H. Diels and W. Schubart (eds.), Berlin, 1904, vol. 12, pp.43ff.

3 Quoted in N.G.L. Hammond, *Philip of Macedon*, London, Duckworth, 1994, p.36.

4 Pliny, *Natural History*, Book VII, chapter 124, as quoted in Prag and Neave, *op. cit.*, p.72.

5 See Prag, Musgrave and Neave, 'The Skull from Tomb II...', *op. cit.*, also J.H. Musgrave, 'Dust and Damn'd Oblivion: A Study of Cremation in Ancient Greece', *Annual of the British School at Athens* 85, 1990, pp.271-79.

6 Herodotus, *The Histories*, trans. Aubrey de Selincourt, Harmondsworth, Penguin, 1954, p.264.

Part III
Introduction

1 Suetonius, *The Twelve Caesars*, trans. Robert Graves, Harmondsworth, Penguin, 1957, pp.94-5.

2 In fact they had cleverly adapted the alphabet of the Greeks.

3 Virgil, *Aeneid*, Book vi, 851.

4 Kenneth Painter, 'Glass in the Making', *Minerva*, January/February 1992, p.42.

Chapter 11

1 Publication is awaited of a major study of Hanunia, edited by Dr John Prag of the Manchester Museum and Judith Swaddling of the British Museum, with contributions from major medical and historical specialists. Meanwhile much of this chapter, particularly the forensic findings on Hanunia, is greatly indebted to chapter 9 of John Prag and Richard Neave's *Making Faces*, *op. cit.*

2 Becker's studies have appeared in *Antropologia Contemporanea* 13-14, 1990, pp.359-69, and G. Maetzke (ed.), *La Civiltà di Chiusi e del suo Territorio*, Florence, 1991, pp.397-410.

3 For general background to the Etruscan religion, see M. Pallottino, *The Etruscans*, Harmondsworth, Penguin, 1955, p.154 ff.

4 For some background see Rex E. Wallace, 'How to Read Etruscan' in *Archaeology Odyssey*, Summer 1998, pp.32-33.

Chapter 12

1 The material in this chapter is based on information in the 1999 documentary 'Bones in the Barnyard' in BBC TV's *Meet the Ancestors* series, and the corresponding chapter of Julian Richards' book of the same title, published by the BBC in the same year.

2 In common with Celts generally, the pre-Roman Britons' metallurgy skills were excellent. See for instance Barry Cunliffe, *Iron Age Britain*, London, Batsford, 1995, also T.G.E. Powell, *The Celts*, London, Thames & Hudson, 1958.

3 For general background on Lindow Man, see I.M. Stead, J.B. Bourke, Don Brothwell (eds.), *Lindow Man: The Body in the Bog*, London, British Museum, 1986; also Prag and Neave, *Making Faces, op. cit.*, chapter 8.

4 Except that, as suggested in Anne Ross and Don Robins, *The Life and Death of a Druid Prince* (London, Rider, 1989), the Celts may have offered him to the gods to supplicate their aid resisting the Roman conquest of Britain.

5 For background on the Celtic gods, see Miranda Green, *The Gods of the Celts*, Stroud, Alan Sutton, 1986; Anne Ross, *Pagan Celtic Britain*, London, Routledge & Kegan Paul, 1967.

6 See for instance P.V. Glob, *The Bog*

People, London, 1969. Also the excellent chapter 'The Bog Burials of Britain and Ireland' by R.C. Turner and C.S. Briggs in I.M. Stead *et al.*, *Lindow Man*, op.cit.

Chapter 13

1 Reported in an article by the Italian journalist Mara Amorevoli in the newspaper *La Repubblica*, 10 February 2000. I am indebted to John Follain of the *Sunday Times* for his kind help in making this article available.
2 Quoted in a report by Richard Owen, 'Ancient mariner rises from the deep', published in *The Times*, 11 February 2000.
3 Keith Muckelroy (ed.), *Archaeology under Water: An Atlas of the World's Submerged Sites*, New York, McGraw-Hill, p.50.

Chapter 14

1 Much of the information about this particular find derives from the excellent Museum of London website, www.museumoflondon.org.uk, and from the BBC's programme about it in the *Meet the Ancestors* series.
2 Dalya Alberge, 'Lifting the lid on a Roman uptown girl', *The Times*, 15 April 1999.
3 Paul Budd, 'Lead lies long in the tooth for the Princess of the City', www.brad.ac.uk.
4 For general background, see Hugh Clout (ed.), *The Times London History Atlas*, London, Times Books, 1991.
5 Simon Tait, 'Roman docks found on Guy's site', *The Times*, 1989.
6 Quoted in *Archaeology Odyssey* September/October 1999, p.9.

Part IV
Introduction

1 R.K. Gordon (ed. & trans.), *Anglo-Saxon Poetry*, London, J.M. Dent, 1926, p.84.
2 In fact the Arabs had acquired some rudiments of the numbering system from the Hindus, but it reached Europe via Arab scholars such as al-Khwarizmi.
3 Robert Clairborne, *Climate, Man and History*, 1973.

Chapter 15

1 See for instance Johannes Brøndsted, *The Vikings*, trans. Estrid Bannister-Good, Harmondsworth, Penguin, 1960, p.115 and pl.23B.
2 See A.W. Brogger and H. Shetelig, *The Viking Ships*, London, Hurst, 1951.
3 Five were found in the 1960s, another nine thirty-five years later.
4 This name has created great controversy, as it was apparently coined on account of the land bearing wild grapes. Yet Newfoundland is far to the north of where grapes might be expected to

grow, even allowing for the Little Optimum. Curiously, an English surgeon, James Yonge, reported 'wild grapes incredible' in southern Newfoundland as late as 1663. The archaeologist of L'Anse aux Meadows, Helge Ingstad, however, has suggested that the Old Norse word *vin* meant pasturage.
5 Anne Stine Ingstad and Helge Ingstad, *The Norse Discovery of America*, vols. I and II, Oslo, Norwegian University Press, 1985.

Chapter 16

1 'Sepultus est rex apud monasterium de Dunfermelyn in medio chori, debito cum honore'. Goodall (ed.), *Scotichronicon cum Supplementis et Continuatione Walter Boweri*, vol. II, p.292.
2 Report by Sir Henry Jardine, extracts from which are given in the *Transactions of the Society of Antiquaries of Scotland*, vol. II, 1822, pp.435-55.
3 For an excellent account of this cast, see Karl Pearson, 'The Skull of Robert the Bruce, King of Scotland, 1274-1329', *Biometrika*, vol. 15, 1924, pp.253-72.
4 E.L.G. Stones (ed.), *Anglo-Scottish Relations 1174-1328*, London, Nelson, 1964, pp.323-25.
5 L. Poulain (ed.), *Les Vraies Chroniques de Messire Jehan Le Bel*, Brussels, 1863, p.47.
6 See Ronald McNair Scott, *Robert the Bruce King of Scots*, New York, Carroll & Graf, 1996, p.242, note VI.

Chapter 17

1 This reconstruction was featured in a Granada TV documentary about the Towton discovery, 'Secrets of the Dead: Blood Red Roses', screened on UK Channel 4, 29 June 1999.
2 For the most definitive recent study of the battle, see A.W. Boardman, *The Battle of Towton*, Stroud, Sutton, 1994. In his Preface, Boardman describes Towton as 'arguably the biggest, longest and bloodiest engagement on British soil'.
3 This figure is given as the tally counted by the heralds, in an attachment to a letter sent by Sir William Paston of Norfolk to John Paston. See James Gairdner (ed.), *The Paston Letters 1422-1509 AD*, 3 vols., 1872-75, vol. 3, pp.267-68.

Chapter 18

1 Casts of the sculpture are exhibited at the Florida State Museum, Gainsville, Florida, and the Xavier De Salas Foundation Museum, Trujillo, Spain.
2 An invaluable account of Pizarro's life remains William H. Prescott's classic *History of the Conquest of Peru, with a Preliminary View of the Civilization of the Incas*, London, Bentley, 2 vols., 1847.
3 H.Ludeña Restaure, 'Versiones

Tempranas Sobre La Muerte de Don Francisco Pizarro', *Boletin de Lima* vol 7, 1985, p.5-32
4 See in particular W.J. McGee, 'The Remains of Don Francisco Pizarro', *American Anthropologist*, vol. 7, 1894, pp.1-25. This incorporates a translation of studies made in 1891 by two Peruvian physicians who described as 'baseless' any doubts that the sarcophagus mummy was Pizarro.
5 William Maples *et al.*, 'The Death and Mortal Remains of Francisco Pizarro', *Journal of Forensic Sciences*, vol. 34, no.4, July 1989, pp.1021-36. I am indebted to Betty Pat Gatliff for an offprint of this article.
6 For a detailed appraisal of all these injuries see the latest study on the subject, Robert A. Benfer, Jr., and Hugo Ludeña Restaure, 'The Identification of the Remains of Don Francisco Pizarro', in Scott I Fairgreaves (ed.) *Forensic Osteological Analysis*, Charles G. Thomas, Springwood, Il., 1999.
7 Betty Pat Gatliff, 'Forensic Sculpture Adapts to Museum Use', *Scientific Illustration – 1986, Selected Papers from the 7th Annual Conference of the Guild of Natural Science Illustrators*, Washington, D.C., 1986.
8 William Maples, *op.cit.*, fig. 8-5B, p.123.

Chapter 19

1 I.A. Soloviev, *Ivan Grozny*, 1898, quoted in M. Gerasimov, *The Face Finder*, p.187.

Chapter 20

1 For much of the information in this chapter I am indebted to the excellent website of the Texas A&M University Conservation Research Laboratory, which is constantly being updated. This can be found at http://nautach.tamu.edu
2 Entitled *Le Temple de la Paix*, this ballet was danced before Louis XIV at Fontainebleau on 15 October 1685.
3 Henri Joutel, *Joutel's Journal of La Salle's Last Voyage*, London, Lintot, 1714, reprinted New York, Franklin, 1968; William C. Foster (ed.), *The La Salle Expedition in Texas: The Journal of Henri Joutel, 1684-1687*, trans. Johanna S. Warren, Texas A&M University Press, 1999.
4 Other details are to be found in the journal of the engineer Minet, and information given by the children Pierre and Jean-Baptist Talon. For these documents in translation see Robert S. Weddle (ed.), Mary Christine Morkovsky and Patricia Galloway (associate eds.) *La Salle, the Mississippi and the Gulf: three primary documents*, trans. Ann Linda Bell & Robert S. Weddle, College Station, Texas A&M University, 1987.
5 A fourth bronze gun was removed sometime in the recent past by unknown individuals.

Postscript

1 Widely reported in world media, 27 June 2000.
2 Anjana Ahuja, 'How seven women founded Europe' and 'So God created woman', *The Times*, 19 April 2000.
3 Stewart Tendler, 'DNA detectives will fit a face to a flake of skin', Report on the Annual Conference of the Police Superintendents' Association in Bristol, *The Times*, 16 September 1998.
4 One cache was found in 1881, the other in 1898. Egyptian priests had gathered up the mummies in haste after widespread looting during lawless episodes in antiquity.
5 See Nigel Hawkes, 'Golden image of boy king goes pear-shaped', *The Times*, 3 August 2000. This reports the textile expert Dr Gillian Vogelsang-Eastwood's deductions that Tutankhamun measured 31 inches (79cm) at the chest, 29 inches (73.5cm) at the waist and 43 inches (109cm) around the hips.
6 See a suggested realignment of the identifications presented in Peter Clayton's report on a Conference on the Valley of the Kings held at Highclere Castle, 15-17 June 1990, published in *Minerva*, September 1990, pp.28-9.
7 Zvi Greenhut, 'Burial Cave of the Caiaphas Family', *Biblical Archaeology Review*, 18, 5, September/October 1992, pp.29-36.
8 Julian Richards, *Meet the Ancestors* London, BBC, 1999, p.8.
9 Natalya Polosmak, 'A Mummy Unearthed from the Pastures of Heaven', *National Geographic*, October 1994, p.99.
10 Howard Carter and A.C. Mace, *The Tomb of Tut Ankh Amen*, 2 vols., New York, 1923 and 1927.
11 R. Rau, 'How James Drury cast the bushmen displayed in the South African Museum', *South African Journal of Science*, 60, 1964, pp.242-44.
12 Laurens van der Post, *The Lost World of the Kalahari*, London, The Hogarth Press, 1980.
13 Donald Thomson, *Donald Thomson in Arnhem Land*, compiled and introduced by Nicholas Peterson, South Yarra (Victoria), Currag O'Neal, 1983, p.77.
14 Carolyn M. Bloomer, *Principles of Visual Perception*, New York, Design Press, 2nd edition, 1990, p.113.
15 David Hurst Thomas, 'Archaeology for the 21st Century: A New Model for Archaeologists and Native Americans', *Scientific American Discovering Archaeology*, January/February 2000, pp.76-7.
16 Quoted in Nicholas Wade, 'The Human Family Tree: 10 Adams and 18 Eves', published on the Stanford University website, 2 May 2000.

INDEX

CREDITS

2, 11 Photo: Bryan Wharton/ *The Sunday Times*, London; 8, 100, 101, 203 Charles O'Rear/CORBIS; 10, 69, 118, 161 The British Museum; 12 193 (bottom); 196 Ian Wilson; 14, 15: National Portrait Gallery, London; 16, 185, 189 Dr. Tatyana Balueva, Laboratory of Anthropological Reconstruction, Institute of Ethnology and Anthropology, Russian Academy of Science; 17 Copyrighted Facial Approximation by Sharon A. Long, Artist/Anthropologist, consulting with Douglas Owsley and David Hunt, National Museum of Natural History. Photograph by Chip Clark of the Smithsonian Institution; 19, 21, 41, 42, 53, 54, 82, 88, 92, 102, 104, 118, 119 (top & bottom), 122, 124, 160 (bottom), 162, 168 (bottom), 170-171 MNWP/The University of Manchester; 22, 58, 59 Photo: Kenneth Garrett/National Geographic Image Collection; 27 South African Museum; 32, 37 C.M.Dixon Photo Resources; 36, 193 (top) Bettmann/CORBIS; 38 Hubert Stadler/CORBIS; 40 Diego Lezzama Orezzo/CORBIS; 44, 76, 112-113, 160 (top), 174, 182 Topham Picturepoint; 46 (top) Collection of the Department of Anthropology, University of Wyoming; photo: Peter A. Bostrom; 50: National Museum of Wales; 52 Andrew Brown; Ecoscene/CORBIS; 55 South West News Service; 60, 62 South Tyrol Museum of Archaeology, photo: Augustin Ochsenreiter; 61 South Tyrol Museum of Archaeology, photo: Marco Samadelli; 74, 77 (bottom) private collection/Bridgeman Art Library, London; 77 (top) The Art Archive/ British Museum; 84-85, 86, 90, 91 (top), 96, 138 The Ancient Art & Architecture Collection; 87, 166, 173 Sonia Halliday Photographs, 91 (bottom); 95 Leeds Museums and Art Galleries (City Museum); 97, 98 (top & bottom) Novosti (London); 105 Archaeological Museum, Thessaloniki/Bridgeman Art Library, London; 106 John Heseltine/CORBIS; 107 Gianni Dagli Orti/CORBIS; 116 Photo: Louis Mazzatenta/National Geographic Image Collection; 121 National Geographic Image Collection; 123 Jane Brayne, 125 Steve Austin; Papilio/CORBIS; 126, 132 Werner Forman Archive; 127 Ian Potts/BBC; 128 AKG London/ Erich Lessing; 130 Soprintendenza archeologica della Toscana; 131 (top & bottom) Professor Francesco Mallegni, University of Pisa; 134, 137, 139 (top & bottom) Museum of London; 144-145 Musee de la Tapisserie, Bayeux, France/Bridgeman Art Library, London; 150 University Museum of Cultural Heritage, University of Oslo; 152, 153 York Archaeological Trust; 154, 157 Jorvik Viking Centre; 158, 164 The Art Archive; 168-169 Andrew Boardman; 172 Reproduced by permission of the Trustees of the Wallace Collection, London; 176, 186 AKG London; 177 (top) The Art Archive/Mireille Vautier; 177 (bottom), 181 (top) Betty Pat. Gatliff; 178 Robert Harding Picture Library; 180 Biblioteca del ICI, Madrid, Spain/Bridgeman Art Library, London; 181 (bottom) Photo by William R. Maples, Ph.D; 190, 195 1996 Robert Clark/AURORA; 200: Archivio Iconografico, S.A./CORBIS; 206 The Saatchi Gallery, London

First published in the United Kingdom in 2001 by Cassell & Co

This paperback edition first published in 2002 by Weidenfeld & Nicolson

Text copyright © 2001 Ian Wilson
Design and layout copyright © 2001 Cassell & Co

The picture acknowledgements on this page constitute an extension to this copyright information.

A CIP catalogue record for this book is available from the British Library.

ISBN 1 84188 194 5

Designed by Nigel Soper
Printed and bound in Spain

Weidenfeld & Nicolson
Wellington House
125 Strand
London WC2R 0BB